September 2002

To Holly and

With Sincere

for all of your
support and friendship
Love
Myra

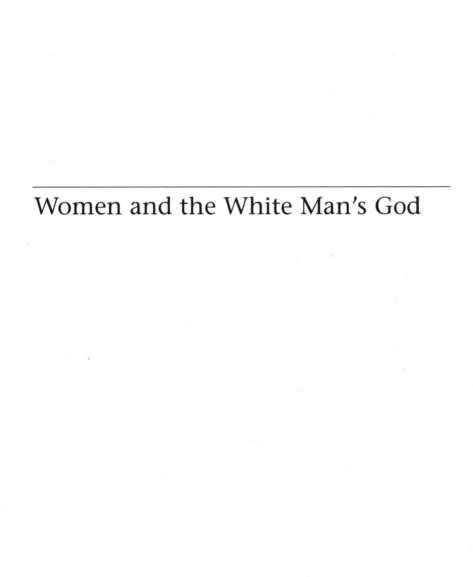

# Women and the White Man's God

*Myra Rutherdale*

# Women and the White Man's God: Gender and Race in the Canadian Mission Field

**UBC**Press · Vancouver · Toronto

Printed in Canada on acid-free paper

**National Library of Canada Cataloguing in Publication Data**

Rutherdale, Myra
Women and the white man's God

Includes bibliographical references and index.
ISBN 0-7748-0904-3 (bound); ISBN 0-7748-0905-1 (pbk.)

1. Church of England – Missions – Canada, Northern – History. 2. Women in missionary work – Canada, Northern – History. 3. Women missionaries – Canada, Northern – History. 4. Native peoples – Missions – Canada, Northern – History.* 5. Northwest, Canadian – Race relations. 6. Northwest, Canadian – History. I. Title.

BV2815.N6R87 2002    266'.371    C2002-910486-6

Canadä

UBC Press gratefully acknowledges the financial support for our publishing program of the Government of Canada through the Book Publishing Industry Development Program (BPIDP), and of the Canada Council for the Arts, and the British Columbia Arts Council.

This book has been published with the help of a grant from the Humanities and Social Sciences Federation of Canada, using funds provided by the Social Sciences and Humanities Research Council of Canada, and with the help of the K.D. Srivastava Fund.

Printed and bound in Canada by Friesens
Set in Stone by Brenda and Neil West, BN Typographics West
Copy editor: Susan Quirk
Proofreader: Barbara Storey
Indexer: Patricia Buchanan
Cartographer: Eric Leinberger

UBC Press
The University of British Columbia
2029 West Mall
Vancouver, BC V6T 1Z2
604-822-5959 / Fax: 604-822-6083
www.ubcpress.ca

*For Rob and Andrew*

*and in memory of my parents,*
*Elizabeth M. (Noseworthy) MacKinnon*
*and Donald J. MacKinnon*

# Contents

# Illustrations

# Acknowledgments

As I write these acknowledgments, I am reminded of how fortunate I am to have been sustained by such supportive family, friends, and colleagues. This book was initially a dissertation undertaken at York University's Department of History, supervised by William Westfall. His belief in this project, his unfailing sense of humour, and his understanding of the Anglican world have been critical to the book's completion. Kate McPherson also deserves special thanks for all the hours she dedicated to reading and rereading drafts at the dissertation stage and for the support she has provided since. Other committee members – Paul Axelrod, Ruth Compton Brouwer, Doug Freake, and Roberto Perin – provided helpful commentary. Before them, I was encouraged by many fine mentors and good teachers at the University of New Brunswick and McMaster University. I thank especially Charles M. Johnston at McMaster, whose senior undergraduate seminar on imperial Britain inspired my interest in empire and colonialism, and Sylvia Van Kirk, whose graduate course on women's history at the University of Toronto reinforced my belief that, to understand the past fully, women's experiences must be removed from the margins.

I owe a debt of gratitude to Dorothy Kealey, Terry Thompson, and Josie DeLucia, all at the indispensable General Synod Archives of the Anglican Church of Canada (GSA) at Church House in Toronto. Jennifer Davis at the Diocese of Caledonia Archives in Prince Rupert was very helpful, especially at the initial stages of this research, as were the archivists at the Yukon Territorial Archives (YTA) in Whitehorse. Anne Morton at the Hudson's Bay Company Archives promptly forwarded very useful material, for which I thank her. Thanks also to archivists at the Glenbow Museum, the Provincial Archives of Alberta, the Provincial Archives of British Columbia, the Vancouver School of Theology, and the National Archives of Canada. I am also grateful to missionary family members who kindly provided me with both memories and additional material. Mary Marsh McWhinney was especially helpful in allowing me access to

Elizabeth Wilgress's diairies, and in discussing her family's commitment to northern missions.

At UBC Press, I want to extend special thanks to Jean Wilson, Associate Director, Editorial. Jean has been a patient editor and a good friend. I appreciate the efforts of Holly Keller-Brohman and Darcy Cullen, who shepherded this book through the final stages, and Susan Quirk, for her adept copy editing. Eric Leinberger produced the maps. Thanks also to the two anonymous readers, who offered helpful suggestions.

I wish to express my appreciation to my friends and colleagues for their inspiration and unfailing kindness. For reading parts of the manuscript in various forms, and for potluck dinners and engaging conversations, I thank Kerry Abel, Jean Barman, Catherine Cavanaugh, Jo Fiske, Mona Gleason, Jacqueline Gresko, Norman Knowles, Lynne Marks, Adele Perry, Katie Pickles, Pat Roy, Ruth Sandwell, Nikki Strong-Boag, and Randi Warne. For their kindness and loyalty, and for listening patiently to repetitions of "Yes, I am just about done," I thank Holly Kavanaugh, Alan Kavanaugh, Joan Buchanan, Larry Woods, Alison Peel, Doug Peel, Shannon Olfert, Deanna Reder, Eric Davis, Fiona MacPhail, Bertha Jarron, and Lyn Riddett. My family – the MacKinnons and Rutherdales – have made this book possible. During my childhood years in Saint John, New Brunswick, my parents instilled in me a desire to understand the past and the love of a good story. I have also been fortunate to have had the extraordinary support and friendship of John, Jack, and Jean Rutherdale, who willingly provided humorous moments, fantastic meals, and child care, among many other things, so that I could get on with this work. My partner, Rob, and my son, Andrew, I have left to thank last, although they know that they are uppermost in my gratitude. Dinner discussions throughout Andrew's young life have often centred on missionaries and history, and he has, for the most part, patiently endured mission stories and his mother being busy with writing. More than this, he has been such a pleasure for myself and Rob. Rob's optimism and friendship have been a model for me. He has never wavered in his belief in me, and for that I thank him.

# Introduction

While on holiday in Devon, England, in 1921, London resident Winifred Petchey listened to a "stirring sermon," which implored young men in the congregation to volunteer to go to Canada for missionary training. Petchey later recalled, "I was seventeen years old and a girl; thus, I was excluded from consideration, but the desire for foreign mission work lay deep within my heart. As I left the Church that summer's night I was angry and resentful."[1]

On the way home, it occurred to her that her friend, Donald Marsh, would be a perfect candidate for mission work and she immediately persuaded her mother to write to encourage him. On her return home to Winchmore Hill, London, a few months later, she learned that Marsh had already sailed for Canada. Subsequently, Winifred Petchey enrolled in courses in dentistry at Bethnal Green Medical Clinic, midwifery at the Mother's Hospital in London, and other medical courses at the Livingstone College in London. She also taught art in north London.[2] In 1933, after several years of correspondence with and brief furlough visits from the Reverend Marsh, Petchey married and joined him in his work at Eskimo Point (now Arviat) in the eastern Arctic.[3] In 1950, the Reverend Donald Marsh was consecrated Bishop of the Arctic, and the family remained in the north until 1973. Winifred Marsh raised three children in the north and became a well-respected watercolour artist. She corresponded regularly from the Canadian Arctic with her family in England and with a wider audience that took an interest in mission news and views. Most assuredly, she also served as a missionary in her own right.

Aspects of Winifred Petchey Marsh's life story were shared by hundreds of Victorian and Edwardian women. British and, later, Canadian churches regularly appealed for young men – but not usually women – to become missionaries. Many women, however, like Winifred Petchey felt drawn to mission work. While some may have felt discouraged because of their gender, others were recruited as single women, or they married missionaries who were on their way to their first posting. Stories of "last-minute" marriages are numerous.

This book examines the perceptions and experiences of Anglican missionaries primarily from the records of one hundred and thirty-two such English and Canadian women, who were part of a mission frontier in northern British Columbia, the Yukon, and Canada's Arctic from 1860 to 1940. My intention was to try to understand why women like Winifred Petchey were attracted to mission work, and how they expressed their experiences of it. I wanted to discover what preconceived ideas they held about mission work, how they described their new circumstances in northern settings, and how they interacted with numerous Aboriginal cultures.[4] I wondered whether they questioned or doubted their religious mission. Did they see mission work as a calling, or were they attracted to it because it offered adventure? I looked for preconceptions these women held about other cultures and whether they remained or changed as a result of contact with Aboriginal peoples. I quickly learned that the women's thinking varied according to individual experience, but realized that a more balanced understanding of the complexities of colonialism in northern Canada could be gained by examining the collective roles of Anglo-Canadian women missionaries. How the north was perceived by missionary women and how they saw themselves interested me most of all.

Winifred Marsh with her daughter at Eskimo Point (Arviat).

As with other studies of cultural contact, histories of missions in northern aboriginal communities have largely focused on men.[5] The important studies by historians John Webster Grant, Kerry Abel, Kenneth Coates, Brett Christophers, and others who have focused on relations between Aboriginal peoples and newcomers have not, unfortunately, documented the specific perspectives and experiences of women. Attention has been paid to male actors who distinguished themselves for either their religious fervour or their eccentricity.[6] A focus on male missionaries is somewhat ironic since, if mission wives are counted as missionaries, then most of the missionaries in the north were women. Their perceptions of gender, racial and cultural differences, the landscape, and religion represent constructions that drew on many sources.

While this book is in part a case study, it is more than that. It shows how preconceived ideas about empire, colonialism, race and culture, travel, gender, and religion were often in conflict with actual experience, and how these were reflected in the missionary discourse. Discourse analysis is applied to the language used by missionaries to discuss their experiences and perceptions. The language charted a territory of consciousness, yet what was said did not always reflect the reality of the mission experience. Gender differences were tested and amended by the mission experience. At times male missionaries attempted to define themselves in terms of masculine dominance over nature while, at other times, they found themselves unwittingly performing tasks that, in England, would have been thought of as the exclusive province of women. Social perceptions of femininity and masculinity became more fluid as a result of the circumstances in which missionaries found themselves. While gender may have been shaped within the Victorian and Edwardian ideology wherein men and women occupy separate spheres, on the mission frontier new spheres were established. Evidence of shifting boundaries could find expression in new forms of self-perception and personal freedom. Ironically, there were also circumstances in which women and men reinstated gender boundaries to suit their aims as missionaries.

Missionaries aimed at religious conversion but were also dedicated to introducing European ideas and practices into the religious frontier. At the same time, however, the colonial context created tensions. Whether because of the new opportunities that missionary women enjoyed away from the constraints of the imperial centre, or because of their relationships with Aboriginal peoples, the experience in the mission field was never one way for these women: they learned much from Aboriginal peoples. Close analysis of the northern mission field prevents us from making generalizations about colonial relations. Notions of race, of both Whiteness and Aboriginality, were constructed and reconstructed in Anglo-Canadian missionaries as relationships were forged and varying needs were met.

## The Anglican Church

This book focuses on the Anglican Church for a number of reasons. In the late nineteenth and early twentieth centuries, it was the dominant Protestant religious institution in northern Canada. The first missionaries came to the north under the auspices of the London-based Church Missionary Society, an institution that developed what historian Jean Usher has called "one of the most efficient and extensive home organizations of the [nineteenth] century, themselves becoming the model *par excellence* for later societies."[7] Missionaries arrived in a region rich and diverse in cultural history; as part of the process of imperial expansion, they also found themselves on what could be referred to as a religious frontier. Their efforts to expand the geographic boundaries of Christianity placed them in unfamiliar settings in which their perceptions became contingent on local conditions. The landscapes of this book comprise a vast variety of geographies and cultures.

The first initiatives of the Church Missionary Society in North America were modest. In 1820, the Hudson's Bay Company, as the civil authority at Red River, offered to pay the salary of an Anglican clergyman. John West was sent as the society's first representative to minister to the needs of the company. West planned to start a school for Aboriginal children in the colony. He was outraged at the conditions in the Red River settlement, describing it as "a Heathen land, which Satan hath held bound, lo! not these 18 years or a century, but probably since the Creation of the world."[8] Yet, Red River was to become what John Webster Grant calls the missionary gateway to the northwest.[9] Thanks to an endowment from a former Hudson's Bay chief factor, the Church Missionary Society's modest beginnings flourished so that, in 1849, with "unfeigned satisfaction" the society appointed David Anderson as its first bishop in North America.

Competition between Anglican and Roman Catholic missions for northern Aboriginal souls intensified throughout the last half of the nineteenth century. Anglican historian Frank Peake claims, with an explicit bias, that the Catholics followed the Anglicans into the field deliberately to "offset the Anglican venture."[10] In the 1840s, the Roman Catholic Church sent missionaries to survey the "religious needs" of the Carrier peoples (Dakelh-ne) of central British Columbia's Gnotuk plateau but no permanent station was established until the 1860s.[11] They also undertook surveys of the Yukon in the 1850s and sent permanent missionaries to the north in the later part of the decade. Beginning in the 1850s the Oblates of Mary Immaculate built a strong rapport along the Mackenzie (Deh Cho) River among the Dene. Anglicans were also active by this time. The Society for the Propagation of the Gospel had, by the 1850s, spread from eastern Canada to southern British Columbia, with its main focus on Vancouver Island.[12] As the Church Missionary Society took root in northern British

Columbia, the Society for the Propagation of the Gospel sent a few representatives but did not gain a strong influence in the area.[13]

By 1900, the Church Missionary Society had an established network of mission stations throughout the Yukon, the Mackenzie valley, and northern British Columbia. While some stations were temporary and some Aboriginal peoples were reached by itinerant clergy, the society's missionaries had worked from the 1870s onward to build permanent mission stations

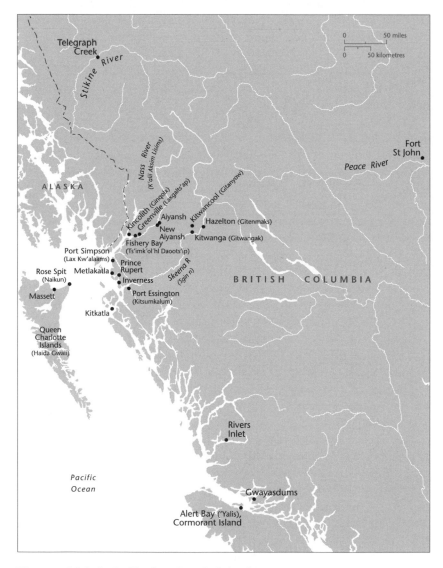

Diocese of Caledonia, Northern British Columbia

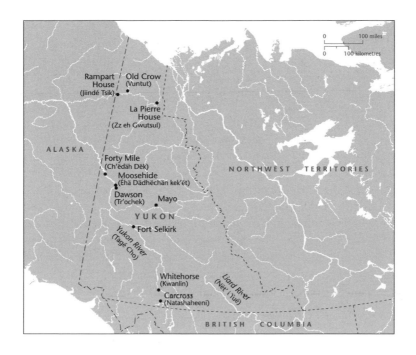

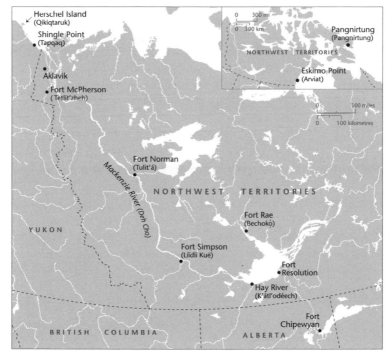

Yukon and Northwest Territories, 1920s

in the north. When Anglican missions began in northern British Columbia, the Diocese of Caledonia included Alert Bay ('Yalis) on Cormorant
Island. Eventually, this diocese stretched over 1.3 million square kilometres, from the Queen Charlotte Islands (Haida Gwaii) to the Alberta
border.[14] The Caledonia mission stations were established and built after
1879, the year the first bishop, the Reverend William Ridley, was consecrated. Prior to Ridley's arrival, work had been started at Metlakatla,
Masset, and Kincolith (Gingolx) largely by William Duncan, Robert
Tomlinson, and the Reverend W.H. Collison. Soon, Aboriginal missions
were established by Bishop Ridley and his co-workers at Alert Bay, Kitkatla,
Metlakatla, Kincolith, Lakkalzap, Masset, Kitwanga (Gitwangak), Aiyansh,
and Hazelton (Gitenmaks). In most of these villages, day schools were
held either by the clergyman, his wife, or a mission teacher. During the
1890s at Metlakatla, the Church Missionary Society opened a small hospital, a boys' and girls' school, a girls' home, and the White and Half-Breed
Home, later known as the Ridley home. By the early 1920s, there were
approximately thirty churches, several of which were non-Aboriginal and
Canadian-sponsored.

Anglican missions in the northern territories were even more dispersed.
The Diocese of the Yukon included all of present-day Yukon Territory.
There, the Church Missionary Society had established nine mission sta-
tions prior to 1920. When formed in 1933, the Diocese of the Arctic
encompassed an area of close to 7 million square kilometres, including
such communities as Hay River (Kátl'odéech), Fort Simpson (Líídli Kuë),
Fort Norman (Tulit'á), Fort McPherson (Tetlit'zheh), and Aklavik in the
Mackenzie valley, as well as Eskimo Point (Arviat) on the western shore of
Hudson Bay and Pangnirtung on Baffin Island.[15] Prior to 1933, many of
these villages had been part of the Mackenzie River Diocese which started
in 1869, and was enhanced in 1880 by a private donation of $5000 from a
supporter in England. Islington graduate William Day Reeve arrived from
England in 1869 and was stationed at Fort Simpson, Fort Rae (Bechoko),
and Fort Chipewyan before he was consecrated bishop in 1891. Throughout the 1890s, missions were established at Herschel Island (Qikiqtaruk) in
the Yukon, and at Fort McPherson and Hay River. With supplements from
the Canadian federal government, the church sponsored a large school
and a mission hospital in Hay River; the school closed in 1937 but the mission was maintained. In the Yukon, the Chooutla School at Carcross
(Natashaheeni), established by Bishop William Bompas, also received federal government supplements, as did the children's hostel at Dawson
(Tr'ochek) which was started in the early 1920s.

The arrival of newcomers in the late nineteenth and early twentieth
centuries rapidly transformed northern communities and less permanent
Aboriginal settlements, and Anglican missions became part of these

changes. Within this vast territory, missionaries encountered many Aboriginal cultures, which varied enormously with respect to customs and traditions, families and clans, ways of life, and beliefs. Some aspects of these cultures became points of conflict between Indigenous peoples and colonizing Christians, while others became a convenient entree for mission efforts. From the perspective of the missionaries and mission boards, these territories were ripe for conversion – they were "heathen lands." The north, in this Eurocentric sense, was perceived as a homogeneous racial whole rather than culturally diverse. This is not to deny that some mission bureaucrats or missionaries made distinctions between cultures and communities, but for most missionaries the common link among these communities was the approach to mission work. The "north" needed salvation.

The Church Missionary Society withdrew from Canada in 1920, at which time the northern mission field became the responsibility of the Missionary Society for the Church of England in Canada, yet many of the methods, ideologies, and mission staff remained the same.[16] Among Canadian mission societies, the Toronto-based mission society was particularly active in promoting ideas about British colonization. The belief that missionaries were on an imperial as well as religious frontier in northern

Bishop William Ridley (1836-1911), first bishop of the Diocese of Caledonia.

Canada was well ingrained. One Canadian missionary reported in 1902 that the Arctic's Herschel Island (Qikiqtaruk) was "the uttermost end of empire." Later, in 1933 the school at Shingle Point (Tapqaq), between Herschel Island and Aklavik, was described as the "most northerly residential school in the British Empire."[17]

Even after the imperial rhetoric began to decline following the First World War, the Anglican Church did not challenge imperialist assumptions. It continued to participate in colonial expansion in the north but, instead of being supported by a British mission society, the Anglican Church of Canada acted in tandem with the federal government to attempt to assimilate northern Aboriginal peoples into Canadian society; in this sense, the church was part of what Kenneth Coates has called the extension of "Canada's colonies."[18] This was most evident with respect to general health care and the education of northern children. "Through the boarding school program," Coates points out, "the missionaries and the government hoped to transform the children into 'better' Canadians, offering the intellectual and technical skills deemed necessary for fuller participation in the larger Euro-Canadian society and the Christian values required to separate the students from their 'heathen' past."[19] The "two arms of colonialism" – church and state – worked together throughout the north.[20] Missionaries were in this way involved in the colonization of the north first as participants of the British imperial project and later through their partnership with government assimilation policies in the north.[21]

The dichotomy drawn by some mission scholars between civilizing and evangelizing was not so evident in the north.[22] The emphasis on civilizing Aboriginal peoples continued, but the rhetoric about the glory of the British empire had begun to decline after the First World War. In spite of the waning of specifically British rhetoric, missionary efforts to provide European-style health care and education continued to serve both religious and colonial ends. The founders of the Church Missionary Society may have lauded Christianization over the introduction of European health care and education, yet in the field there were not always such clear distinctions. By the 1920s, education and health care were well integrated with the dissemination of Christianity. For example, nurse Mildred McCabe from Coxheath, Nova Scotia, wrote to the woman's auxiliary of the mission society in 1933 to describe her experience while at the Aklavik hospital between 1928 and 1933. Her report offers some insight into the mixing of Christianity and health care by northern missionaries: "Last but not least is the spiritual side of the medical work. There are times when all human efforts seem hopeless, but in some mysterious way the Great Physician of body and soul intervenes and restores His child to health and strength. During my term of service in that northerly hospital oftimes the unseen world seemed very near, and I was reminded of the presence of the risen Lord ever ready to help his children who call upon Him. Truly 'His touch has still its ancient power.' The natives nearly always ask for the Minister to come and pray for them when they are sick."[23] Health care and education were inextricably linked to Christianity and missions in the north. During the 1920s nurses and teachers were more often employed than were women missionaries without these skills.

The Anglican church was a useful choice for this study because its archives include an abundance of mission documentation on women. Like other societies, the Church Missionary Society and later the Missionary Society for the Church of England in Canada (MSCC) allowed women a degree of freedom that extended beyond the private sphere. As institutions, the British and Canadian mission societies provide an opportunity to examine the place of women in the missionary enterprise. The societies expressed numerous views about the roles of women and employed them in increasing numbers – in seeming contradiction to the church's public pronouncements on the place of women. In this book, I have attempted to balance official and public statements with private correspondence that is part of this missionary literature.

In the nineteenth century, missionary accounts became popular reading material for a wide audience at home. They combined a sense of the exotic with notions of benevolent evangelism, which was connected to the romanticization of mission work strengthened by the publication of Livingstone's African exploits of the 1850s. Jean and John Comaroff argue that "accounts of missionary 'labour and scenes' had by the late nineteenth century become an established European literary genre, taking its place beside popular travel and exploration writings, with which it shared features of intent and style. This was a literature of the imperial frontier, a colonizing discourse that titillated the European imagination with glimpses of radical otherness – over which it simultaneously extended intellectual control."[24]

The Church Missionary Society had a large number of publications which fit into this genre. According to Jean Usher, missionary accounts provided the "European public with much of their information about aboriginal peoples and their social environment. The colourful accounts of heroism and stories of exotic cultures of all kinds enjoyed a great popularity in Victorian homes."[25] The society itself claimed that "our knowledge of foreign lands, and the habits and manners of distant nations has been amazingly increased by the researches of Missionaries."[26] Missionary accounts were often thought of as accurate depictions of Aboriginal lives and environments and were meant to inspire confidence in the mission movement and, thereby, to attract more funds. Portrayals of Aboriginal cultures were thus placed within a discourse that combined extreme destitution and urgency with horror and fascination.

Public missionary accounts and actual experiences in the mission field were often disparate. Daily tasks and personal relationships were not always included in the rhetoric of the civilizing Christian mission. This makes it difficult to judge the veracity or representativeness of the vignettes and anecdotes of life in the north presented in the public documents. On the other hand, it is precisely because the published letters and texts were designed to capture the attention of British and southern Canadian audiences that they presented the most extreme discourse of colonization generated by missionaries in northern Canada. This discourse could contrast with private correspondence that reflected immediate observations and actual experiences of women in the mission field. Personal diaries reflect direct observations and sentiments of women in the field. Private letters written to parent committees or friends and family can provide candid perceptions not always found in public letters written to church publications. Public letters and reports to the societies' woman's auxiliaries written by women in the field are also assessed here. Informative and written in a narrative form to reveal persistent images of mission work and Aboriginal cultures, these reports nevertheless expose the ambiguities of the mission experience. These sources represent the written perceptions of Anglican women on the northern mission frontier. This analysis is based on an assumption that the process of writing about their perceptions and their experiences helped them to make sense of their lives. Identities were formed from a number of positions. Of course not every missionary woman who worked in the north left detailed accounts: in some cases only names and dates of tenure can be ascertained.[27] Another important body of materials for this book includes journals, letters, biographies, and official correspondence by male missionaries. They tell us much about the personal objectives of individual missionaries, perceptions of women missionaries, and the division of labour along gender lines within the mission field. Taken together, these sources offer some discernment of the formal and public discourse being relayed to Canadian and British audiences along with the private perspectives of women missionaries.

## Women, Colonization, and Religion

Writing in the early twenty-first century about the experiences of these women allows for reflection on current debates concerning postmodernism, post-colonialism, and gender identities. As June Purvis observes, women's historians have gone, in a span of about twenty years, from including the contributions of "women worthies" in their narratives to questioning whether the category "womanhood" is a legitimate analytical tool.[28] Denise Riley, in *Am I That Name*, argues that "any attention to the life of a woman, if traced out carefully, must admit the degree to which the effects of lived gender are at least sometimes unpredictable and fleeting."[29] Riley asks if anyone can "fully inhabit a gender without a degree of horror? How could someone 'be a woman' through and through, make a final home in that classification, without suffering claustrophobia?"[30] Indeed, women did suffer claustrophobia because of constructed boundaries, but this does not preclude the discernment of certain similarities shared by women. Purvis notes that "to study women as women is not to claim, as poststructuralists assume, that all women's shared experiences have been shared equally."[31]

Race, ethnicity, class, religion, and culture are undoubtedly crucial determinants in assessing experience. A consciousness of these determinants can lead to a legitimate analysis of how a particular group of women expressed their actual experiences. In this context, the language these missionary women used is powerful and resounds with the discourse of imperialism. A close reading shows that experiences in the mission field were given meaning by the multiple positions that the women themselves inhabited. The mission women in this book were White, mostly middle-class, Anglican, and British or Canadian. Their religion, class, ethnicity, and gender were central to their perceptions. They had several cultural traditions on which to draw to describe their encounters. Language helped to shape the meaning of their experiences as it reflected and affected their feelings of superiority over Aboriginal peoples.

The arguments presented in this book draw from three related bodies of scholarship. The first is in the area of imperial relations, especially colonial discourse analysis. Edward Said's work of literary criticism, *Culture and Imperialism*, marked a shift from the traditional studies of imperialism and colonization (i.e., the gun-boat diplomacy school) to consideration of cultural perceptions of empire.[32] Said argues that discursive strategies adopted by cultural elites in the nineteenth century – later reinforced by European academics – have been integral in shaping perceptions of empire. Texts describing imperial settings and life modes, often written with little knowledge of the subjects under consideration, have served to reinforce the economic and political imperatives of empire. Said's interpretation of the culture of imperialism offers insight into a reading of missionary texts to reflect the shaping of evangelism by imperialism. Flags and paraphernalia for Christian celebrations were not incidental to the mission experience but communicated and represented European culture. Such aspects of the mission experience undoubtedly reflected the British empire. Missionaries frequently linked their religious mission and work for the empire. The women repeatedly declared that they were working in the farthest northern outposts of the British empire. In 1933, for example, Canadian-born Mildred McCabe described her nursing experiences in what she called the "most northerly hospital in the British Empire."[33] The women learned the language of imperialism before they went to the north and they used it often to describe and identify places and experiences in the mission field. Placing Anglican missions within an imperial context supports an understanding of missionaries' perceptions of the north as an imperial frontier. However, this analysis alone, like some of Said's conclusions, does not provide the full insight into the complexities of the mission experience, as it risks leaving an impression of static representations that do not consider the shifting boundaries of human relations.

The importance of local context and the potential ambiguities in colonial relationships are reflected in Homi Bhabha's work.[34] Bhabha's method of focusing on the contact zone itself provides a way to go beyond the colonized/colonizer dichotomy. Analyzing the specific sites and spaces of colonization disrupts this binary. Missionary sources can offer an understanding of both the local and the fluid nature of colonization. The missionaries' reliance on Aboriginal knowledge provides a clear example. Winifred Marsh, for instance, relied on a Padlimiut Caribou (Pallirmiut) woman identified as Nellie to prepare warm clothing for her child. Many missionaries relied on Aboriginal peoples to provide clothing, food, travel guidance, translation, and health care. Such instances demonstrate the complexity of human relations that goes beyond imperial hegemony and reinforces the ambiguity of colonial relations, and the nature of cultural hybridity. While Bhabha and Said have changed perceptions of the history of colonization, ironically neither pays much attention to the roles of women.[35]

The second field of scholarship on which this book draws is the growing area of gender and imperialism. Like others in this genre, the focus on women provides a corrective to the assumption that the northern mission frontier was dominated by men. Within popular culture, the north was a male frontier and mission boards built on this culture when recruiting men for the north, often overlooking the presence of a large number of missionary women. Scholars have recently started to reassess the role of women in the imperial movement, challenging the long-standing assumption that the empire was strictly a men's club where White women were unwelcome. Throughout the 1980s, popular culture has undergone what critic Vron Ware calls a "reconstruction of historical memory" in visual representations of women and empire.[36] Studies on women's roles in imperialism have undergone a substantial growth over the past few years. Nupur Chaudhuri and Margaret Strobel argue that, until recently, most research has "consciously or unconsciously [accepted the] 'masculine' attributes of colonialism [and has] simply excluded or marginalized European women from the focus of their studies."[37] Historians, as much as the imperialists they study, have largely overlooked the role of women in the imperial process.

Presenting women's imperial work disturbs conventional liberal assumptions about women's positive contributions and a global sisterly womanhood. In fact, it opens new questions about race, class, and power relations. Anne McClintock's view is that White women imperialists were in positions of power over both colonized men and women: "As such, White women were not the hapless onlookers of empire but were ambiguously complicit both as colonizers and colonized, privileged and restricted, acted upon and acting."[38] Vron Ware asks whether "Kipling's White Man could exist without White Woman somewhere at his side"? Ware argues that "gender played a crucial role in organizing ideas of 'race' and 'civilization' [in which] women were involved in many different ways in the expansion and maintenance of the Empire."[39] Given the complex relationship between race, gender, and empire, how should White women's roles in imperialism be approached? Are we, as Antoinette Burton has suggested, to indict them because "they collaborated in the ideological work of empire" and say that they have handed on to Euro-Canadian feminists and historians a legacy of colonization and destruction?[40] Or should Ware's caution prompt historians to seek neither to create new heroines nor to "bring white women to account for past misdeeds" but, rather, to determine their roles in gender and race relations in their new settings?[41] Recent literature on such women's organizations as the Canadian Imperial Order of the Daughters of Empire and the British-based Girls Friendly Societies demonstrates the deep influence of imperial ideas on women's individual and group identities. Julia Bush maintains that thousands of Edwardian women "answered the call," with their involvement in "the Primrose League, the British Woman's Emigration Association, and the Victoria League as the leading imperialist organizations that provided ladies with a platform and a proving ground for the powers of womanly imperialism."[42] Missionaries were integral to the imperial movement, although their primary goals were not necessarily colonization. Yet their views were often similar to those of other White women in colonial contexts.

Taking my lead from Vron Ware, I too wish to avoid the glorification of the experiences of these Anglican missionary women. They were neither "women worthies" nor heroines, despite contemporary references to them as such. My purpose is not to glorify their lives nor to reinscribe their perceptions, but to reflect on the meaning of their work and the significance of their relations with Aboriginal peoples. Taken collectively, their responses to women's places within the patriarchal structure of the Anglican church, and to Aboriginal cultures and lifeways, gender relations in the mission field, travel, motherhood identities, and religion add considerably to previous knowledge of the contested and dynamic process of colonization in Canada's north.

The third area of historical inquiry addressed here is that of women and religion. In Canada, and internationally, a number of historians have focused on questions concerning religious women and most agree that they achieved a certain amount of freedom through their work in religious institutions. One of the first full-length studies in Canadian women's history to address the question of women's roles in an institutionalized Christian context was Marta Danylewycz's 1987 work, entitled *Taking the Veil: An Alternative to Marriage, Motherhood, and Spinsterhood in Quebec, 1840–1920*. Danylewycz argues that women who entered Québec's convents between 1840 and 1920 were surprisingly able to secure a good deal of independence, power, and respect. Danylewycz concludes her book by saying that: "Under the protection of their vocations, women pursued life-long careers, wielded power, and on occasion entered the public sphere."[43] Danylewycz challenged the myth that women in Québec society were forced to enter convents because they were unable to find marriage partners and, on entering, were rendered obsolete and powerless.

Similar challenges have been issued about English Protestant women who pursued foreign mission work. Ruth Compton Brouwer and Rosemary Gagan have undertaken the most substantial work on Canadian Presbyterian and Methodist women missionaries. Brouwer argues that women's mission work became acceptable to Canadian society because it was assumed that it would not radically alter commonly held perceptions of womanhood.[44] The rhetoric of separate spheres still existed but, ironically, a large number of women were asserting themselves in the mission field and assuming careers that did significantly change women's roles. While gatekeepers of the status quo moralized about women's roles, many "new women" were transgressing social expectations. Gagan draws similar conclusions in her treatment of Canadian Methodist women missionaries at home and in Asia, arguing that the women who had the courage to join the Woman's Missionary Society often found that they gained more in terms of self-fulfilment than they gave to the mission work. Gagan reports their experience as generally positive, as the leap from middle-class comfort to mission work, while potentially risky, was usually rewarding. This was true for all except the few women Gagan examines who stayed in Canada to work in northern British Columbia's Port Simpson (Lax Kw'alaams) mission station: "Many women stationed among the Indians quickly became disenchanted with their chosen vocation. They hated living and working in semi-isolation among the native-people; they excoriated native culture and dismissed native religion as paganism. In short, the degree of personal adaptation and privation required for Indian mission work seems to have been more acute than for missionaries in Japan and China."[45]

Historians of women and religion seem to agree that religious work, whether voluntary or paid, provided opportunities for women to advance themselves and exert a limited degree of power. Under the auspices of the various churches in Canada, they could step beyond the Victorian boundaries of constrained womanhood. Evidence ranges from the Salvation Army's Hallelujah Lasses preaching in the streets to Catholic Sisters taking courses in engineering. It is important to acknowledge, however, that not all historians agree. Patricia Grimshaw's account of American wives of missionaries in nineteenth-century Hawaii questions the idea of mission work as emancipating.[46] Grimshaw finds that the mission field was anything but liberating for the mission wives in her study. According to her findings, missionary wives were so preoccupied with domestic tasks they had no time to participate in the public aspects of mission work, and many felt isolated, frustrated, and unhappy in their new circumstances.

To date, very little has been written on missionary women who either came to or stayed in Canada, and even less has been said about Anglican women. Only recently have historians turned to questions concerning women's roles within the Anglican Church. Wendy Fletcher-Marsh and Brian Heeney, for instance, place women's church work within the context of separation and subordination.[47] In Britain and Canada, women progressively took on more responsibility and demanded more recognition for their work but were often left outside of the official power structure. This was especially evident for women who worked at the home base of the mission societies. In the field, however, gender boundaries were tested and challenged, certainly by the women in this book.

Ambiguities in Euro-Canadian attitudes can be seen in each analytical category from race, gender, and landscape to motherhood and religion. Chapter 1 chronicles how the Anglican Church responded to feminization and how missionary women struggled to overcome their subordination as women. Working within a context of separation and subordination, women nonetheless carved out an area in which they could expand their roles in the church and subsequently in the mission field. The rhetoric of subordination was most often in contrast to women's actual experience.

In Chapter 2, I argue that racial boundaries, which began for many missionaries as formidable barriers to cultural understanding, gradually became eroded through the experience of living in the north. Missionaries were usually aware before they went into the field of the language used to describe racial differences and frequently relied on it to express their own experiences. Within their correspondence, however, are clear signs of ambiguity. While they may speak of their revulsion toward their new circumstances, they might reveal shortly after that they enjoy close relations with Aboriginal peoples. The process of writing about their experiences itself defined categories of difference between missionaries and Aboriginal peoples, and simultaneously reinforced a new awareness of the connection.

The third chapter argues that the mission field, conceived by the patriarchal church as a masculine frontier, offered some opportunity for the liberation of women. Neither images of masculine Christianity nor those of Victorian femininity proved useful as metaphors for understanding how women and men related to one another in the mission field of northern Canada. Rather, gender boundaries shifted. Men had to perform domestic tasks or act as nurturers, and women frequently had to adopt masculine practices to cope with the demands of their environment. Women sledded, canoed, or rode on horseback to travel long distances, sometimes alone; some shot and skinned animals, did carpentry work, carried water, cared for children, taught school, nursed, and held Sunday services. The mission field occasionally provided both a physically freeing and fluid space for experience and empowerment. Placed within the context of a higher calling, both women and men transcended gender boundaries. Women, in particular, led lives that would have been unusual in southern Canada or in Britain. Even when they left the north, missionaries demonstrated their new skills by communicating their experiences to Anglican audiences.

Preconceived ideas about Aboriginal cultures were often imposed onto northern landscapes, areas thought to be empty and wild before the missionaries travelled through them. Efforts to reconstitute physical and social space, considered in Chapter 4, involved transplanting familiar material objects and symbols. These objects gave women a connection with their past and, just as importantly, allowed them to communicate European culture to Aboriginal peoples. Women's relationships with the land, whether based on a spiritual interpretation of the landscape or on comparisons to British countrysides, were contrasted with the necessity of developing an appreciation for how Aboriginal peoples interacted with the land, particularly to procure food and clothing. Living in the north – becoming northerners – became an important part of the identity of missionary women, while many maintained an identity as an outsider, a southerner, a person from civilization.

The desire to create familiar settings alongside northern identities paralleled efforts women missionaries made to cast themselves as benevolently superior to Aboriginal women in motherhood roles, the subject of Chapter 5. Images of motherhood were ubiquitous in the nineteenth-century feminist movement; in the mission field, this identity took on interesting meanings. The motherhood identity provided missionary women with the freedom to expand their work in the north. It also projected missionary women as strong, brave, and, most importantly, kind and nurturing. This identity had several ironic meanings, as within the church, women were rhetorically described as mothers while they were expanding their roles as ministers well before women were ordained. Many of the women who took on the identity, ironically, were not mothers themselves: some undoubtedly chose their careers to escape from traditional gender roles.

Religious mission, like gender and racial preconceptions, could also be redefined in the field. The final chapter demonstrates how initial strategies were reshaped by local conditions and local cultures. Conversion did not always mean what missionaries anticipated, as practices and interpretations rested with Aboriginal peoples. Conversion had many meanings and was never straightforward, as, despite the wishes of missionaries, Aboriginal peoples continued to practise their spiritual traditions. The continuation of the potlatch and medicine making – two traditions frequently condemned by missionaries – is a clear example of the resilience of Aboriginal cultures in the north. It is argued here that Aboriginal peoples were active agents in their choice to adopt Christianity. The theme of Aboriginal agency has been central to the development of the historiography of relations between Aboriginal peoples and newcomers over the past twenty years.[48] The concept of having Christian Aboriginal converts minister to their own people is certainly important to understanding the relationship between religious missions and Aboriginal communities. So too is it important to recognize that some Aboriginal peoples saw missionaries as potential middlemen between themselves and government agencies. Clarence Bolt's biography of Thomas Crosby, a Methodist missionary to the Tsimshian between 1874 and 1897, demonstrates that Crosby was expected by local people to represent their views with respect to land claims. When the Tsimshian land dispute was ignored by Ottawa they slowly dropped away from the mission and Crosby eventually left Port Simpson.[49]

In a similar way, Kenneth Coates argues that, in the Yukon, Anglican missionaries acted as middlemen between Aboriginal and government agencies: "the few protections the Natives of the Yukon did enjoy, in the form of land and harvesting rights, medical care, relief programs, and education were extracted from a reluctant government by the active and committed missionaries of the Anglican church."[50] Though this admission tends to shift the balance of power away from Aboriginal peoples, some Aboriginal leaders apparently saw missionaries as potential mediators between themselves and far-off governments, at least when it came to issues that fell more and more under state control. Although this argument portrays Aboriginal peoples as active agents within a changing cultural context, it also implies that they needed the help of others to cope with the new order. The idea that missionaries could mitigate the enormous problems caused by European settlement has prompted rethinking about Aboriginal agency – not to challenge it but to decentre its Eurocentric location. Aboriginal peoples had coped with various environmental and human stresses and changes before the arrival of Europeans. This is not to imply that White settlement did not cause severe disruption. But, as Bolt reminds us, we must not assume that Indigenous cultures were ineffectual in coping with change or willing to look to Europeans to solve problems that Europeans themselves introduced. As John Webster Grant and Kerry Abel have demonstrated, Aboriginal peoples often took from Christianity only what they chose. Religion was a syncretic interface where traditional practices and beliefs were often incorporated, if not fully retained, depending on many factors.

Syncretism is central to this book. Missionaries did not always understand that two originally different systems of belief could be blended. Most argued instead that more work had to be done to eradicate all vestiges of the past. They held strongly to their assumptions and resisted Aboriginal tendencies to blend Christianity with their spirituality. Impatience with the slowness of conversion was tempered with a feeling that success was inevitable in the long run and that faith, above all, had to be maintained. Despite their resistance to blending, over time, missionary assumptions changed. With contact and familiarity, missionaries began to view syncretism differently. After the Second World War, the first steps were taken toward accommodating Aboriginal culture within the church. In the 1950s, the Anglican Church permitted priests to incorporate traditional dress and to display Aboriginal art in their churches. This accommodation is symbolic of the stubborn persistence of cultural barriers.

From the Inuit women in Pangnirtung who used the woman's auxiliary to carry on their traditions of social interaction and craft production to the enthusiastic revivalism of the Church Army, cultural hybridity and syncretism were evident. Indeed it is this hybridity that lends complexity to the mission experience.

Anglican Church at Metlakatla, British Columbia.

# Women and the White Man's God

# 1
# Breaking Down the Barriers: Gender and the Anglican Church at Home

The Reverend James B. McCullagh saw mission work primarily as men's work. Originally from Newry, Ireland, McCullagh went in 1883 as a missionary to the Nass River (K'alii Aksim Lisims) valley in British Columbia, in the Diocese of Caledonia. In 1915, while McCullagh was on furlough in England and engaged in promotional work, he declared his preference for missionary meetings for men far more than drawing-room meetings for ladies:

> Personally, I love men; I love to see men at missionary meetings, particularly business men. It interests me to interest them, and show them that missionary work is a man's work. In some places special efforts are made to get men together. With the greatest success, which goes to prove that men can be interested, and are ready to respond, if approached in the "man" way.[1]

The Reverend McCullagh felt that drawing room meetings with leading ladies of various parishes were effective and "beautifully English," yet he most enjoyed talking to men about his work. Though a number of messages were suggested here, the most apparent from the perspective of gender issues was that missionaries were men in a men's world. The ideal missionary was conceived of as a male who could endure discomforts bravely for the sake of his work. Yet, according to the Anglican *Church Missionary Intelligencer*, women outnumbered men in the mission field: "The latest statistics of all Protestant Missionary Societies, British, Continental, American &c., give no less than 2576 unmarried women missionaries. The male missionaries are given as 5233, and as these have 3641 wives, the total number of women, married and unmarried, exceeds that of men by just a thousand."[2] Eugene Stock, the Church Missionary Society Secretary and official historian, claimed that in 1899 the Church Missionary Society staff in northern British Columbia comprised "nine clergyman, three laymen, nine wives, and eight other women, total 29."[3] Missionary work was nonetheless thought of as men's work.

This misconception seemed to be reinforced in popular and church literature. In 1904, Norman Tucker, first General Secretary of the Missionary Society for the Church of England in Canada, suggested that, since it was becoming more difficult to find new male recruits for the north, women be sent: "Owing to the great lack of men for the ministry and the unlimited field for workers in the territories and western provinces, it is necessary that trained, efficient, God fearing women should stand in the gap."[4] Tucker typically overlooked the fact that women had been working in the north for years. In fact, especially after the turn-of-the-century, most Anglican missionaries in the north were women.

Masculinity, empire, and religion were intricately linked and outwardly manifest in the origins and early practices of the Church Missionary Society. The views of the founding fathers of the Church Missionary Society resonated throughout the nineteenth century and were important in shaping the nature of mission work in northern Canada. In their efforts to raise mission funds, encourage new recruits, or form church policy, the Church Missionary Society administrators and the missionaries themselves frequently emphasized the manliness of their work, much more than other contemporary Protestant mission societies based in Canada or the United States. The Church Missionary Society itself was created at a time when notions of masculine identity and religious practicality were being contested. So too was women's status within the church.

In its original discussions and organizational meetings, the Church Missionary Society did not include women. The organizers could not imagine, or chose to ignore the fact, that women too would want to go overseas to work as religious missionaries. Inevitably, though, the Church Missionary Society would have to come to terms with this oversight. Throughout the nineteenth century, determined women continually pressed for women's participation, insisting that they be given the opportunity to pursue mission work. By the 1880s, the Church Missionary Society could no longer resist their demands. In fact, the irony is that, while women's status within the Anglican church was continually being redefined and contested, it was women who supported and maintained missions through their volunteer efforts within home mission societies and later through their work in the mission field.

## The Church Missionary Society, Masculinity, and Empire
The central question addressed by a select group of men on 18 March 1799, in a meeting of London's Eclectic Society, was: "What methods can we use more effectually to promote the knowledge of the gospel among the Heathen?"[5] Participants in the meeting were Josiah Pratt, John Venn,

W. Goode, Charles Simeon, Thomas Scott, and a handful of other evangelical Anglicans, many of whom were members of the Clapham Sect.[6] The Eclectic Society, which consisted of clergy and laymen, had been holding regular meetings since 1783 in the vestry of St. John's Chapel, Bedford Row. They sought to explore the aims of evangelism, propose projects to spread Christianity, and establish philanthropic bodies. One of their prime concerns was missionary work. Over the years, ways to "enlarge the place of thy tent," or spread Christ's message to the heathen beyond England had often been considered.[7] The Eclectic Society supported the formation of the Baptist Missionary Society in 1792 and the nondenominational London Missionary Society in 1795. Two Anglican missionary societies active before the late eighteenth-century – The Society For The Propagation of the Gospel (SPG) and The Society For The Promotion of Christian Knowledge (SPCK) – were seen by the Eclectic Society as too closely tied to the "high" church. From the perspective of the evangelicals, the "established" church was not properly represented in the mission field. Following considerable planning and preparation, the public was invited to a meeting on 12 April 1799 to witness the formation of the Church Missionary Society.

At the heart of the philosophy of this society was the idea that the mission must represent "the Church – principle, not the high-Church principle."[8] The fact that John Venn distinguished between high and low church was crucial to the establishment of the society and later to the endurance of the Church Missionary Society in Canada. The founders thought it quite acceptable for evangelicals with similar goals to work outside conventional Anglican structures. One of the central principles of the Church Missionary Society was that missionaries did not have to be ordained, something the SPG and SPCK for the most part could not accept. In fact, Simeon was in such a hurry to get the society off the ground that he said it was "hopeless to wait for missionaries, send out catechists." Again, this reflected the evangelical desire for what William Wilberforce described as "real religion."[9] The evangelicals wanted a different kind of Anglican Church, one which was more in touch with its parishioners.

The establishment of the Church Missionary Society took place during the struggle in the Anglican Church between high Churchmen and evangelicals, and in an atmosphere that was critical of status and prestige. The evangelical movement itself was part of the eighteenth-century revival associated with Methodism.[10] At the parish level, according to historians Leonore Davidoff and Catherine Hall, the Anglican evangelicals called for more active and visible clergy as opposed to the traditional "scholarly cleric immersed in esoteric theological debates."[11] In his comprehensive study of the evangelical movement, D.W. Bebbington presents a similar view of the parish clergy: "The hunting, shooting and fishing parson was a common type. It was the evangelical movement that prompted the clergy to greater diligence especially in cottage visiting."[12] Evangelicals disrupted conventional patterns of exclusive behaviour and moved religious worship outside of customary structures.

Evangelicals perceived themselves as active proselytizing clergy and not members of the gentry. Most evangelical clergy believed in the importance of individual conversion, the need to spread the gospel, the centrality of the Bible, and the importance of Christ's sacrifice. Evangelicals such as the Church Missionary Society founders Henry Venn and his son John, as well as Charles Simeon, believed not only in justification by faith but that grace be properly manifested in public religious works and not restricted to the physical trappings and traditions of the Anglican Church. Practical Christianity and self-reflection were emphasized over questions of doctrine.

Mission work in Britain and throughout the British empire was inextricably linked to the late eighteenth-century evangelical revival. In typical evangelical discourse, the eminent writer Hannah More claimed at the dawn of the nineteenth century that "action is the life of virtue and the world is the theatre of action."[13] The world, or at least the British colonies, were rapidly becoming theatres of action for missionaries. The Church Missionary Society founders did not wonder how the missionaries would be received in these imagined heathen lands or the world theatre. They did not – and could not be expected to – doubt the wisdom of the mission movement. Nor did they discuss the place of women, who were also absent from their organizational meetings and their plans. The Church Missionary Society was created by men who did not question England's imperial endeavours, who wished to reshape Anglicanism to include a more practical approach, and who felt that men were entitled to spread the gospel while women were not.

Anxieties over masculinity were especially apparent in the discourse surrounding the growth of evangelism. If the shooting, hunting parson was an object of criticism for evangelicals, then what model of masculinity would replace him? As Davidoff and Hall show, the evangelical clergyman "risked his masculine identity" by emphasizing action, emotion, and sensitivity. Public displays of weeping, singing, and praying drew criticism from high church Anglicans. This tension was resolved by the midnineteenth century when emotionalism as an expression of religious conversion began to decline and was replaced by a new emphasis on control as a manly virtue. Graham Dawson argues with respect to India that Christian, and specifically evangelical approaches to empire, became especially popular in the early nineteenth century: "A moral critique of the old imperialism expounded against its characteristic forms of masculinity: the Empire had attracted 'the wrong kind of Englishmen and brought out the wrong tendencies in them.' Training for the [East India] Company service began to propound the virtues of a new kind of 'Christian English-man' – a righteous, energetic reformer who would be dedicated to the establishment of a virtuous and rational Raj."[14] One aspect of the late eighteenth-century evangelical manhood that did not disappear was a focus on work and action. Work was elevated and God's work was especially distinguished.

The distinctive features that marked the founding principles of the Church Missionary Society were evident in northern Canada. An evangel-ical background was important, especially in the north where optimism, adaptability, enthusiasm for visiting, and itinerant outreach were crucial characteristics for the success of individual missionaries. These principles were well exemplified in two early missionaries sent from England to the north in the nineteenth century, William Duncan and the Reverend William C. Bompas. Both appeared to be suitable candidates to represent the evangelical beliefs of the Church Missionary Society. And both found scope in their new mission fields to interpret and shape evangelism. They were attracted to what Bebbington called the "empire of philanthropy" offered by the nineteenth-century marriage of evangelism and world mis-sion and, like many others, they were captured by the endless appeals heard in English churches in the 1850s and 1860s to join the mission movement.

A strange twist of fate was responsible for the arrival to the Yukon territory of the Reverend William Bompas.[15] Anglican Christianizing of Aboriginal peoples in the Yukon through missions had begun under the guidance of Bishop David Anderson, the first Church Missionary Society bishop. Under Bishop Anderson's instructions, the Reverend W.W. Kirkby was sent from Red River to Fort Yukon in 1861 to become the first Angli-can missionary to contact the Gwich'in Dene. Although he only stayed a week, the Church Missionary Society reported that Kirkby had "prepared the way for a missionary who was about to appear on the scene, settle down and establish a mission among these Indians."[16] The Reverend Robert McDonald, described by the Church Missionary Society's official historian as an accomplished "country-born missionary trained at Bishop Anderson's collegiate school at Red River" settled at Fort Yukon in 1862.[17] Indirectly, McDonald's ill health – or at least the report of it – was respon-sible for the Reverend Bompas's arrival.

Born into an evangelical London Baptist family, William Bompas con-verted to Anglicanism as a young man and served as a lay worker in a working-class parish in his home city. He was an avid supporter of the Church Missionary Society and felt comfortable with its evangelical prin-ciples. Bompas volunteered for mission work after hearing a sermon in London's St. Bride's Church in 1865, given by Bishop Anderson, who had just retired to England. He read an appeal from McDonald, whom Bishop Anderson feared was about to succumb to an illness, with pleas that someone "come forward to take up the standard of the Lord as it drops in his hands." The Reverend Bompas left almost immediately for the Yukon, arriving on Christmas Day 1865 to find McDonald much recovered.[18] As historian Kerry Abel has argued, the Reverend Bompas "was determinedly idealistic about the promise of salvation through the realization of sin and the acceptance of true faith. He felt church rituals such as crosses, candles, incense, and processions were insults to God."[19] Exceedingly evangelical, the Reverend Bompas wanted nothing to do with high church trappings. He stayed in the north for forty-one years, serving first as a missionary and later as a bishop, first of the Diocese of Athabasca, then in the Diocese of Mackenzie (Deh Cho) River, and finally in the Diocese of Selkirk.

Nearly a decade before the arrival of Reverend Bompas, a mission was established by William Duncan for the Church Missionary Society on the northern coast of British Columbia. Like the Reverend Bompas, Duncan was swept up in the missionary movement in its golden age. Many Sunday services during the mid-nineteenth century featured guest missionaries on furlough who came to speak to congregations about the benefits of mission work. According to his biographer, Duncan was attracted to the Church Missionary Society in the "golden years of missionary fervour. Livingstone's exploits in Africa had captured the public imagination and created publicity for the whole movement. The glamour and excitement surrounding missionary work exerted a strong pull on the troubled young man."[20] Duncan was certainly troubled. He was embarrassed by his working-class background and ashamed to be labelled illegitimate. At twenty-one, Duncan heard an appeal from a clergyman from York, who was at the Beverly Minster promoting the Church Missionary Society. Duncan applied and was sent to the society's Highbury College in London, England. Two years later he was recommended by the society for a posting at Port Simpson (Lax Kw'alaams).[21] Both Duncan and the Reverend Bompas had strong evangelical beliefs, were attracted to the work by Church Missionary Society recruiters, and would ultimately contribute to the mission field as a masculine endeavour.

Male missionaries from Britain generally trained at Highbury College or Islington College in London, which attracted men without university education. Historian John Webster Grant claims the Islington men were "tough if uncultivated graduates."[22] Many of the Canadian male missionaries who went into the northern field trained at Wycliffe College in Toronto. In describing the type of men Wycliffe hoped to recruit, principal T.R. O'Meara claimed as late as 1927 that they wanted masculine spirited men: "We must have good men. The future students in preparation for the sacred work of ministry must be physically sound, manly and virile. The time is long past when the weakling of the family can be set aside for the work of the church."[23] The masculinity that took root in the north was a curious amalgam of the premodern and modern, in which the masculine outdoorsman combined with the evangelical visiting clergy who attempted to reach out to convert as many people as possible. Ironically, while many of the male missionaries were from the lower middle class, they portrayed the image of the "squire parson" in their self-reflective correspondence, as though in their transplantation from Britain or southern Canada, they had risen in social status.

There were many models for this type of manhood, found especially in popular boys' literature from the mid-Victorian era through to the early twentieth century. According to historian Patrick A. Dunae, boys' literature "reflected the missionary zeal and the pragmatic materialism associated with empire during the last decades of the nineteenth century."[24] The middle- and upper-class discourse of empire and masculinity employed such terms as "virile," "manly," "muscular," and "forceful" to convey such assertions. *Tom Brown's School Days*, a mid-Victorian novel written by Thomas Hughes, personified this tradition with special poignancy. Tom Brown was exemplified as an example of a new type of masculinity: muscular Christianity. A contemporary of Hughes described Brown as "a thoroughly English boy. Full of kindness, courage, vigour and fun – no great adept at Greek and Latin, but a first rate cricketer, climber and swimmer, fearless and skillful at football and by no means adverse to a good fight in a good cause ... [his] piety is of that manly order, that not even an ordinary schoolboy of the present day will find himself wearied of it."[25] Brown became a symbol of the muscular Christian: physically strong, able to protect the weak, ready to fight for a good cause, and, above all, responsible to God. Historian J.A. Mangan describes Brown as a blend of piety and machismo.[26] The idea of muscular Christianity was popularized through such writers as Hughes. Another mid-Victorian writer, Charles Kingsley, preferred to call this combination of manliness and Christian responsibility "Christian manliness."

Historians John Mackenzie and Allen Warren have considered the related emergence of the Boy Scout movement and place it firmly within the context of popular manliness and the formation of many of Britain's imperial masculine images. Lord Baden-Powell's manifesto, *Scouting for Boys*, encapsulated many representations of young men drawn from popular images of the period. Scouts were ultimately frontiersmen whom Baden-Powell claimed were found all over the empire: "The 'trappers' of North America, hunters of Central Africa, the British pioneers, explorers, and missionaries over Asia and all the wild parts of the world, the bushmen and drovers of Australia, the constabulary of North-West Canada and of South Africa – all are peace scouts, real men in every sense of the word."[27] The so-called peace scouts were strong and plucky, adept in the wilderness and, according to Baden-Powell, prepared to sacrifice themselves for the sake of their mother country.[28] Masculine representations of missionaries as much as trappers, hunters, and explorers followed noticeably similar lines. Masculine Christianity and the sporting sense of recreation found in the scouts fused to produce an image of masculinity associated with empire. Missionaries were considered an integral part of this masculine culture. Bishop Du Vernet of Caledonia asserted that he knew exactly the type of men needed for his diocese: "they must be men of the right kind. Men who are willing to tramp the trail in advance of the train. Men who can find a joy in carrying the Gospel to the lonely settler. Men who with simple reverence can lead in the worship of God a congregation of ten in a neighbor's shack. Men who count it a privilege to be pioneers for Christ and His Church."[29] In fact, a remarkable amount of the missionary recruiting literature of the nineteenth and early twentieth centuries produced by the Anglican Church used this masculine rhetoric to appeal for male missionaries.

Similarities between male missionary correspondence and memoirs, and the texts of late nineteenth-century adventure writers are striking. The language of masculine adventure was evident in the writing of two Caledonia-based missionaries, each of whom served in northern British Columbia for over twenty years. Bishop William Ridley's book, *Snapshots from the North Pacific*, and Archdeacon William Henry Collison's evocatively entitled work, *In the Wake of the War Canoe*, epitomize masculine Christianity in their mission work. Bold undertakings involved long canoe trips, with risky portages and harrowing weather conditions. Strength and endurance were exhibited by hunting or building log houses, churches, and schools. Organizing crews for extended travel required manful leadership.

In 1876 the Reverend Collison set out from Metlakatla to the Queen Charlotte Islands (Haida Gwaii). In his account, Collison invoked images mindful of Haggard or Henty, recalling an arduous journey, involving large squalls that "nearly tore our sail to pieces." "Off Rose Spit," continued Collison, "a large sea lion harassed us by following the canoe, and coming up and down now on one side and again on the other. My crew feared it might upset us, and although we were sailing very fast, we could not outdistance it. So, acting on their advice, I seized my rifle, and as it again emerged very close to the canoe, shot it through the head."[30] Similarly, the Reverend William Ridley, first Bishop of Caledonia, who arrived at Metlakatla in 1879, described a trip up the Skeena River (Sginn) in a steamer that entered a treacherous stretch of water: "the swiftness is a difficulty rather than a peril. Not so the whirls and cross currents at the confluence of some of the largest tributaries. At these points skill and nerve are summoned to the contest, and exciting it really is."[31] The thrill of battling nature drew from masculine images of adventure.

In the descriptions of their conquest over the whirls and currents, Collison and Ridley employed the masculine rhetoric of the public school and scouting traditions of Victorian and Edwardian men. They appear to be conscious of the links among mission, masculinity, and British identity. In his hopes to attract more men to his diocese, Ridley reflected on this nexus:

Have you found that the "regions beyond" are always an attraction to missionaries? Thirty years ago I chafed behind the frontiers of the Punjab, as if the British side had not difficulties enough! Then the spirit of adventure bred in British bone might have had a large share in this yearning to go forward; but now I am too old to be carried away by that – I had nearly added "that nonsense." It is not nonsense, however, but a national quality God has implanted for set purposes. A worn-out charger puts on war-like airs in his paddock at the bugle's call, and we applaud his quenchless spirit. So I fancy even worn-out missionaries will say in

"Bishop Bompas helping
to work a raft."
A photograph of a
drawing with this title by
John T. Campbell.

their hearts, "Go ahead, boys," as they see in young soldiers of the Cross a desire to break through old lines right and left ...

I want an enterprising but determined bachelor, very self-contained, yet full of the Spirit as the chief qualification. He will want a log-cabin first, and later a larger building for church and School purposes. Within a few weeks he will do as another did when he showed me his hands blistered through using his axe. I could only comfort him saying, if he stuck to it his hands would harden.[32]

The masculinist discourse was not strictly reserved for the "British side." Similar language was employed by Canadians involved in northern mission work. A school history produced to mark Wycliffe College's jubilee celebrated men who had taken up mission work. In this edition, Canon Gould, secretary of the Missionary Society for the Church of England in Canada, recalled when Isaac Stringer and Tom Marsh had been recruited for northern work. Bishop Reeve, a Church Missionary Society missionary originally from Harmston, England, and the second bishop of the Diocese of Mackenzie River, visited Wycliffe in the fall of 1892 and, as Canon Gould described, his meeting with potential recruits was a rousing affair:

On a certain eventful evening, which the writer well remembers, in the month of November, 1892, the Wycliffe students, with 'Ike' Stringer presiding, were addressed by one of the stalwarts, in physical form and missionary spirit, of the Church in Canada, the Right Rev. William Day Reeve, Bishop of the diocese of Mackenzie River. Bishop Reeve presented a plea for two men for service in the far northwest of the Dominion, one to ascend the Liard River from its junction at Fort Simpson with the Mackenzie, and establish there an Indian Boarding School; the other for the evangelization of the Eskimo dwelling in the Mackenzie Delta, westward along the Arctic coast to the border of Alaska, on Herschel Island, and eastward along the same coast to Ballie Islands. The plea was answered, the Chairman of the meeting volunteered for the Eskimo, and husky Tom Marsh, the man that no student could lick in the trial of physical strength, for the Liard River. Thus the Spirit of Missions, whose sources none can determine and whose flow none can control, burst out in fresh forces of life, quickening the zeal, of the whole body of students and inspiring the ever widening constituency of supporters to larger conceptions of the work and to increased liberality for its support.[33]

Bishop Reeve as well as Stringer and Marsh were seen by Gould as hardy representatives of Christianity in the north. Their physical strength and passion for mission work stirred the enthusiasm of other men. In fact, on a visit to the north in 1916, Gould was reminded yet again of Marsh's masculinity: "Of the many and interesting things the General Secretary of the MSCC saw ... none attracted him more than the log house, the first home of the school, which its founder and first principal had hewn out of the forest and erected for the most part, with his own hands."[34] Among men such as Bishop Ridley, who admired a man with blistered hands, Marsh had asserted his masculinity by hewing wood to build a log house.

For the Reverend Isaac Stringer, hunting expressed his masculine identity. In 1893 and 1894 he wrote a series of letters to his fiancée Sarah Alexander outlining his recent activities. On a journey to Rampart House (Jiindé Tsik) from the Peel River mission, he told of his first hunting expedition: "We had some good hunting on the way and I shot my first deer. Had a wild chase after it. The snow was quite deep and at times it was difficult travelling." He boasted that he had become "a regular Husky in nearly everything."[35] In a more colourful narrative and self-representation of the hunter, Stringer offered Alexander the picture of a masculine hero,

Bishop Isaac O. Stringer beside the bear he killed en route to Forty Mile (Ch'ëdäh Dëk) in a rowboat.

just home from the hunt: "Deer hunt shot one. But wasn't I lionized after the hunt. You ought to have seen how the people came out and expressed their admiration as I walked home through the village with my portion of that deer on my back. They were pleased at my success and I think it helped me in gaining an influence over them."[36] Stringer thought his display had won him respect among the Inuvialuit, hoping that masculinity signified by proven success in killing a food animal could be influential. While it might be argued that Stringer's hunting experiences were necessary for his basic survival, the language of lionization also suggests a certain power gained through his hunting conquest.

The Church Missionary Society and the Canadian missionary society appealed frequently to masculinity to attract recruits. And these images of missionary men continued to be reinforced by those already in the field. Whether shooting rapids or being heralded as great hunters, male missionaries appeared in their correspondence to revel in the glories of the outdoor life of masculine Christianity. John Webster Grant observes: "Protestants were more inclined to think of hardships as obstacles to be overcome in the athletic spirit of British Christianity."[37] Found in private letters, autobiographies, and public mission newspapers, the strength and persistence of images of the virile masculine missionary provide a recurrent motif. These constructions offer a significant background to the experiences of women missionaries who operated in the same institutional structures and physical surroundings.

### Women in the Church Missionary Society
Given the juxtaposition of masculinity with mission work, it should come as no surprise that the Church Missionary Society was resolute in its opposition to sponsoring women missionaries. Nevertheless, during the nineteenth century, hundreds of single women in Britain asked to be sent abroad as missionaries. Frequently women with an interest in mission work married missionaries so that they could pursue their own goals. The society insisted that, if a woman was to partake in mission work, she had to marry a male missionary or go into the field with a close relative, usually a brother or a son. This rule guaranteed that women would stay within the family. In 1864, a number of letters from women were heard by the Church Missionary Society candidate's committee, which remained convinced that its duty did not include promotion of women's mission work.[38] Yet, an emerging consensus among missionaries was that women were needed, for, as one observer put it: "only women missionaries can gain entrance to the Zenanas of India, where millions of purdah women spend their lives."[39] Until the 1880s, the Church Missionary Society would not be persuaded by this argument, believing instead that the Zenana work was being adequately carried out by other mission societies.

According to Brian Heeney, during the first half of the nineteenth century most Anglicans believed that women were subordinate and should remain within the private sphere: "Victorian Anglican defenders of subordination found a powerful biblical base for their view of women."[40] This context of subordination was largely responsible for the fact that women were refused the opportunity to pursue mission work.

Maternal feminism, however, with its emphasis on the moral and ethical superiority of women and the social need to bring characteristics learned in family life to the public sphere, was a strong and growing force in Victorian society. An especially important aspect of maternal feminism was its relationship to the growing influence of women within Protestant denominations. Barbara Caine's history of Victorian feminism argues that the maternal ideology was both binding and liberating for Victorian women: "Feminists found in early Victorian domestic ideology not only a set of ideas which they had to combat, but also one which helped them to negotiate with liberalism and with the gendered nature of the public sphere."[41] Caine connects evangelism to an extended idea of domesticity, which ultimately provided women with a wider sphere: "From a statement of their limitations women face and their necessary domestic confinement, it thus moves to the demand that women carry first into their homes and then into the wider society something of the religious zeal and fervour which other missionaries were taking to the heathen in the foreign lands."[42] Domesticity and maternalism were not always limiting ideologies for women; rather, they could be used as deliberate strategic identities to extend women's influence.

In this vein, Ann Douglas argues that religion in American society throughout the nineteenth century became increasingly a women's domain, in a process she identifies as the "feminization of religion."[43] As fund raisers, volunteers, and chairs of women's church committees, women were active agents within religious institutions. While ministers recognized and welcomed their participation in parish work, this enthusiasm had its limits: "At the other extreme, in the realm of fact, ministers blocked the practical implementation of those feminine virtues they lauded so energetically in print. Ministers opposed the outright and by definition unholy demands for political equality posed by the women's rights movement, but they also bitterly feared and fought feminine assumption of conspicuously Christian tasks. Clerical hostility was a form of territorial imperative springing from an uneasy sense of a too cramped common space."[44]

While the church was increasingly a place in which women contested their place, a significant feminization of religion was also occurring in Britain during the same period. By the end of the nineteenth century, the male-dominated domain of Sunday school was largely a female preserve.

Women had their own deaconess houses, sisterhoods, mothers' unions, local clubs, and study groups. Women's increased activism within British religious life was connected to the rise of evangelism, which reinforced separate spheres and created opportunities by challenging conventional occupational and religious roles. Although a clear consciousness of the ideology of separate spheres for each gender had emerged, under evangelism women found themselves transcending prescribed roles. Justified in terms of family strategy or religious work, women increasingly entered the public sphere.[45] Yet, only grudgingly and gradually did Victorians accept unmarried women missionaries.

In taking advantage of the marital status of missionary men, the Church Missionary Society, with no conscious plan to do so, consequently paved the way for single women missionaries. An observer noted years later in the *Missionary Herald*, "it is the missionary's wife who, by years of endurance and acquired experience in the foreign field, has made it possible in these later years – the years of the Women's Missionary Societies – for unmarried ladies to go abroad and live and work among the people of Eastern lands."[46] Although the author was likely referring to India, the duties of missionary wives were similar in Canada's north. In an endorsement of the valuable work done by missionary wives, this writer goes on to say: "I never yet saw a missionary's wife whose companionship did not double her husband's usefullness [sic]."[47] Given irrefutable evidence of the usefulness of women in the mission field, by the 1880s, the Church Missionary Society could no longer reject appeals from single women. Other denominations were opening their doors to missionary women and the Church of England had already sanctioned societies under its auspices to send women abroad. Eugene Stock, the Church Missionary Society's official historian, asserts that opening its doors to women was a move which the Church Missionary Society "never formally or designedly entered upon." Instead, it gradually acquiesced to the opportunity women presented. No specific rule laid out this change in policy: the Church Missionary Society was compelled to follow the lead of other mission societies. For this reason the growth of the society was marked by an increased number of women: from 1887 to 1894, some 172 single women joined as missionaries and, by 1898, there were 253 single women on the Church Missionary Society roll.[48]

The Church Missionary Society moved rapidly from the exclusionary position it had held for most of the century to the imposition of high standards for women missionary candidates. Potential missionaries were to exhibit their qualities throughout a rigorous application process. In a speech on women's church work, Georgina A. Gollock, the Lady Secretary of the new Church Missionary Society Women's Department, whose role was to oversee the training of women missionaries, discussed the appropriate credentials for candidates and outlined the recruitment process: "Definitions are rarely satisfactory, but it may be well to state that our minimum standard of acceptance would include evidence of true devotion to Christ and subjection to the Holy Spirit; some experience and earnest purpose in seeking the salvation of souls; clear and intelligent Bible knowledge; distinct and well grounded doctrinal views; loyal attachment to the Church principles dear to us; as well as sound bodily health."[49] The recruits first completed a formal application. If accepted, they took a set of oral interviews with a six-member panel. Each panel generally consisted of three men and three women. Even this process was embedded in preconceived ideas about women's distinct nature. Gollock proudly proclaimed: "the women interviewers naturally deal more with questions of character and temperament, the Clergy with points of Scriptural knowledge, doctrine and Churchmanship, but all seek humbly and in entire dependence upon the Divine spirit to discern the presence or absence of the all-important spiritual qualifications for the work."[50] Future missionaries would then enter a training program at Mildmay or Highbury deaconess house in London.

The deaconess movement, with its origins in Germany, began in England in the 1860s and represented the culmination of three features in Victorian society: the growth of evangelism, the anxiety over so-called redundant women, and a pronounced moral panic over a decline in social conditions.[51] Evangelism was significant to the deaconess movement since it allowed for a public display of religion beyond institutional strictures. On the other hand, women in high church Anglican communities were cloistered. The deaconess movement allowed middle-class evangelical women to filter their energies into respectable religious charitable work and to put into practice the Victorian belief in *noblesse oblige*. Reverend William Pennefather, the founder of the first deaconess house in England claimed that his motivation for opening Mildmay was to provide religious women with equal educational opportunities:

> It seemed strange that, while training institutions and colleges are deemed essential for men who are to be used either as medical missionaries or as preachers of the Gospel, there should not be institutions where women may acquire that knowledge of the bodies and minds of their fellow-creatures which would render them capable of fulfilling their high destiny as help-meets to man.[52]

While the Reverend Pennefather wanted women to have an opportunity to train for religious work, he also believed that they were meant to use their training as subservient "help-meets to men." Yet, Mildmay and other deaconess houses offered evangelical women the chance to become professional full-time church workers, which itself represented a step forward for such women.

Deaconess training lasting between one and two years was meant to enhance skills deemed necessary for local parish work and, later, for the foreign mission field. Courses were offered in Bible study, nursing, cooking and other domestic arts, as well as bookkeeping.[53] Under the auspices of the local clergy, deaconesses in training worked with orphans and "rescued" women and did home visits in East London. Students were to participate in morning prayers and dedicate at least one hour of each day to either meditation or religious study.[54] The Toronto Church of England Deaconess and Missionary Training Home initiated in February 1892 took Mildmay as its model. Sybil Wilson, the first principal, studied at Mildmay and, on her return, published a leaflet to advertise Canada's first deaconess house with a two-year training program.[55] Lectures were offered in church history, Bible study, and the prayer book. Practical work in local parishes would also be undertaken. The goal of the house was to prepare deaconesses for work as home or foreign missionaries:

> The true vocation of a deaconess is to try to lead men and women to Christ, and for his sake to help them in all possible ways. That such trained workers, giving up their whole time, will be an invaluable help to overworked clergymen in town and country, no one can doubt. The committee also hope that many of the deaconesses will become missionaries, both in the Northwest, where such able helpers are sadly needed, and also in foreign fields, where the labourers are so few and the field so large.[56]

Deaconess training was constructed within the framework of Victorian norms about gender. In form, the course curriculum in nursing and domestic arts did not challenge gender hierarchies. Yet, in terms of field practice, the deaconess movement represented a significant step away from the private sphere and into an independent life for many Victorian women.

Deaconesses exercised very little power in the Anglican hierarchy. Although their order began in 1861, official guidelines about their status were not established until the early 1920s. The Lambeth Conference of 1897 sanctioned the order, but failed to give it any formal power within the Church of England. In 1919, a report of women's status in the Church of England claimed that "there is no official recognition of the status and duties of a deaconess in the English Church, nor any one authorized form of ordination."[57] Even the seemingly official category of deaconess, which could have granted a degree of power to women, was ambiguous and subordinated. By the end of the nineteenth century, however, women had broken down the exclusionary barriers imposed by church mission societies.

Mission training was available, although the context of subordination undoubtedly continued to impede full equality of opportunity. In Canada, there was some debate between church women who saw their role as subservient to male clergy and those who wanted to take full credit for their contribution to the Anglican mission enterprise.

### Canadian Women and Anglican Missions

In 1885, Canadian Anglican women began to organize an extensive network of voluntary workers to support missions. The catalyst behind the formation of the national woman's auxiliary was Elizabeth Roberta Tilton. She was influenced by the leading Episcopalians and Anglicans she met during her extensive travels when she toured deaconess houses in London, England, and attended woman's auxiliary meetings in the United States.[58] Tilton felt that Canadian women should organize a similar auxiliary and in April 1885 she and six local Anglican women addressed the board of the Domestic and Foreign Missionary Society at a meeting in Ottawa. Tilton proposed the creation of a national woman's auxiliary. She appealed to the board by stating that from Victoria, British Columbia, to Sydney, Nova Scotia, there were potential talents that could aid in the Lord's work: "And knowing this, we ask, that as the Apostles of old recognized the women of their day as labourers with them, you our beloved Fathers in Christ, may recognize the women of the Church of Canada, and give your hearty and earnest consent that there should be established, in connection with your Board, a Woman's Auxiliary."[59] The board approved the proposal, stating that they welcomed the "co-operation of all our Christian sisters [in] carrying out the noble object of our Missionary society."

The purpose of the organization was to encourage women's work at the parish level and to promote missionary zeal by writing to missionaries and by gathering and sending clothes to mission stations for dispersal among converts. In April 1887, the national woman's auxiliary merged with Toronto's Church Woman's Mission Aid, the first Anglican woman's society, formed in Canada in 1879. At the annual meeting of 1887 the Reverend Dr. Mockridge from Hamilton expressed delight that these two societies were joining together and that women were "gladdening poor missionaries with practical sympathy and substantial help." He admitted that "women's work in the Church had perhaps not been enough considered in times past."[60] His comments mark the beginning of an official recognition of women's participation in Canadian Anglican mission work. But as with women's experience in Britain, the theme of subordination continued to shape the discussion.

Mrs. Harriet Von Iffland, who addressed the Richmond Conference in 1893, was a staunch proponent of the doctrine of woman's auxiliaries as subsidiary to the main work of the church.[61] She issued a warning that women must be thankful to be allowed to participate in the work. Suggesting that women "guard against the innate love of independence" and work closely under the "direction of our Bishops and those spiritual guides who are set over us,"[62] Von Iffland believed there was a place for women in the mission field and claimed pride in women Zenana workers and medical missionaries in India, Japan, and northern Canada. She recognized the need for "women teachers and healers of body and soul," but insisted upon women's continued deference to church leaders.[63] Von Iffland's statements were made to a group of women, some of whom probably still believed that gender hierarchy was part of an ordained or natural order. However, as Von Iffland was making her proclamations, women had already started to carve out independence for themselves in the mission field. And for those women who worked as mission bureaucrats at home, there were also widening spheres of independence and power.

Support for home missions began slowly. In 1894, an article in the woman's auxiliary newsletter, the *Letter Leaflet*, argued that the woman's auxiliary had a moral obligation to support domestic missions. Assuming that charity should begin at home, the author of "The Duty of the Woman's Auxiliary towards Missions in the north-west" was convinced that the woman's auxiliary should make the northwest a "specially chosen field for our Missionary effort."[64] The woman's auxiliary was prompted to support the north earlier by Jane Ridley, in Metlakatla in the Diocese of Caledonia, who asked that the woman's auxiliary consider her diocese when making their pledges: "What I should much like is to be drawn closer to the Church people beyond the mountains, and to feel that we belong to each other. As it is now, England seems nearer to and more necessary to us than other parts of Canada ... Our great difficulty is to obtain funds for the rapidly expanding work. Could we be included in the area assisted in your auxiliary?"[65] Ridley's request may have been provisionally addressed, but it was not until 1904 that the woman's auxiliary began to take an active interest in Caledonia, claiming that until then the diocese had been maintained by the Church Missionary Society or private contributions.[66] By the late 1890s, the woman's auxiliary also started to recruit, train, and send women missionaries, as well as material and financial aid, to the Diocese of the Yukon and the Diocese of Mackenzie River.

Woman's auxiliary workers contributed substantially to mission work in Canada's north. Corresponding secretaries, in consultation with other woman's auxiliary executive members, had a great deal of influence over the distribution of finances and materials. Bishops made constant appeals to the woman's auxiliary, stating their needs and desires, and the woman's auxiliary responded accordingly. Funds were pledged by the parochial branches for specific projects and passed on to the bishop of the chosen diocese. Funds for sponsoring missions were largely collected through local donations and sales of handicrafts and baked goods generally known as "sales of work." As Alan L. Hayes notes, by the 1920s, the woman's auxiliary was an impressive and efficient Anglican Church organization. Not only did their members collect vast amounts of money for mission work, they also sponsored social work in Toronto: "By the 1920s, with women still excluded from the councils of the 'official' Church, the woman's auxiliary became almost a para-church, in which women could plan budgets, identify ministries, develop programs, appoint workers, gather for worship, and publish religious literature."[67] In 1923, it was financing 43 per cent of the church's domestic and foreign mission work, claimed a membership including young children of 75,000 throughout Canada, aided bishops with material support, and paid the salaries of women missionaries.[68] This was comparable to the Methodist Church Woman's Missionary Society which, according to Rosemary Gagan, by 1925, had a membership of 61,049.[69] The woman's auxiliary contribution for mission work in 1923 amounted to $169,000 out of the $406,000 spent by the entire Canadian church on missions.[70]

In November 1923, the woman's auxiliary national treasurer, Mrs. D.B. Donaldson, spoke to the annual meeting of the dominion woman's auxiliary held in the Diocese of Algoma. She pointed to the importance of the work of the woman's auxiliary, noting that its contribution was undervalued by the clergy:

> I have often felt that I should like to suggest to the leaders of our Anglican Theological Colleges that a few lectures on the W.A. and its work would be a helpful addition to the curriculum in those halls of learning. If all the clergy of our Church when taking up parochial work, only understood what the W.A. really was, and what it did, and the work and worry it saved them, they would with one accord rise up and call us blessed – instead of the reverse, as has been known to have been done.[71]

Donaldson cautioned that there must be co-operation and unity between the mission society and the woman's auxiliary; she also suggested that the clergy should be aware and appreciative of the contribution to mission work by the woman's auxiliary. These points mark a considerable change from the more humble approach taken by women like Tilton and Von Iffland in the late nineteenth century. As women's work became more essential to the Anglican Church, women began to demand greater recognition. Home bureaucrats and missionaries alike had to promote their work and make sure that it was recognized.

The mission newspaper of the women's auxiliary, *Letter Leaflet* (later called *The Living Message*) attempted to inspire women to join the Anglican missions. In 1920, for example, an article appeared under the heading "Another Call for Nurses." In this article, the woman's auxiliary candidate's secretary claimed that, while the suffering of the heathen in "Christless lands" was painful to witness: "one need not look ever so far afield, for at our very doors within our own Dominion there is a crying need for the ministrations of strong, Christian nurses." The stated aim was to place a nurse in each of seventeen residential schools. To qualify as mission nurses, women had to be "members of the Anglican communion, preferably but not necessarily between 30 and 40 years of age possessing sound health, adaptability to unusual conditions, capacity for co-operating harmoniously with fellow workers and ability to live contentedly in a small community with little opportunity for social pleasures."[72] The call for nurses concluded with an anonymous poem to remind readers of the needs of those still in spiritual darkness:

Why is it that our souls are not on fire
With zeal to raise our brother higher,
To lift them from their lives of sin and shame,
Of degradation, misery and pain?
Is it because we do not realize
The veil that hides Thy glory from their eyes?
Because we do not see and feel their need
That they for help and comfort vainly plead?
For surely if we knew our hearts would be
Filled with a wealth of sympathy.
And love would not be idle but would move
In constant, zealous ways itself to prove;
For love must always thus itself be proving
And all true work for God is just love moving.[73]

While this poem has a ring of conventional rhetoric, it demonstrates a significant difference in approach to recruiting than was evident with male missionaries. The nurses had to be strong, but the language reflected a concern with the emotional aspects of the work more than with physical strength. There was no discussion here about building log cabins or tipping canoes. Love of God was deemed to be of central importance. That such messages had a distinctive tone, quite different from that found in the muscular Christianity idealized for the male recruits, is indisputable.

Once more in 1924, *The Living Message* summoned women to join in mission work. Again the need to be able to demonstrate a deep love of God was demanded. This time, however, women from a variety of backgrounds were being encouraged by the Anglican Church:

For the girl who has always lived in the quiet precincts of home, there is the vivid and sometimes awful realization of the way in which other less fortunate folk live ... For the business girl there is the initiation into the necessities and manifold duties of a home with its all-absorbing problems of how to preserve fruit, or how long to bake a cake, all of which practical training is taken in the spring term. The nurse, perhaps only recently from the environment of the hospital ward, realizes that there are other angles of life than that of the medical, and that sometimes sick souls are harder to cure than sick bodies. The teacher with a previous knowledge of kindergarten work, or older children, begins to tackle "Mothers" or to learn something of the art of nursing, and to her too comes a broader and bigger vision, while the university girl comes out of her books and applies her accumulated knowledge to practical affairs. The older woman perhaps accustomed to independence and authority, learns to hold her experience back, to learn new ways, and perhaps watch other younger ones blunder – sympathetically. All learn that without the true Christian spirit the keenest brain, the most efficient and untiring worker is of little avail, that every bit of ability must be subordinated to the leading of the Holy Spirit, and that without love it is nothing.[74]

While versatility was valued the language used in this article was crafted to appeal to the gentler side of women's domesticity, rather than a realistic representation of the duties and responsibilities of mission work.

Other than these appeals, the *Letter Leaflet* – and later *The Living Message* – increasingly throughout the 1920s printed stories about women missionaries that were meant to solicit funds and to encourage women to join in the work. Some women were also persuaded to take up mission work by their local clergy. For example, Bessie Quirt, who was raised in a family that operated a lumber business in South River and Orillia, Ontario, was convinced of the value of mission work by her local clergyman, the Reverend J.R.S. Boyd, a former China missionary. She graduated from the North Bay Normal School and taught school for four years before she started courses at the Anglican Women's Training College in 1928. Like others, Quirt had worked in another field before she took her mission training. This was not so unusual, since most unmarried women who entered the mission field were over the age of twenty-five. Teaching or nursing experience were key qualifications.

Others, such as Deaconess Louise Topping, professed always to have been committed to doing God's work. She was raised in the Canada/United States border town of St. Stephen, New Brunswick. Her father was a bookkeeper for a local furniture manufacturer. She recalled her fondest childhood memories as rambling on her maternal grandmother's farm.

When she was at the appropriate age, she started Sunday school, then church, and claimed to be very devoted at a young age. She referred to her early years as a "wonderful Christian foundation [which] had much to do with choosing [my] life's work." After she finished high school, she took a business course and worked as a stenographer with the Canadian National Railway in Moncton for five and a half years. She then applied to the Anglican Church, where she had already served as a Sunday school teacher and president of her local woman's auxiliary. She attended the deaconess house for three years, declaring them to be the happiest years of her life. Like other women, she took theology at Wycliffe, social service courses at the University of Toronto, nursing courses at various Toronto hospitals, and teaching courses at Toronto's Normal School. She worked in the northern mission field mostly as a teacher from 1930 until her marriage in 1943 and, after that, continued to serve the church as a deaconess in Yellowknife.[75]

Significantly, the training and experiences shared by many of the women like Quirt and Topping were carried out within a separate-sphere ideology. Training in business, nursing, and teaching would lead to socially acceptable occupations for women. Of course, during the late nineteenth century, women were challenging professional barriers by entering law and medical schools. But, for the most part, women who wanted to pursue careers in Canada and Britain before 1940 were encouraged to work as teachers, nurses, or stenographers. Nonetheless, women were told that they could blend their previous experience in those fields with mission work.

While the social and educational backgrounds of the women missionaries varied, many trained either as nurses or teachers before they went to northern Canada. Thirty-four of the women were trained nurses. During the 1920s, the number of trained nurses increased and their training was in many cases more substantial and specialized. Others were hired as missionary teachers or, as in the case with missionary wives, were expected to teach. Two women, Susan Mellett and Maria Lucas, had taught in Ragged Schools in Britain, and Adelaide Butler had nine years' experience as a teacher in England before she departed for the Shingle Point (Tapqaq) School. Canadians Kathleen Martin-Cowaret, Mrs. Fry, Blanche Nesbitt, Bessie Quirt, Dorothy Robinson, and Mary Samwell were trained and experienced teachers. Four Canadian women had taken general arts courses at university. Mary Crocker had been a student at Dalhousie and Ruth Hamilton at Trinity; Emily Pontifax Hughes took a post-graduate course in social services after her nursing degree; and Margaret Peck held a bachelor of arts degree from Oxford. Such a well-educated woman as Peck, however, was rare. She was raised in a prominent Montréal family and attended a private girls school before university. According to Archibald Fleming, the first bishop of the Arctic, Peck did not want her colleagues at the school in Aklavik, where she taught in the 1930s, to know her background:

> At Miss Peck's own request no one at Aklavik knew that she was a graduate of Oxford University with honors in history, and came from a well-known family in Montreal. Few knew that only after much intellectual struggle had she attained the Christian position that allowed her to radiate love while performing the ordinary duties of life. Her faith, education, and culture enabled her to interpret to the children, but even more especially to the older girls and younger mothers, what is meant by one's duty to God, and to one's neighbour.[76]

While Peck was unusually well educated for mission work in any area, there were others who were equally well trained for the work. Another college-trained woman who dedicated most of her life to the Anglican Church was Mabel Jones. Born in Toronto in 1895, Jones attended high school at Harbord Street Collegiate and then studied at the deaconess house. On graduation in 1921, she went to Saskatchewan to work with the Reverend Lloyd among recently arrived immigrants. In the late 1920s, she returned to Toronto to take courses at Wycliffe College, where she graduated in 1931 with a Licentiate in Theology, the first woman to receive this degree. From there she went to the first school for Inuvialuit children at Shingle Point.

Women missionaries on their way to the north. *Standing, left to right:* Miss Cox, Marion Harvey, Margaret Peck, and Mrs. Peck. *Sitting, left to right:* Mildred Rundle, nurse; Blanche Nesbitt, teacher; Mildred McCabe, nurse; and Louise Topping.

In general, however, Anglican women missionaries who went to the north were not exceedingly well educated. In this they differed little from their male counterparts. There was only one woman doctor and, while many of the women had studied at the University of Toronto or Wycliffe under the Deaconess and Missionary training program offered by the Anglican Church, there were still very few university graduates.[77] However, the majority of women who went into the northern mission field had some measure of training in either education or medicine. This included missionary wives. Of all the women, forty-four went into the field as married women.

Missionary wives engaged in a variety of tasks in the mission field and their experiences before leaving for the field were diverse. For example, Sarah Stringer, whose parents were farmers from Kincardine, Ontario, took a nursing course at Grace Hospital in Toronto and spent time at Toronto's Deaconess and Missionary Training Home before she departed for Herschel Island (Qikiqtaruk) in 1896.[78] In a talk given by Stringer to the Woman's Missionary Society of the United Church in Toronto she reminisced about how her preparedness before going into the field was so useful to her: "After I was engaged to be married my husband went to the north and I entered a hospital here, Grace Hospital, and graduated a nurse. This was so I might be a help in the mission field. It was of untold benefit to me in my work out there. It is an excellent thing to go prepared and fitted for the task. It gives me confidence for emergencies. My course was of tremendous benefit. It gave us a stand amongst those people and made them more willing to listen to the good news or the Gospel that we had to tell them."[79] Similarly, Marion Goodwin, who married the Reverend William Henry Collison and served in the Diocese of Caledonia for forty-nine years, was a trained nurse.[80] Not all the women who claimed to have medical training, particularly in the early years, had completed a regimented course in nursing; in some cases, they had received only minimal training.

More rare were those who had no training whatsoever before entering the mission field. For example, in 1868, seventeen-year-old Alice Woods married Robert Tomlinson, a Church Missionary Society doctor posted at Metlakatla. En route to his post, Tomlinson stopped at Victoria to visit the Irish Anglican, the Reverend C.T. Woods, who was Alice's uncle. Apparently Tomlinson met Alice on this visit and asked her father if he could marry her. Richard Woods made his views clear: "Go up there and find what you're takin' a woman to, and if in a year you're of the same mind, you come down and my answer might be quite different. But you're not taking Alice up there at this stage of the game."[81] Tomlinson returned one year later to marry Alice and one assumes that she had some choice in this matter. As she had never done housework and was unable to knit or sew, she was somewhat unprepared for the work that lay in front of her. But she quickly learned and became skilled in outdoor living.[82] Although she was formally unprepared, Woods had obviously grown up in a pious household which emphasized religion. One can infer that she had observed her aunt in her role as wife of the Archdeacon of Victoria.

No matter what their previous experiences or preparation for the mission field, all women had to be versatile, combining teaching, nursing, and ministering. The initial reluctance of the church to accept women as missionaries produced a certain tension and impression that the mission field was a male endeavour. Women's status as church workers, whether voluntary or paid, was particularly ambiguous. Ironically, because of this ambiguity, there was potential for women to carve out careers in mission work and ministry that were both unofficial and creative.

*Back row, left to right:* Reverend Harry S. Shepherd, Rt. Reverend Archibald Lang Fleming, and Reverend Thomas Umaok with Shingle Point (Tapqaq) staff members Ethel Hewer, Mabel Jones, D. Somers, and Adelaide Butler, 1934.

# 2
# Perceptions and Interpretations of the "Other"

In October 1895, just before Christine Carleton departed for northern British Columbia, she was given a letter by the Church Missionary Society stating that she had been well prepared for what she was about to encounter:

> You dear Miss Carleton, after having passed through an experience of work and training both at Highbury and in the large parish of Aston are now assigned by the committee to go forth in your master's name to the North Pacific Mission. The knowledge which you have acquired as a nurse will, the Committee doubt not be utilized to the full in the mission field. Use it even as a blessed instrument of winning the confidence and affection of the natives so shall they be the better prepared to receive and welcome from you the great message of salvation to communicate which is the great object of your missionary life. The Committee heartily sympathize with you in turning your back for Christ's sake upon all the special privileges which you have enjoyed in an English home and parish. You go forth to grapple with much indifference, with gross superstition, with much which will shock your whole soul.[1]

Shortly before missionaries went into the field, they might receive such instructions including a statement of what the mission society expected them to achieve. Instructions usually emphasized the religious goals of the mission and, at times, might point to the specific training that missionaries had taken before their departure in order to remind them that they were well suited. The Church Missionary Society also wanted to ensure that missionaries had a strong sense of what their duties were. In Carleton's case, her training as a nurse was important to her prospects as a missionary. The underlying assumption was that, if medical missionaries could prove the value of European medicine, they might thereby devalue traditional Aboriginal medicine. If Aboriginal peoples would turn to nurses and doctors for medicinal remedies, missionaries could then discuss Christianity and the merits of their medicine. The committee's choice of words shaped some of the preconceived ideas held by missionaries. Carleton was notified that she was leaving the "special privileges" of her English Anglican community behind. Warned to be prepared for what would possibly shock their entire soul, missionaries formed preconceptions of and assumptions about difference while in training.

Many women who came to the north, either as missionaries or missionary wives, had preconceived ideas about their superiority rooted in their identities as members of a White Anglo-Saxon middle-class Anglican community. They were, in other words, familiar with the discourse that surrounded mission work. Representations or images of otherness – perceptions of difference through the imperialist gaze – demonstrate some of the apparent tensions that developed in the mission field, tensions which were perhaps an inevitable result of contact between Euro-Canadians and Aboriginal cultures. Yet, women's narratives also indicate an ambiguity which emerged in their daily lives. Personal relationships sometimes softened preconceived notions about Aboriginal peoples. Many women, once settled into mission stations, wrote letters, either personal or for use in church publications, using language redolent with these perceptions of otherness. At the same time, however, they had to establish relations with Aboriginal peoples that were much more immediate and direct than their correspondence suggests.

Nineteenth-century missionary zeal, especially within the Church of England, went hand in hand with enthusiasm for the British empire. Typically, the British portrayed themselves as civilized, White, and Christian, whereas Aboriginal peoples were said to be uncivilized, dark, and heathen. Commenting on what he called the "ethics of empire," nineteenth-century author H.F. Hyatt expressed this contrast in the popular periodical *The Nineteenth Century*: "To us – to us, and not to others, a certain definite duty has been assigned to carry light and civilization in the dark places of the world; to touch the mind of Asia and Africa with the ethical ideas of Europe; to give to the thronging millions who would otherwise never know peace or security, these first conditions of human advance."[2] The moral duty of missionaries and others involved in imperial expansion was to free the "thronging millions" from their state of ignorance and enlighten them to God's way, which was synonymous with the European way. Metaphors of light and darkness were especially prevalent in evangelical discourse.

Dichotomies that juxtaposed civilized with uncivilized places popularized by imperialist supporters, as well as missionaries, left little middle ground between colonizer and colonized. Aboriginal cultures could not be described as civilized, nor could civilizers be represented in any way as uncivilized. Albert Memmi argues that, while a variety of stereotypical images of the colonizer can be found, there were far more for the colonized. A "mythical portrait of the colonized," according to Memmi, included images of Aboriginal peoples as excessively lazy, wretched, backward, weak, and dishonest: "Nothing could better justify the colonizer's privileged position than his industry and nothing could better justify the colonized's destitution than his indolence."[3] Memmi observes that colonizers were often in positions of economic, social, and political power and the key to maintaining this power was that the colonizer had to remain ideologically isolated from the colonized. In other words, the characteristics of the Aboriginal culture had to be undervalued and the quality of the colonizer's culture and customs upheld and glorified. Because the colonizer and colonized could never be equal – for then the colonizer would no longer have a raison d'etre – the colonizer usually resorted to racism.[4]

Dichotomies, however, are frequently dangerous and unstable. Frederick Cooper and Ann Stoler note that colonial discourse which drew on such dichotomies failed to recognize the fluidity and changing circumstances of cultures facing colonization: "Here lies the basic tension of empire: the otherness of the colonized person was neither inherent nor stable; his or her difference had to be defined and maintained; social boundaries that were at one point clear would not necessarily remain so."[5] While perceptions of colonizers and colonized, such as those described by Memmi, were pervasive, there was at the same time a tension related to maintaining differences between the two.

This awareness does not invalidate or deny the Euro-Canadian obsession with altering Aboriginal peoples. Hayden White argues that Europeans fixated on Aboriginal peoples "by viewing them simultaneously as monstrous forms of humanity and as quintessential objects of desire." They were the other, simultaneously frightening and fantastic, and they were heathen, without Christianity. "But even more basic in the European consciousness of this time," White suggests, "was the tendency to fetishize the European type of humanity as the sole possible form that humanity in general could take."[6] Education, European medicine, thrift, and sobriety were inextricably linked to European humanity and the remaking of the "other."

### Could They Look Like Europeans?
While the priority for missionaries was to have Aboriginal peoples worship Christ, they had by extension a desire to change the peoples' physical appearance and consciousness. Missionaries assumed that they could effect such changes to transform and remake Aboriginal peoples. Personal appearance – the way Aboriginal peoples looked – was a central concern for many women missionaries working among northern Aboriginal peoples. In her analysis of colonial discourse, Anne McClintock observes that soap and

cleanliness were fetishes for colonizers: "Victorian fascination with clean, White bodies and clean, white clothing stemmed not only from the rampant profiteering of the imperial economy but also from rituals and fetish. Soap offered the promise of spiritual salvation and regeneration through commodity consumption, a regime of domestic hygiene that could restore the threatened potency of the imperial body politic and the race."[7]

Most missionaries in northern Canada described the appearance and behaviour of Aboriginal peoples as if viewed through what Mary Louise Pratt has termed "imperial eyes."[8] The deeply embedded Victorian sentiment that "cleanliness is next to Godliness" was held by many women missionaries and, according to them, left Aboriginal peoples quite far from salvation. The introduction of European or Anglo-Canadian conceptions of personal and domestic hygiene were central parts of the mission's function. And concerns about cleanliness appear to have had a strong resonance with the readers of missionary accounts. The ease with which many missionaries drew on derogatory terminology, and the patterns in which this was applied to northern Canada and other mission settings, indicate a discourse of difference that was well established before they went into the field.

During her first two years at Fort Simpson (Líídli Kuë) in the Northwest Territories, Charlotte Selina Bompas acted as a school teacher, nurse, and mother. Born in 1830 to Charlotte Skey and Dr. Joseph Cox in London, England, she spent most of her childhood in Italy as a result of her father's asthma. She grew up in émigré gentility, spoke fluent Italian, and loved the classics. According to her niece "even as an old lady she always carried her Dante in her pocket."[9] Cox remained single until age forty-four, when she married her cousin, William, then the first Bishop of the Mackenzie River (Deh Cho) Diocese. In her early years, Selina hardly held romantic notions of marriage to a missionary: "My brother who was Vicar of Bishop's Tawton, Devonshire, used to hold missionary meetings at the vicarage, and I remember thinking them the dullest affairs, and the clergymen who addressed us ... I looked upon as the most dismal old slow coaches it was anyone's unhappy fate to attend to."[10]

Bompas arrived at Fort Simpson, at the confluence of the Liard (Net'i Tué) and Mackenzie rivers, in September 1874. From the outset, she taught an afternoon class for Dene children. School routine was described in terms reflective of the imperialist gaze: "I go in and make them sing and do calisthenics exercises. Before this I preside over an ablutionary department [religious cleansing] and then send them outside with a comb by which their black shaggy manes are reduced to order."[11] Bompas expressed grave concern about the condition of Dene women's hair. A woman she met in her evangelical travels near Fort McPherson (Tetlit'zheh) was described as a "shriveled and grimy" old witch whose "frizzled hair [was] flying about in all directions" so much so that Bompas said "you can not fancy that it had ever seen a comb."[12] Despite their efforts, Dene women could never quite meet Bompas's standard. On one occasion she was asked to serve as a sponsor for two little boys who were being baptized: she recorded that "the mother had done her best to make them, as well as herself, neat and presentable, but Indian faces have a perverse habit of grimness, and Indian hair is ever thick and shaggy and rough."[13] Many years later, while teaching school at Fort Yukon, Bompas maintained that: "in spite of all the difficulties the children are getting on by degrees and taming down, for a wilder and more undisciplined set of ruffians than they were at first it would be hard to find out of the zoological gardens."[14] Black and grimy, with rough manes, these Aboriginal women and children were exposed to Bompas's harsh gaze and criticism.

This obsession with appearance blinkered the imperial eyes of missionary women, especially on first contact, throughout the years from 1860 to 1940. On a stopover in 1894 at Alert Bay ('Yalis) in British Columbia, Florence Appleyard recorded her first impressions of the Kwakwaka'wakw. At the time a twenty-nine-year-old nurse from Finsbury Park, England, Appleyard described her initial reactions in self-revealing terms: "We happened

Charlotte Selina Bompas. Note the formal pose with a timepiece prominently displayed on the front of her dress.

to arrive just as a wedding feast was taking place and the women with painted faces were sitting in rows singing and clapping hands. They looked wild and terrible and some of them were really very ugly. I can realize now more than ever before how full of love one must be in order to teach these poor creatures whose faces betray that they know not the Lord Jesus. It is very sad to see these poor Indians and know how ignorant they are and to hear the missionaries say 'We are so short handed.'"[15] Appleyard's first glimpse of the people she describes as "poor creatures" suggests a tone of fear, almost of repulsion. Her apprehensions diminished over time but did not entirely disappear.

Mary Mellish, a school teacher originally from Prince Edward Island, wrote to the woman's auxiliary discussing her progress with the students and commenting on her impressions of her work at Carcross (Natashaheeni), Yukon: "My school work is going on as usual. I have good attendance sometimes I wish there were fewer, as the atmosphere is not-very-sweet when a number of them are together and when the weather is cold we cannot have the door or window open long."[16] Mellish was uncomfortable about the smell of her pupils. Body odours were a common complaint from missionary women. Evelyn Merritt held the same concern when several Aboriginal people visited her small mission house in Bernard Harbour: "This summer there have been about seventy in camp here. The sickness has brought us all closer together, but we want a room where the people can be accommodated. When we invite them to service, or they come to visit, there is scarcely air enough for one to breathe and is most uncomfortable for a white person, to say the least."[17] Her comments were somewhat ambivalent. Merritt was now living and working in intimate contact with Aboriginal peoples, but positioned herself possibly for the first time in her own view, as a White person who could not tolerate the smell of others.

Another woman who worked in the Peace River Region in the Diocese of Caledonia and who was at first appalled by local conditions was Monica Storrs. She arrived at Fort St. John on the Peace River in 1929. Most of her work involved establishing Sunday schools and girl guide and boy scout troops among the young British and European settlers of the region. However, Storrs travelled extensively on horseback and kept a diary of her excursions. On one trip, about fifty kilometres north of Fort St. John, she came on what she described as a "squalid little camp" of members of the Dunne-za: "all the Indians of our district are pretty debased, more or less like Gypsies, and speak hardly any English. They don't do any sort of work, but only hunt bear and moose and barter their meat with the white men for vegetables and butter."[18] The analogy to gypsies and Aboriginal people's apparent lack of employment clearly reflected the perspective of a newly arrived European in the north, in this case of a woman from a relatively privileged background. Before the end of Storrs's departure on this particular outing she recalled in her diary that she "grinned at the women and children and gave them some chocolate."[19]

The description of Aboriginal peoples living in squalor was expressed by other missionaries, including Adelaide Butler, who began her mission work in 1932. Butler, originally from Reading, England, was serving as a school teacher at Shingle Point (Tapqaq), when she recorded a trip that she and her companion, Marion Harvey, took to Herschel Island (Qikiqtaruk). On their way, weather conditions forced them to stop overnight at King Point, about thirty kilometres from Shingle Point. Butler described a dwelling and two families who "came out to meet us and they looked deplorable dirty and half-clad ... Sarah the elder is very ugly and primitive, but is not nearly so fierce as she looks ... Harvey went inside their house but the outside was enough for me; it was made of sods and looked like a shelter for animals more than for human beings."[20] Images of the other were constructed in many such passages that support Memmi's observations.

Many missionaries expressed superiority through the alleged lowly condition of Aboriginal peoples, who were the objects of their mission. Local people were uncivilized in spiritual and other cultural practices; the missionary's responsibility was to save souls and introduce a new order. Had Aboriginal peoples been civilized, Christian, or respectable, the missionaries

*Back row:* Alberta and Reverend Tom Marsh with congregation at Hay River (Kátl'odéech), Northwest Territories, late 1890s.

would have been without purpose. Missionary work was perceived to be all the more important because of Aboriginal conditions. Anne McClintock argues that many attitudes expressed toward Aboriginal cultures were similar to those by which the underclass in Britain was described by those in upper classes. She compares the references of slovenliness and idleness to a long-held rhetoric, which was particularly strong in the nineteenth century, linking poverty to laziness: "Colonialists borrowed and patched from British discourses and couched their complaints in the same images of degeneracy, massing animal menace and irrationality familiar to European descriptions of the urban underclass."[21] McClintock focuses on British Victorians, but the same ideas were presented by Canadian reformers and missionaries.[22]

## To See God's Marvellous Light

As if missionary accounts of the appearance and lifeways of Aboriginal peoples were not shocking enough, they frequently portrayed Aboriginal cultures as excessively dark and evil. One aspect of this theme, which emerges in the correspondence and diaries of the women missionaries, is murder. Aboriginal peoples were often described by missionaries as being murderous prior to Christian contact. This was considered evidence of their moral debasement and, when applied to their physical appearance and daily habits, greatly magnified negative images. As Hayden White observes, depictions of "radical otherness" could be evoked in surprisingly excessive terms.[23] Described in ways intended to titillate, murder could be used to measure the success or failure of Christianity's civilizing influence.

Elizabeth Jane Soal, originally from Lewisham, England, arrived at Metlakatla in 1901 after two years training at Highbury deaconess house to start her work as a teaching missionary. She worked briefly at Metlakatla and was then transferred to Hazelton (Gitenmaks). In describing her experiences, she related that the couple with whom she was stationed, the Reverend and Mrs. Field, had worked at Hazelton for thirty years and had witnessed "marvelous changes": "My knowledge of the Indian goes back for a period of ten years only but those who have lived here for many years say that he was highly excitable, very noisy, easily angered, cruel, a gambler, dog eater, slave driver to his wife, and a firm believer in evil spirits ... The Potlatch of the old days, which as a rule led to poverty and frequently to murder, is forbidden by law, but the natural craving for some excitement has been substituted [by] the funeral feast."[24] Soal believed that the combination of Christianity and the abolition of the potlatch had transformed these Aboriginal people from barbarous to semi-civilized. This view of a slightly reformed other was shared by Canadian-born missionary Sarah Stringer. In 1898, she moved to Herschel Island, where she and her husband worked and lived for five years. During the late 1920s and early

1930s, when Stringer was invited on many occasions to give public talks in southern Canada on her experiences as a missionary in the north, she usually chose to speak of her years at Herschel Island. In one such address in 1927, Stringer recalled that, prior to their arrival the Inuvialuit had been "a heathenous and superstitious people. Murder was common amongst them. Whenever an Eskimo became angry his first instinct was to kill his opponent so it was best to act in a wise and judicious way with them." In another lecture delivered in October 1930 to the United Church Woman's Missionary Society in Toronto she described how the Inuvialuit came to visit her when they lived on the island: "The Eskimos at that time were a treacherous ignorant people and always carried a knife in their hand or in their bootleg to be prepared. It was not pleasant to have them come to my house with a knife in their hand. One had to go on and pretend they were unconcerned though not always feeling quite comfortable. If it were not for the fact we had God with us we could not go on day after day."[25] Such a description evoked strong images of the barbaric, of lives encountered where fear and danger were constant companions. Of course, as Stringer undoubtedly realized, the Inuvialuit carried knives for eating, carving, and hunting, not for striking one another from fear.

Similar references appear throughout the diaries and correspondence of other missionary women in the north. Cannibalism and scalping were added to the gory image of Aboriginal peoples. Miss F. Copeland, a missionary school teacher, related in the *North British Columbia News* that Kincolith (Gingolx) was known as "the place where they scalp" before the arrival of missionaries. She added that: "thanks to the glorious gospel and to those who have preached it and lived it out there in the 'Far West' for so many years, scalping is now a thing of the past."[26] According to their own accounts, missionaries and their Christian message had offered some measure of improvement. But, as no missionary had actually witnessed a murder, this language seems to represent little more than an artificial and created sense of change. A dark savage past being overcome by the light of Jesus and the true God was standard missionary rhetoric but, in the retelling of these stories, Aboriginal peoples are historically barbarous and moving toward salvation. Readers were to be impressed with hard-won apparent improvements, however slight, and were to be inspired to continue giving financial support to the work that left so much to be accomplished.

One of the most pervasive themes in missionary narratives was the enduring heathenism and primitiveness said to characterize Aboriginal cultures. In effect, missionaries acknowledged few redeeming qualities within Aboriginal cultures. On his first trip to the Mackenzie River delta, Bishop Bompas described the Gwich'in Dene as good crafts people, kind, and obliging but "lazy and sleepy, and addicted to lying, stealing and even stabbing." He said that their religion consisted mainly of "heathen dances, songs and conjuring." However, he at least recognized that they believed in a "tradition of Creation" and worshipped the Sun as a "good spirit" and an evil spirit called "Atti," which represented cold and death.[27]

Just as Bishop Bompas was critical of medicine making and the Dene religion, William Ridley, Bishop of Caledonia, was horrified by the potlatch. In describing the unconverted Tsimshian of the Skeena River (Sginn) villages, Bishop Ridley presented an image similar to the one used by Bishop Bompas:

> The heathen are dirty, ragged, dispirited, and jealous of the Christians. To avoid treading in filth one must walk on the crooked trails with circumspection. The children stand at a distance huddled together. I have seen two even in the biting blast of winter wrapped in a single piece of blanket, their only covering. The houses are rotting propped up and patched. Squalid within and dismal without they truly show the moral and physical condition of their ignorant and superstitious inhabitants. These cling with a passionate resolve to the *yaok*, or potlatch. "That is our mountain say they our only joy dearer than life. To prison and death we will go rather than yield." Yet this is their ruin.[28]

Bishop Ridley linked the physical appearance of the Tsimshian to their moral or spiritual condition. As Monica Storrs and others would later conclude, Aboriginal morality, or lack thereof, was somehow visible in their appearance.

Missionaries consistently expressed opposition to the potlatch and medicine making, Aboriginal cultural traditions that they believed simply had to be eradicated. The language used may have reflected the missionaries' view that they were bringing light to a dark and heathen land. Metaphors of simplistic dualism described complex colonial relationships. As Memmi points out, Indigenous practices and beliefs were seen as corrupt and debased, whereas European institutions were desirable and glorified. Evidence for this took many forms.

Christine Carleton departed from England for Alert Bay in October 1895. She spent her first month at Alert Bay, then in December she and another missionary, Edith Beeching, went to teach school and hold services at Gwayasdums, a village about twenty-five kilometres to the north. Writing to the Church Missionary Society in February 1896, Carleton expressed great satisfaction with her work, although she admitted that she found teaching "trying at times" because, as she said: "One cannot expect the little untrained heathen children to be as obedient and as fond of learning the ABC's as English children." Carleton noted that the people abandoned the village to attend "their business which is the distribution of blankets

and is termed 'the potlatch' at the same time they are practicing their heathen rites, etc. which are connected with this potlatch and are most dis-
tressing."[29] One year later and still contented with her work, Carleton
admitted to doubt concerning her impact, stating in typical evangelical
discourse that she would be delighted to see the people "come out of darkness" to see God's "marvelous light." Like her co-workers, she was experiencing a sense of disillusionment, bolstered at times only by conviction.
Missionaries feared that unless the potlatch and medicine making could be
undermined such spiritual darkness would continue.

During their time at Herschel Island the Stringers tried to weaken the
position of medicine makers, or "conjurers," as they called them. In
November 1897 Sarah Stringer wrote of the sadness she felt after visiting a
sick child in a snow house. She had witnessed traditional medicine and
described the practice: "When the child lies still and they think it is not
breathing the doctor breathes life into it (so they say) and sings some
Eskimo song. It is sad to see the hold superstition has on them." She went
intending to visit this child again before it died, but did not go into the
house because "the doctor was there making a wild noise and all was darkness within."[30] Stringer recorded several incidents when apparently, out of
desperation, members of the Aboriginal community came to the mission
house seeking medicine. One very ill boy was brought to their home only
after the parents had invited five different medicine men to attend to him.
At first, the Stringers were reluctant, then insisted that "no native doctor or
in fact anyone else have anything else to do with the treatment of him."
Within a few months the boy recovered and, as Stringer noted, his parents
"feel very grateful for our care of their son, and it certainly will have its
influence." They offered medical aid in the hope that their success would
lead the Aboriginal peoples to "give up their evil and superstitious ways"
and abandon the tradition of medicine making.[31] Mission accounts, especially during the late nineteenth century, consistently expressed intolerance
for Aboriginal spirituality and attached little value to Aboriginal traditions.
Most missionaries had little respect for the fact that the Aboriginal peoples
had their own cultural practices passed on for generations. Although Sarah
Stringer, for example, occasionally tried to describe the medicine-making
process, she failed to understand or to appreciate its significance from an
Aboriginal perspective.

In cases where Aboriginal peoples seemed more willing to accept medical assistance, missionaries continued to express disappointment at the
outcome. Selina Bompas acted as a nurse in Fort Simpson, although she
found this work disappointing because, in her view, the "poor Indians"
were helpless. In the face of illness their response was to "watch and kiss
and fondle and cry out in agony, but not stir to provide the least remedy,
and if you give them medicine, the chances are they will not use it."[32] Mary

Ellis, a British-born school teacher and matron at the Carcross school from 1901 to 1908, found that Aboriginal peoples would comply as long as she was there to instruct them: "We have had much sickness in the camp: two young women have died, one I am almost sure I could have saved if I had her here, but the Indians are so apathetic, and even when they see remedies, and the good effect produced, they never think of doing the same things themselves."[33] At Moosehide (Éhä Dädhëchan Kek'ét), some twenty years later, another British missionary found the same thing with the Tr'ondek Hwech'in. Mrs. Bentley found the "poor ignorant people" very much in need: "It is really funny if it were not so pathetic. One poor dear went to the doctor and returned with four different kinds of medicine. There seemed to be some doubt in her mind about them so she brought the whole lot to me to see if I thought they were all right. When I assured her they were quite all right and would most likely make her better she went on her way rejoicing. Poor souls! They need all our help and prayers."[34] This same frustration was expressed by Adelaide Butler, who at the time of a measles epidemic at Shingle Point said that the "Eskimos are more like children," because they failed to realize the seriousness of the disease and refused to comply with her wish that they stay away from the mission if they were ill. Reading between the lines, one is reminded by these examples that Aboriginal peoples made choices to accept or refuse medicine and treatment, based on their own needs.

Besides wanting to introduce European medical treatment and eradicate the potlatch, missionaries offered new names to those being baptized. Jean and John Comaroff call this practice in South Africa a "colonization of language." They suggest that there is a "general tendency of imperialisms of all stripes to impose themselves by redesignating people and places."[35] The evidence available for the northern mission frontier suggests that baptismal names were chosen by missionaries. At Herschel Island, for example, Sarah Stringer knew a young Inuvialuit boy called David Copperfield. Canadian-born Bessie Quirt spoke of a baptismal service at Shingle Point where a young Inuvialuit girl, Too-kul-u-wok, became Mary, while another little girl was baptized Margaret-Ann.[36] On a visit that the Stringers made to Fort Selkirk, a village located between present-day Whitehorse (Kwanlin) and Dawson (Tr'ochek), it was noted that the bishop baptized a number of children: "There were children to be baptized, but before they could be baptized Mrs. Stringer and Miss Martin [the resident missionary] had to assist the Bishop in selecting names that would be acceptable to the mothers. This was finally accomplished to the satisfaction of all and the Bishop baptized twenty-one native children."[37] Even one of the founders of the Church Missionary Society, Henry Venn, was memorialized by the baptism of Henry Venn Keste, a man in La Pierre's House who eventually became a Christian leader in his community.[38] The use of Old Testament or English names to help change culture paralleled efforts to change physical appearances and belief systems. The extent to which Aboriginal peoples chose to be renamed is difficult to assess.

Explorers and fur traders commonly renamed landscapes and rivers. Many place names that missionaries used were designated by these earliest Europeans in the north. In reference to the topography south of Great Slave Lake, for example, Bishop Bompas commented that one of the falls had been named after British royalty: "The Hay River, falling into Great Slave Lake contains a beautiful water-fall, which has been named the Alexandra Falls, in honour of the Princess of Wales."[39] Renaming individuals and places, educating local people to European ways, and attempting to eradicate Aboriginal traditions and undermine spirituality were integral and interconnected parts of the Christianizing process. Symbolically, such steps marked a rejection of the past and reflected broad aims for implementation of a new order.

## Could They Mimic Europeans?

The pathos evident in missionaries' efforts was that, even when Aboriginal peoples imitated their behaviours and rituals, their attempts were criticized. Inevitably, they were still viewed as inferior somehow. Performances which drew on both the cultural referents of the participants and new rituals introduced by missionaries have been analyzed by post-colonial writers as a process of mimesis. Aboriginal people who tried to mimic or behave like missionaries risked being considered inherently inadequate. The objective of colonial mimicry, as Homi Bhabha discusses, "is the production of a reformed, recognizable other, as a subject of difference that is almost the same, but not quite."[40] The colonized might have attempted to participate in institutions and ceremonies that formed part of the colonizer's cultural baggage, but the colonizer's racial perceptions commonly judged that they could not quite succeed. Examples from Selina Bompas and Adelaide Butler illustrate this pattern.

Bompas's first Christmas at Fort McPherson was memorable. Her husband had left the fort shortly after their arrival in the fall of 1874, and Bompas busied herself making toys for the Aboriginal children and preparing a festive meal. She confided in her diary that she "had planned a Christmas dinner for twelve old Indian wives. Dear old things! They did their best to get themselves up for the occasion, and some of their leather dresses were quite smart, profusely ornamented with beads, with fringes of leather and tin tassels. I had dinner prepared in the schoolroom, the cloth spread and knives and forks etc. But these proved useless for though some of the women did try to use them to please me, their efforts were quite ineffectual and they were soon forced to lay them down and take to nature's implements."[41] The Aboriginal women described here, it seems, could not meet Bompas's expectations of cleanliness and, despite their efforts to behave in a civilized fashion, they failed. In Bompas's view, they were too close to nature and not elevated enough to use another culture's eating implements. Bompas also provides a glimpse into how the colonizer attempted to remake the colonized in their image. For about sixteen to eighteen months, she had been training a servant named Julie:

> She was becoming an excellent servant and I thought very well of her in most points but she left me a week or two since without any warning or intention, and the worst of it is she took with her many of my things, in true Indian fashion. I was greatly startled and grieved when this came out as I hoped better things of my little maiden, but one has to remember that these are savages – wild Indian girls – who like their camps and wild camp life in spite of all its miseries and privations, far better than the white man's home with its comparative luxuries and restraints. The Indian infirmities too are not easily overcome and uprooted.[42]

Again, a case is presented of an Aboriginal woman who was almost acceptable but ended up, in Bompas's myopic vision, just like the rest of them. Bompas had done her utmost to remake Julie, but the young woman ultimately resisted and departed. She could have been but was, in Bhabha's words, "not quite/not white." While a degree of understanding developed between Bompas and Julie, this temporary relationship, at least from Bompas's viewpoint, disintegrated and she was left again with a low opinion of Aboriginal peoples and continued to refer to them in derogatory terms.

A more striking example of colonial mimicry can be found in Adelaide Butler's account of what she described as a Husky [Inuvialuit] "wedding" that took place at Shingle Point during Christmas 1932.[43] The couple being married were a woman by the name of Mabel, and Alec Stefansson, the son of a local woman and the Arctic explorer Vilhjalmur Stefansson. Mabel was depicted as a nice girl, "careful of herself and sport[ing] a silk dress and gold wrist watch and bracelet just like any 'tunik' [White person]." Butler felt, though, that the wedding left much to be desired: "You would never have thought that a marriage was about to be solemnized." She described the event in a letter to her friend in England:

> The Bridal couple was sitting among the rest of the congregation not together and there were no bridesmaids, no confetti, no fuss, no nothing! The minister called the bride, groom and Allen, the bride's father, forward. The service was in Husky, and after Allen had done his part and disposed of his daughter he left them to get on with theirs. They knelt down on the hard wooden not very clean floor, and did not go up to the altar rail. Mabel had no bridal attire, only the usual "atikluk" [atige cover]

of some inexpensive cotton material, and not very clean, no head cover-
ing ... After the ceremony was over the bride and bridegroom got up and
went back to their previous seats until the service was over; we had a service about Holy Communion not marriage and they did not even go out
of the church together.[44]

Butler was not impressed. She expected a more familiar experience, with
confetti, bridal attire, and bridesmaids. She anticipated that the bride and
groom would leave the church together. The wedding to her was a disappointment. As a ceremonial ritual, it was "not quite/not white."

## Ambiguous Relations

It would be inaccurate to assume that all missionaries held exactly the same
views, but the persistence and similarity in commentary on appearances
and traditions in missionary correspondence is remarkable. There was also
more complexity than these descriptions reveal in the relationships
between Aboriginal peoples and the above-mentioned missionaries. In
their correspondence, both Selina Bompas and Sarah Stringer show occasional moments of appreciation or at least ambiguity about Aboriginal
culture. However strong the dominant discourse used to construct the
other may appear, it is clear that there were many important moments
in the mission field when racial barriers broke down. Evidence of friendships between missionaries and Aboriginal peoples, and of moments when
British or Canadian missionaries appeared to appreciate or understand

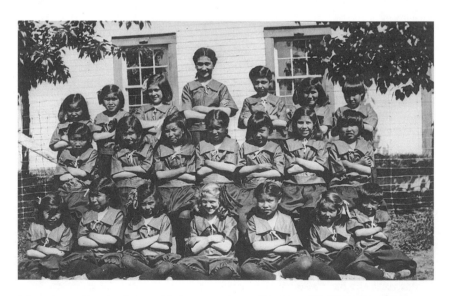

Mary Samwell and mission girls in gym suits at Hay River (Kátl'odéech), 1924.

Aboriginal culture suggest that ambiguity might have been characteristic of the Aboriginal/missionary relationship.

Stoler and Cooper argue that a complex tension existed in colonial relationships purely because social relations were far from fixed. This was quite apparent in northern Canada. Once individuals became familiar with one another, missionaries might change some of their preconceived ideas about or images of Aboriginal peoples. Living and gaining experiences necessitated responses that differed from public missionary rhetoric. This was especially true for missionary women. Women spent more time at mission stations and were in closer individual contact with Aboriginal peoples. With respect to the American missionary experiences in China, Jane Hunter has pointed out that male missionaries concentrated on preparing for and meeting with their congregations, or travelling, while women met with individuals on a more regular and immediate basis. Hunter has interpreted women's ministry as more "socially intimate" than that of men's.[45]

Prior to their five-year assignment at Herschel Island (Qikiqtaruk), the Stringers were itinerant, travelling between Peel River and Herschel Island. On their first trip they stopped at an Inuvialuit encampment at Kittygagzyoort.[46] They were greeted on shore by several members of the community, then were invited to the Council House. Sarah Stringer summed up her impressions by stating that "their appearance and actions seemed odd and laughable to me while I daresay I seemed just as ridiculous to them as I was the first white woman who ever visited them therefore they scrutinized me very closely & judging by their grimaces they were much amused." She expressed a notable degree of sensitivity in suggesting that they had gazed at each other through cultural prisms. She described those she visited as warm and good-natured, and added that "sometimes too when leaving to go home after a visit one of the women would put her arm about my waist in an affectionate manner and walk out a short distance with me."[47] Stringer found the women especially kind. She recalled a tense situation when "the Chief was intoxicated and wanted to kill some of us. They [the women] came to the door of my tent took my hand and smoothed it over and tried to assure me that everything would be all right."[48]

Selina Bompas described a time during the Christmas of 1876, shortly after moving to Fort Chipewyan, when she became ill while her husband was out on a circuit which could take as long as seven months. Bompas had met a Cree woman from Saskatchewan named Madeline. She felt the Cree were different from the Chipewyan, as their faces "exhibit a great deal more intelligence" and they were "better looking than the Chipewyans." Yet, she claimed the Cree "of all ranks are proverbially light fingered, and many of them are incorrigible thieves."[49] Bompas and Madeline developed a close relationship during a serious food shortage at the fort. As it turned out, Madeline supplied Bompas with food from her husband's traps. In exchange, Bompas reluctantly surrendered her treasured red shawl. When Bompas became ill, her woman servant abandoned her and for quite a long period of time she was left alone ill and caring for an adopted baby. Eventually Madeline learned of the illness and went to her. Bompas recalled that "she came and stood by my bedside, and said in kind, almost remonstrating tones: 'You are ill; why not send for me? I work for you; I do anything for you; wash clothes for you; nurse baby for you'."[50] Bompas was thankful for Madeline's assistance. Gratified, she was compelled to take Madeline's "small dark-coloured hand ... and stroke and press it while I thanked God for putting into the poor woman's heart to come to me in my extremity."[51] Bompas claimed to have slept soundly the night that Madeline stayed with her, waking only once to observe a very comforting and calming scene with Madeline whistling to Jennie who was "propped upright between blanket and pillow in a manner peculiarly Indian." She returned to sleep confident that, as she expressed it, "my little wife" had settled Jennie and provided a relaxing atmosphere.[52]

Sarah Stringer visits with an Aboriginal woman.

This particular episode may be interpreted in several ways, with due caution. For an "unpredictable and fleeting" moment, as Denise Riley would have it, Bompas saw herself as having a "wife."[53] Bompas was, in this sense, imposing one of the categories of "woman" onto Madeline. Whether she saw herself as a man being nurtured by a woman, or a woman being nurtured by a woman, or neither, is difficult to say with any certainty. Nonetheless, Madeline was portrayed as her "little wife." Bompas still viewed her as a Cree woman with a "small dark-coloured" hand but may also have claimed a new self-perception and gender in her intense closeness to Madeline. Intimate relations were not part of the dominant colonial discourse, but the context of living in the mission field allows for a challenge to the preconceived ideas held by missionaries.

Augusta E. Morris, the first of the Church Missionary Society single women sent out to live and work with Selina Bompas, reported a similar relationship with a Dene woman known to her as "Old Tiger." In April 1883, Morris was ill in bed at her mission house at Fort Resolution (Denínu K̨), but was well enough to have visitors. According to her diary, the visit from Old Tiger was a mixed blessing:

> Old Tiger, the oldest Indian, who is supposed to be nearly 100 years old, came to see me yesterday. She is a dreadfully grimy old thing, her blanket & c. are in a filthy state, her hair all about her face & c. so although she meant to be kind I was not altogether pleased particularly as she generally kisses one. However I resolved she shouldn't so when she came to the bedside I shook hands but that was not enough she must needs push out her poor old dirty face & wouldn't be satisfied until she had given a kiss of peace. After she performed that operation to her satisfaction she seated herself on the floor, saying "now I was her sister!"[54]

As in the case of Madeline and Selina Bompas, Augusta Morris described an important moment of intimacy between herself and Old Tiger. Certainly, Morris was obsessed, as other women were, with cleanliness and appearance but, beyond these fetishes, was a relationship which the Dene woman appeared to enjoy and even cherish. Old Tiger offered Morris much more than a handshake in her "kiss of peace." One can just imagine the satisfaction that Old Tiger felt as she sat down to continue with the visit. To spare Old Tiger's feelings Morris deliberately veiled her concern with appearance and allowed the intimate kiss to occur.

Finally, a degree of admiration for Aboriginal peoples' approach to the physical environment was occasionally expressed. For example, in an advice article for prospective northern settlers, Selina Bompas suggested that White women should learn to appreciate some Indigenous traditions: "It should not need many hours of argument to convince you that an

Indian baby in a moss bag is a far happier and warmer creature than a poor little white baby with its whole outfit of cotton and wool, etc. for the little Indian's moss is the cleanest, softest, most absorbent of substances, and needs only occasional change to keep the baby as tidy and sweet as the baby should be."[55] Bompas went on to say that despite the fact that the Aboriginal peoples were in her view a "phlegmatic race," who would not be "inconvenienced by anyone, least of all by a 'Ciciaco' [newcomer, many of whom were goldseekers]," one must still treat them with patience and kindness. After all, she noted perceptively, "the white man has invaded their territory, cut down their fine forests, slaughtered or driven away their moose and caribou, and is fast possessing himself of their hidden treasure, is it asking too much of his wife or sister to bear patiently with the Indian's idiosyncrasies to deal gently with their failings, and above all to show towards them under all circumstances in the summer calm of golden charity."[56] Still located in this segment are signs of denigration and images of Aboriginal peoples as passive individuals. Bompas also ascribed homogenous characteristics to a diversity of cultures around which she lived. But she did recognize that some Aboriginal traditions should be valued, and that resources which had, even in her mind, belonged to the Indigenous peoples were being exploited by Europeans.

A similar tone comes through in one of Sarah Stringer's public talks on the Inuvialuit. She said that they are "a very clever people in their own way. They could quite easily do without us." She went on to describe how they built their boats with whale bone, ivory pegs, and deer skin thongs rather than nails. She admired their artistic clothing, fashioned by "clever needle women," and concluded that they were intelligent in their own way, "but it was hard for them at first to get book knowledge as they had known nothing about books up to that time."[57]

Ambivalence within the relationship between Aboriginal peoples and missionaries was particularly evident during the 1920s and 1930s. As was the case with Selina Bompas, some missionaries recognized their ambivalent position in the early part of the period under consideration. After the First World War, the focus on difference was still evident as indicated in the correspondence and other writing of such women as Storrs, Bently, Butler, and others. Missionaries still spoke and wrote about the primitive, poverty-stricken living conditions in the north but these comments could be tempered with less negative images by this time. The extent to which the Canadianization of the mission field was responsible for this change is difficult to assess. Statements made by some Canadian missionary women do not necessarily reveal a deeper appreciation of Aboriginal cultures but, at times, they challenged observations that were less sensitive. For example, the wife of the Reverend J.A. Shirley wrote to the national woman's auxiliary newsletter, *The Living Message*, a number of times in the mid-1920s, describing her encounters in the Yukon. At one point she wrote about a journey from her station at Whitehorse 725 kilometres north to Dawson. While there she visited Moosehide (Ёhä Dädhĕchan Kek'ét), just outside of Dawson, and attended a service in Tukudh (a term derived by the Rev. McDonald to indicate written Gwich'in) held by Bishop Stringer. Songs were sung in Aboriginal languages and English, provoking Shirley to comment "as the enthusiastic Indian Lay Reader led in the singing of such a hymn as 'In the Sweet By and By We Shall Meet Again on that Beautiful Shore,' there was a sort of thrill through us as we realized very forcibly the oneness of the human race and the common destiny of us all, no matter what colour or language."[58] Shirley was aware of the difference in "colour and language" but focused more on the common experience shared by all at the service.

Mildred McCabe also revealed ambivalent perspectives. McCabe started her mission career in 1928 at Aklavik. In the fall of 1928, she wrote to *The Living Message* to describe her trip and first impressions. She visited a number of mission stations on her way to Aklavik, including Hay River (Kátl'odéech), Fort McPherson, and Fort Norman (Tulit'á), where she called on several residents and afterwards claimed that she was "beginning to enjoy the society of Indians."[59] When she arrived at her destination, the hospital was in the midst of an outbreak of influenza. Even with the stress of this emergency, she was optimistic: "I am having a unique experience, and have made acquaintance with the natives in a way that I could not otherwise have done."[60] McCabe stayed at Aklavik for four years before being posted at Fort George; in 1936, she was sent to Old Crow to nurse and teach school. Here again she claimed that she liked to visit the Aboriginal peoples: "I enjoy visiting in the homes, for one gets to know the people more intimately, and understand more clearly their problems and living conditions."[61] At the same time, she observed that, although some of the children were "fairly well dressed," many were very dirty with vermin "very much in evidence." She also claimed that "immorality is prevalent here, affecting the native life, physically, mentally, and spiritually." Some, on the other hand, were said to be clean and tidy. One year later she wrote again to the woman's auxiliary expressing her concerns about the continuation of "primitive treatments" and "semi-pagan ideas," but added that "we also have some devoted earnest Christian people who are true friends, and the 'salt of the earth' letting their light shine in their own and humble way."[62] McCabe also discussed her fear for the young children who had returned to the village after being away at school: "When Mission school pupils return home their lot is not always an easy one as they are expected to return to their old way of living – cutting wood, tanning skins, packing water, driving dogs, etc., and many other things they do not learn at school. They must begin again; it takes time and they sometimes are open to ridicule by their ignorant people."[63] McCabe offers a focus on issues that went beyond physical appearance and the supposed impoverished living conditions. There were still descriptive passages which pointed to the perseverance of traditions, but more complexity comes through. McCabe avers that she is quite comfortable with some of the villagers and was careful not to give the impression that they were all heathen. The difficulties children faced on having their traditional learning disrupted by attendance at residential schools were also apparent to McCabe.

Valenis Ottaway, who nursed in Hay River in the mid-1920s, portrayed a similar ambivalence. She attended the local woman's auxiliary meetings regularly and wrote to the home office occasionally. In the winter of 1926, she reported her first impressions and claimed that the Deh Cho Dene in her care were not as decrepit as others might claim: "The Indian's home is usually a teepee, and not such an uncouth sight as the white folks imagine."[64] Ottaway's report was unique, however, and on balance the discourse, while less negative in the 1920s, still portrayed Aboriginal peoples as helpless, passive, and unable to look after their own health and welfare.

Reading missionary narratives usually reveals far more about the individual missionaries and their social backgrounds than they do about Aboriginal cultures. British and Canadian notions of cultural superiority and their tendency to reduce Aboriginal peoples, whether by appearance or

"God Bless Our School." A classroom at the St. Peter's Residential School, Hay River (Kátl'odéech), Northwest Territories.

by daily habits, or at the extreme, by their alleged savagery, to an alien construct is complicated by recurring ambivalence and ambiguities. Their feelings and reactions to direct interaction with individual Aboriginal peoples could challenge gazes fixed by more limited contact. And the discourse adopted in mission accounts, especially those written by British missionaries, was very similar to that used to reflect class differences in Britain. It is important to remember that images of northern Aboriginal cultures were often presented to British and Canadian audiences to garner continued financial support for the mission movement. These messages often constituted the only information that non-Aboriginal readers were exposed to with respect to Canada's Aboriginal peoples. It is unlikely that contemporary reading audiences discerned the ambiguous nature of these descriptions, which nevertheless form important evidence of the relationship between Aboriginal peoples and missionaries: they suggest a more complex pattern than the colonizer/colonized dichotomy presented by Memmi. While the dominant discourse demonstrated the construction of racial and cultural differences, relations in the mission field were not static. Daily experiences necessitated relationships of reliance provoking, for missionaries, a peculiar tension – the need to maintain difference that intersected with a desire to eradicate difference. Neither aim, in the end, could be sustained or achieved.

# 3
# "I Wish the Men Were Half as Good": Gender Relations in the Mission Field

The first married woman missionary in the Diocese of Caledonia sent by the Church Missionary Society, Mrs. Lewin S. Tugwell, came out from Britain in 1860. The Reverend and Mrs. Tugwell, arriving at Victoria in August, were greeted by Caledonia-based William Duncan, who at that time was the main connection between the Church Missionary Society and the Tsimshian. On the journey north, Duncan began to resent the honeymooning Tugwells and to doubt their commitment to the work: "I see that wives after all may be a great hindrance to a man in diverting his mind from the work before him."[1] On their arrival at Port Simpson (Lax Kw'alaams), the Tugwells started to unpack their possessions. Duncan quickly informed Mrs. Tugwell that he and the Reverend Tugwell could manage the baggage, but asked her to prepare biscuits. To Duncan's surprise, she replied that she had never made bread in her life. Many years later Duncan recounted this anecdote to one of his co-workers and, at that time, added: "What do you think of that? The C.M.S. had sent more than five thousand miles, some one to help me teach the Indians Christian home life, and here I was, obliged to make bread for her myself."[2] Duncan was shocked that Mrs. Tugwell was unprepared to meet the customary expectations of a gendered division of labour. Evidently however, prior to Mrs. Tugwell's arrival Duncan had managed his own bread-making quite efficiently.

Images of masculine and feminine conduct were well ingrained in those who ventured into the mission field. Gender norms were conceived from within an ideology of separate spheres for each gender, in which masculinity and femininity were thought to be dichotomous.[3] Women were to be the moral guardians of society with their influence centred on the domestic or private sphere; men were masculine arbitrators over matters deemed to be public, including business and government. Mission societies assumed that conversion depended to some extent on the model of the "mission family," a model which was essentially patriarchal in structure.

Catherine Hall describes Baptist male missionaries in Jamaica as exemplars of patriarchy: "The missionary's role in the family enterprise was in part defined by his fatherhood – head of household, father of the family, father of the congregation, father of the children in his schools."[4] In the mission field, however, conventional gender identities were disrupted to some extent and both sexes were required to transcend gendered boundaries that had been established in their home settings. Gender boundaries among missionaries were fluid.

### Disrupting the Mission Family

Since women were integral to the "mission family," mission societies invariably expected that they would themselves become missionaries and, more particularly, share their partner's work. They generally assumed that missionary wives would work just as hard as their husbands, but without remuneration. The *Canadian Church Magazine and Mission News* of January 1897 commented that the work done by missionary wives was not always mentioned in reports to the parent society but that their contributions were nonetheless "valuable items of solid missionary usefulness."[5] In fact, mission societies were likely to comment on the appropriateness of particular marriages. When the Reverend William Collison was preparing to leave London for Metlakatla he was told that since there was no lady missionary there it would be advisable for him to marry, and he did so three weeks prior to sailing in September 1873. In his instructions from the Church Missionary Society, the committee applauded his choice, Marion Goodwin, and expressed their sincere satisfaction that he was about to marry a nurse and a woman that they were convinced would be a "true helper to you in your work, and a true mother to the infant church at Metlakatla."[6] Goodwin was herself a deaconess. She had a wealth of nursing experience, from assisting wounded soldiers on the battlefields of the Franco-Prussian War to establishing a hospital for incurables at Cork.[7] The extent to which such last-minute marriages were of convenience is open for speculation. Prior to his departure from England for the mission field in 1869, William Day Reeve married Emily Parker. After years in the field, she was described as a missionary herself: "Mrs. Reeve has been a devoted missionary herself, sharing her husband's dangers, wanderings, and privations many a time they have actually been face to face with starvation."[8]

Local bishops also came to appreciate the importance of missionary wives. Writing to the Church Missionary Society in 1895, Bishop William Bompas described the type of man he wanted in the north: "I may say that I prefer a married Missionary or if not thus, then one engaged to be married to whom his wife may be sent without his returning to fetch her."[9] He was satisfied, for instance, when the Reverend J. Naylor, a McGill University graduate, was on his way to the Yukon with his wife Ada Mount-Naylor, also from Québec. In the summer of 1896, Bompas wrote to the Reverend Naylor to tell him how anxious he was about their arrival: "I cannot tell you how earnestly I have longed for additional help and I still cannot but hope that you are bringing with you a second recruit for our work besides Mrs. Naylor to whom please to offer our best respects, and who will I doubt not be an important acquisition in our Mission field."[10] Bishop Bompas clearly viewed Mrs. Naylor as an "acquisition," but in his strained circumstances it is perhaps understandable. He was constantly demanding more recruits. The Reverend Isaac Stringer, consecrated Bishop of the Yukon in 1905, also prefered married couples. In a letter of recommendation for the Reverend W.H. Fry who worked at Herschel Island (Qikiqtaruk) for four years, he applauded both the Reverend and his wife: "Mrs. Fry is an excellent helpmeet possessing all the qualities that a clergyman's wife should possess – tactful and judicious, a good housekeeper and interested in the work of the church. She was formerly a school teacher, and did good work as teacher at the school at Herschel Island."[11] Underlying such praise was the fact that the mission society was getting two workers for the price of one.

Just as one of the central images of male missionaries was connected to masculinity, women were expected to display femininity through the exhibition of their domestic arts. Missionary wives in particular were seen as helpmates sent to the mission field to teach their disciples how to act like "proper ladies." Beneath the performance of womanly rituals rested an assumption that the British/Canadian woman's way was the only way, and that Aboriginal women were somehow lacking in skills necessary to maintain households and raise children. Their standards of cleanliness, child-rearing, and family life in general came under close scrutiny and were found wanting. However, for White women, the mission field also provided the opportunity to stretch the boundaries of gender that, ironically, they were attempting to impose on Aboriginal women.

Selina Bompas was well aware of what was expected of White women in the north, particularly Christian women, and did not hesitate to provide her views on propriety. In November 1907, after many years of living in the north, she wrote an article for the *Canadian Churchman* concerning the type of women who should settle in the north. She was referring, principally, to mission work, but made it clear that school teachers, housekeepers and dressmakers were also badly needed. Furthermore their behaviour, from dress to manners, should set an example for Aboriginal women. "Dear sister-settlers amongst the Indians," Bompas urged, "there is power given you from on high which is intended you should use among them or any other race with whom you may be placed – it is the power of *influence* ... In your Christian households, in your modest demeanour, in your fair dealings with all let them see what they should seek to copy more than the jewels and costly attire which in their eyes are all that is needed to consti-tute a lady."[12] The implication was that Aboriginal women needed White role models so that they might learn to behave like "proper ladies." That Aboriginal women had their own cultural traditions related to gender roles, including care giving and domestic form, was rarely acknowledged.

Expectations about the duties and demeanour of missionary women were especially apparent to male missionaries. When the Reverend J.B. McCullagh's second wife, Mary Webster McCullagh, joined him in his work among the Nisga'a of the Nass River (K'alii Aksim Lisims) valley, he wrote to the Nisga'a Missionary Union to report her success and to boast about how she was so "capable of understanding the why and the where-fore of their racial limitations and imperfections, as well as of appreciating their good points of which they have not a few."[13] McCullagh listed the duties of both his daughter and wife, which included the "daily cooking, washing up, brushing and dusting rooms, washing, starching and iron-ing, and every other thing that has to be done in a house." He recognized that this routine tested the missionary spirit and admired the way Mary McCullagh went about her work: "Looking at her amongst a crowd of Indian women, teaching them to cut and make up articles of wearing apparel, my wife is a source of intense joy and astonishment to me. When one considers how difficult it is to 'handle' Indians, the tact, patience and self-forgetting spirit it requires, to say nothing of the demand on one's physical energy, it is a wonder to me to find her put in two solid hours of this work, and then come away as fresh as the proverbial daisy."[14] The rhetoric of the "Angel in the Home" was easily transferred into the mission field. Imperialist discourse and the ideology of separate spheres for each gender were intricately connected in many accounts of relationships between colonizer and colonized.

Miss F. Copeland, who arrived at Kincolith (Gingolx) in the Nass River valley in 1907, described the work of Marion Collison, a veteran of twenty-six years, in similar terms. She acknowledged that one must know the character of the Nisga'a to appreciate all the "patient, loving toil" the Col-lisons had supplied. She gave Marion Collison credit for raising a number of young Nisga'a women in her own home, resulting in several of them learning how to "clean and scrub, wash and bake, sew and knit, and last but not least, how to bring up their children to some extent in the fear of the Lord."[15] Attempts to export Christian domesticity were characteristic of the global mission movement. Jane Hunter suggests that women mission-aries defined themselves within the context of an "expansive domesticity, endeavouring to embody traditional notions of nurturance, gentility, and affection which distinguished them from men."[16] The goal of teaching Christian domesticity was to encourage women to convert to Christian-ity but, like other peoples targeted by missionaries, Aboriginal women did not necessarily convert because of their new knowledge of European housekeeping.

While modelling domesticity was standard for women, very little was said in the official correspondence about teaching Aboriginal men how to be "proper gentlemen." The act of consciously modelling gentlemanly behaviour was uncommon among male missionaries, as there was not the same concern for teaching men manners. Men had to be "civilized," but not to the same extent as women. Male missionaries, on the other hand, sought Aboriginal knowledge from their guides and translators, hoping to learn skills that would make them more adept at travelling and living in the outdoors. This is not to say, however, that they ever refrained from their sense of urgency in modelling what to them seemed like proper domesticity. One observer noted, after hearing a sermon at Aklavik, prescribing and modelling went hand in hand for some missionaries: "Archdeacon Whittaker, with an interpreter, preached a short sermon on the duty of men, who should do hard work and leave light work to women, taking the line of 'When I want wood I don't send my wife, and, what I say to you, I say not only with my tongue but by what I do.'"[17]

Despite the seemingly rigid categories of femininity and masculinity, when we look at the relationship between missionary men and women in the field the boundaries of gender often appear to be shifting. At times, men had to do what might be traditionally considered women's work while women often had to go beyond what Victorian society would have construed as appropriate womanly behaviour. At times, too, it was necessary to overlook the rhetoric if not the practice of true womanhood altogether. When the Reverend Isaac Stringer wrote to his fiancee Sarah (Sadie) Alexander, then in nurse's training at the Grace Hospital in Toronto, he suggested some areas of medicine to which she should pay particular attention: "I must just mention that syphilis is one of the common diseases amongst the Eskimos. It may seem out of place to mention this to a lady but in our circumstances we must be practical and the mention of this may lead you to study up the different forms of the disease."[18] The Reverend Stringer thought that it would be impractical to shield his future partner in the mission field from the reality of what would soon face her, even if society might not sanction any discussion of sexuality.

Separate gender spheres were not always practical in the mission field. Husbands and wives in many different ways had to eschew tensions between masculinity and femininity and face the daily realities of their work. Dealing with prolonged absences stands out, perhaps because of the extended period of experimentation that they required. Selina Bompas complained bitterly at times about being alone, although, luckily, she was spirited enough to overcome periods of loneliness.[19] So too was Jane Ridley in the Diocese of Caledonia. In 1884, Bishop Ridley went to Ottawa to present his interpretation of the Duncan uprising, when the controversial William Duncan chose to ignore the bishop's requests and carry on without the advice of the Church Missionary Society. Ridley found himself in an awkward position regarding Hazelton (Gitenmaks), where the Church Missionary Society had just established a station. The missionary there was forced to return to England because of his wife's ill health and Ridley did not want to leave the station unattended. Instead, Jane Ridley volunteered to stay behind while her husband went to Ottawa and then on to England. As the *Church Missionary Intelligencer and Record* reported in March 1884:

> Mrs. Ridley can have no idea of his having come on to England. He had left her at Hazelton, the interior station at the Skeena Forks, vacated by the return to England of the Reverend W.J. Faulconer on account of his wife's illness; and there she is spending the winter and carrying on the work of the station entirely alone. We cannot but be too thankful for the self-denying courage with which she has thrown herself into the breach, and for the happy influence she evidently exercises upon the Indians.[20]

Jane Helmer Hyne had married the Reverend William Ridley in 1866, just prior to their departure from England for four years of service in the province of Peshawar in India. They returned to England because of Ridley's ill health and stayed for nine years before he was consecrated the first Bishop of Caledonia in July 1879. Little is known of Jane Ridley's life before her marriage and few of her own written records have survived. After her death, the *Canadian Church Magazine and Mission News* called her a "Missionary Heroine" because she had so successfully maintained the Hazelton station in the winter of 1884.[21] Bishop Ridley declared that she enjoyed her mission and was popular among the Tsimshian. On the scene of her deathbed, he wrote a very melodramatic testimony for the Church Missionary Society: "crowds of Indians hung round her bed and she was delighted ... In her death she, by her beautiful and tender words, and patient endurance of agony at times through choking, drew more souls to Jesus than ever. It was victory on victory, triumph on triumph. Quite two hundred souls shared in the blessing."[22] In the end he gave her body over to the Tsimshian. Bishop Ridley was using the hyperbole commonly adopted in missionary obituaries but it does appear that, during the death of Jane Ridley, her husband believed that souls were saved. The Reverend William Collison attended her funeral and was also swept up in the emotion: "She bade farewell to all the Zimshian native Christians individually and gave to each a parting charge. She was thus enabled by the divine grace to set a seal on the teachings of a life consecrated & devoted to the service of the master amongst the Zimshians."[23] In the fashion of missionary eulogies, Jane Ridley was reconstructed as a heroine.

While traditional gender roles reflected in the discourse applied either to men or women in the mission field, descriptions of certain religious identities could blur gender distinctions. In the case of Jane Ridley an apparent freedom from the normative constraints of gender was implied in her higher calling, or what the *Church Missionary Intelligencer* called her "self-denying courage." Within the context of a Christian calling, Ridley's gender could at times appear subsumed. In a subsequent tribute to women missionaries, Bishop Ridley stated that women "work hardest and by their example fire the men with emulation. There is not one married woman among us who would think she was free to devote nearly all her time to domestic economy. The wife is as much called of God to be his instrument in soul-winning as the husband."[24] From Bishop Ridley's perspective, the Christian calling was not gender specific. This is not to say that he would necessarily have supported the ordination of women, but with respect to "soul-winning," he tended to cast men and women as equals.

As much as a higher calling could serve as a strategic category for women, in terms of the mundane realities of mission life, it was important for both sexes to experiment with traditional spheres of masculinity and femininity, if for nothing else than immediate necessity. Women were often left on their own to maintain the mission station. And, men certainly had to know how to cook and do other household chores. One minister in the Arctic, the Reverend G. Neilson, attracted the compliments of British-born Florence Hirst and Canadian nurse Prue Hockin because of his capable shortbread cookies and doughnuts, although they agreed that "men don't look right cooking doughnuts somehow."[25] Another, the Reverend Alfred Price, stationed at Kitwanga (Gitwangak), wrote to the Church Missionary Society complaining that the Aboriginal woman hired to help his wife in the delivery of their child had abandoned them as the date approached: "there was no one to do the washing; I had to do everything even to delivering the child."[26] The first child delivered to the Prices died, and Bessie Price chose to go to Victoria for the delivery of their next.

Childbirth in the mission field posed new challenges for missionary couples. Like the Prices, the first child born to the Tomlinsons, who arrived at Kincolith in 1868, also died. Alice (Woods) from Victoria, British Columbia, had married the Irish-born Robert Tomlinson when she was seventeen. When stationed at Kincolith in the summer of 1871 Alice Tomlinson, who was expecting her first child, contracted typhoid fever. Fortunately, her husband had some medical training and was with her throughout her most critical period. The child survived only a few hours. In a report to the parent committee Tomlinson expressed his isolation and mourning: "It is hard for those living among sympathizing friends to realize the trials of those more isolated. On this day I had to fill the place of Father, Husband, Mourner, Doctor, Nurse, Clergyman."[27] All these roles required a sympathetic individual rather unlike the image of the rugged frontiersman or masculine stereotype. The trials of marriage and childbirth in such cases could result in the recasting of gender boundaries.

Sarah Stringer had her first two children when she and her husband were stationed at Herschel Island (Qikiqtaruk). In her diary, she recorded the birth of their first child, Rowena, on December 14, 1896. Until the birth, Stringer kept active, mentioning that she had taught school, gone for walks, and held choir practice. In the tone of her diary she appeared very calm about her pregnancy. Ten days after the delivery she wrote that she had been "an invalid for the past few days Mr. Stringer being my physician he was also my nurse also Mr. Whittaker helping and cooking me many dainty dishes. He excelled in this much to my pleasure." The Reverend Whittaker was a former Wycliffe College classmate and was sent to the north in 1896. The Reverends Whittaker and Stringer cared for Mrs. Stringer and were able to manage the household while she was recovering from childbirth. They not only coped, but actually cooked fancy dishes. One month after Rowena's birth Sarah Stringer was teaching again.[28]

Her attitude might be attributed to her medical experience as a nurse and perhaps to her personality. She rarely complained about isolation or loneliness in her letters and diaries. However, she could be critical of those who did. Emma Hatley arrived in July 1898 to marry the Reverend Whittaker and work with him at Peel River. She was originally from London, England, and had been in the north since 1895 assisting her sister Maria Hatley Lucas at Fort Chipewyan. Mrs. Stringer gave her away at their wedding and soon returned to Herschel Island for the winter.[29] Next summer, the Stringers visited Peel River, just after the delivery of the Whittakers's first child. Apparently, Emma Whittaker felt nervous and was reluctant to return for a visit to Herschel Island with the Stringers. In a letter to her friend back in Ontario, Sarah recorded her impressions of Emma: "Mrs. Whittaker does not know whether she will go or not. She fears this that and the other so I do not know if she will go ... She is rather delicate."[30]

The challenges of adapting to a new environment, married life, and a new baby all at the same time were great, as the Reverend Whittaker himself acknowledged. In a letter to Toronto's woman's auxiliary, he boasted of having a new companion but cast some doubt on Emma's adaptability: "Personally, you will be glad to know that I have now some one of my own to get a lunch for me if I come in late. My wife enjoys life here very much, although it is rather hard for one delicately reared."[31] Indeed, in describing his marriage proposal he spoke of the practicality of the arrangement. Emma had, according to Whittaker, "responded to my invitation to be co-helper in the mission."[32]

Many years later the Reverend Archibald Fleming, first Bishop of the Arctic, recalled the trials of the Whittakers and other pioneer missionaries when he visited a church in Fort McPherson (Tetlit'zheh): "Memorial brasses in the Arctic are somehow much more poignant than those in the south. I suppose it is because they represent suffering remote from the comfort of friends. Here in St. Matthew's church this experience is told so eloquently and yet so briefly on three small brass plates each bearing the name of a child born to Archdeacon and Mrs. Whittaker. Two had died at Herschel Island and their bodies were carried two hundred and fifty miles by sledge and dog team to Fort McPherson for burial; the third died up the river."[33]

Life in the north presented unique sets of challenges. For some mission couples these challenges were unbearable, forcing early resignation from the field. As it turned out, the Whittakers were in the north until 1921, but not everyone could adapt to their new conditions. Mrs. Tugwell stayed for only two years. The next couple sent out to help Duncan, the Gribbells, lasted only six weeks.[34] In each case, it was claimed that the woman's health was too delicate to prolong their stay, a frequent explanation when couples chose to leave their assigned station earlier than anticipated.

Emma Whittaker on Herschel Island (Qikiqtaruk) with a boy, his mother, and grandmother.

Women missionaries had to be physically and emotionally able to endure life in the north. The challenges of survival, particularly in areas thought to be isolated, may have been impossible for some women and undoubtedly for some men as well.[35] Others may have found it impossible to adjust.

Newcomers especially complained about the lack of privacy. When the Collisons moved to the Queen Charlotte Islands (Haida Gwaii), they immediately faced this issue. Privacy in living spaces is a cultural factor which, according to the Reverend Collison, was not shared by the Haida. As he related in his memoirs, it became quite a chore to demand it even for his wife in their hut:

> The Haida, many of whom had not seen a white woman, crowded into our little shanty in their paint and feathers, and squatted down on the floor, so closely packed together that there was no room to move ... Not knowing their language, I could not convey to them our desire, or had I attempted to drive them out, I might have been ejected in turn, or subjected to even rougher treatment. I concluded therefore that what could not be helped must be endured. Day after day this continued, so that it was impossible to get near the stove to prepare any food. Any article of wearing apparel within reach was freely made use of. Hats, coats, and boots were passed from one another, each one trying them on and inviting the opinions of the others as to the appearance or otherwise.[36]

The Reverend Collison's recollections suggest that the mission was so tenuous he feared offending their visitors in asking them to leave. His hospitality meant that it would be difficult to spend any uninterrupted time with his family. Writing to Bishop Stringer in 1922, Catherine Hoare, stationed at Aklavik with her husband, expressed similar concerns: "I often wonder how you people managed about eating etc. We had quite a time of it. They even sat in the bedroom and watched us dress. One hates to offend them for they mean no harm."[37] The Bishop replied to Hoare that it was most important that they treat their unwanted visitors delicately, but in his view they should not sit in the bedroom to watch the Hoares dress. He even suggested some phrases they could try to encourage them to leave without offence.[38]

Mission houses were never private homes. They were living spaces where visitors, wanted or not, often crossed family thresholds. Some missionaries encouraged Aboriginal peoples who were preparing to abandon their villages for winter to leave their children so that their wives could teach them English. Mission homes were, in many instances, converted into schools during the day. The issue of privacy had an impact on both men and women, but one could argue that because the running of the household was deemed a woman's responsibility the lack of privacy had more of an effect on women. In negotiating this living space, as well as determining other duties related to mission work, marriages in the mission field had to be partnerships or a couple's failure in the mission field would be certain.

### Unmarried Women Missionaries

Like their married sisters, unmarried women missionaries were also expected to participate in all aspects of mission work. In 1896, Bishop Ridley wrote to tell the Church Missionary Society the type of women that he wanted for his diocese. He insisted on "ladies accustomed to refined environments," believing women from privileged backgrounds had proven more willing to agree to perform undesirable tasks. Scrubbing and cleaning children often "crawling [with] things" were listed as tasks that "servants or unrefined women" would not perform. "I want ladies," Bishop Ridley concluded, "who for Christ's sake will undertake anything in the path of duty." He also argued that women who "are not refined in thought and behavior ... would not meet with the same unreservedness socially as others who are refined."[39] Although he employed the rhetoric of traditional womanhood, when he turned to practical issues, his definition of the ideal woman changed dramatically. Bishop Ridley expected ladies to be something quite different from "proverbial daisies." He demanded they be prepared to do absolutely any work that lay "in the path of duty," including much that might otherwise be seen as undesirable. Women who would

Bishop Stringer and the Reverend Charles Whittaker (upper right) at a confirmation class in 1916.

respond to "higher claims," despite the expectations of gender norms, were considered essential.

Bishop Ridley was pleased with the first unmarried missionary women in his diocese and wrote to the Church Missionary Society in October 1898 that "We do get splendid lady workers for this place. I wish the men were half as good."[40] Eleanor Dickenson from the Isle of Wight arrived in June 1890 and was instantly in demand. According to Ridley, her list of duties was extensive:

> She is secretary to the ladies prayer union and Bible reading union ... she is always ready to go to the rescue when trained nursing is required at the hospital. This is her forte. She would have taken charge of it but that I feared her energy (which is great) would have brought her into collision with our doctor who though much improved of late is not and never will be energetic. She attends to the sick at their homes and so has won the hearts of all the mothers in the place. Her chief work is the girls home. She has nine girls with her.[41]

Her hard work had earned her much respect among the other missionaries and, because she would never rest, Bishop Ridley said that he had to insist that she submit to the "curb." In his estimation Dickinson was an excellent worker but she had to be warned not to overdo it, which is what he meant by submitting to the curb. He was afraid that Dickinson's energy would show up the doctor's lassitude.

His descriptions of male missionaries, on the other hand, showed no fear of this. The Reverend Alfred Price, missionary for Kitwanga, was portrayed by Bishop Ridley as "very intelligent but no student ... He is a man of action full of self reliance and muscular strength."[42] In describing the Reverend Price, Bishop Ridley employed the familiar rhetoric of nineteenth-century self-reliance combined with a reference to muscular Christianity. Women missionaries by contrast were often chided to restrict their enthusiasm and energy. Margaret West, for example, who arrived the summer after Dickinson, was described with typical concern: "You have sent us in Miss West a most charming candidate for missionary honours and I think she will win these provided she submit to the curb. It is indeed refreshing to see one so eager to work for Christ. This is the secret 'she loveth much.'"[43]

While there is ample evidence to suggest that women missionaries spent much of their time committing, as the Church Missionary Society put it, "the performance of everyday common place duties," it is also apparent that they were not perpetually trapped in the traditional category of "women."[44] They often did the same work as their male counterparts and experienced similar moments of adventure in the outdoors. In *Discourses of Difference: An Analysis of Women's Travel Writing and Colonialism*, Sara Mills argues that women travel writers of the eighteenth and nineteenth centuries "were restricted as to the type of language they might use and the sort of 'experience' they might depict, and thus their work was judged to be limited compared to the relative freedom of male novelists."[45] Mills focuses on travel writers, but the same can be said of women missionaries. Their letters and diaries do not contain the masculine discourse of Haggard and Henty, or muscular Christianity's emphasis on action. Women were not conditioned as were their male counterparts to glory in the adventure of tipping canoes or chopping wood. Yet their experiences indicate that they shared equally in the outdoor demands of missionary work. They were called on to perform tasks in the outdoors that were similar to those experienced by male missionaries.

An incident which illustrates this point was reported in the official Church Missionary Society history, compiled by Eugene Stock under the ironic title *History of the Church Missionary Society, Its Environment, Its Men, and Its Work*. Bishop Ridley reported that during the summer months many women missionaries worked at the coastal canneries. In the summer of 1893, Margaret West was stationed at Inverness, about twenty kilometres from Metlakatla, but she also taught school at Sunnyside, another fish cannery. She rowed her own boat back and forth despite the treacherous tidal currents and rough landings. Bishop Ridley claimed that

> she pursued her steady course, so that she has become an expert sailor, handling her 16 foot boat all alone as well as any man on our staff. She had it all to learn to her cost. Once she got into serious difficulties, being capsized in deep and rough water, and was half drowned before she could climb back into the boat. It was a risk to appoint a lady to such a station single-handed where there are some hundreds of Indians, Chinese, Japanese and a band of white men unaccustomed to social or religious restraints.[46]

By the end of the summer, according to Bishop Ridley, West had proven the effectiveness of what he called "true womanliness" combined with "self sacrificing service for Christ." It is striking that, although she could handle a boat as well as any man in the mission, she was still characterized by Ridley as having the distinctive features of "true womanliness."[47] Her accomplishments were described as work for Christ with little reflection of the fact that she had gone beyond traditional gender boundaries.

Edith Beeching and Christine Carleton had similar experiences in their work at the mission stations near Alert Bay ('Yalis). Originally from Dover, Edith Beeching arrived at Alert Bay in the summer of 1894. The following year, she was sent for three weeks to a fishing station at Rivers Inlet, fifty miles north of Alert Bay. While there she kept a diary which she subsequently sent to the Church Missionary Society. Her job was to visit the two canneries, which were separated by a river one-and-a-half kilometres wide. She visited house to house and held meetings with Oweekeno girls and women in the fields outside the canneries where they prayed and sang together. Beeching used a small church belonging to the Methodist mission where she held services with the members of the community. On July 14 Beeching recorded in her diary: "I spent the afternoon sewing for a woman ... I don't know when I felt so happy just sitting in that little cabin of hers, and talking of Jesus to her, I remember wishing to do this when I was in England and now I have the opportunity."[48] In her moment of happiness at the cottage Beeching was doing just exactly what she imagined her work as a missionary would entail. Her visits to the canneries presented considerable physical challenges and in her physical freedom, her travelling, and in leading meetings Beeching had temporarily achieved a freedom from the specific gendered constraints of most women in mission stations.

On her return, however, Bishop Ridley expressed some dissatisfaction to her immediate supervisor the Reverend Albert Hall for the fact that she had been sent unchaperoned. As a result, the following year she was joined by Christine Carleton. Carleton and Beeching worked together planning and conducting services: "we have two services in the vernacular one at 11am and the other at 3pm. Miss Beeching giving the services and I playing the harmoniums. We use part of the Prayer book service sing several hymns read and explain part of the chapter from one of the three gospels which we have translated into the vernacular."[49] Teaching school and conducting services were two of the most common jobs that women found themselves doing in northern missions. But they were also expected to do a little bit of everything.

Bessie Quirt's diary revealed this expectation clearly. Originally from Orillia, Ontario, Quirt was the first school teacher at the new Anglican residential for Inuvialuit children at Shingle Point (Tapqaq), which opened in 1929. Quirt's diary reminds us of the range of activities experienced by missionary women. In a four-month period she spoke of the joy of "taking the new canoe out for a wonderful paddle," the excitement of a visit by the bishop, at which time she "acted as a scullery maid at the mission house," and the pride of the first day of school: "I couldn't help feeling thrilled as I walked over to school that morning feeling what a privilege was mine being the first teacher."[50] She also recorded some humorous moments: "Flossie and I will never forget Christmas eve and Christmas morning hacking, sewing and cutting at that Caribou to make it into Christmas dinner ... We certainly could see the funny side of it and stopped to enjoy the novelty of it quite often."

From piling wood to canoeing to experiencing her first Arctic winter, the novelty for Quirt did not seem to wear off quickly: "I can scarcely realize at times yet that it is actually the Arctic ocean over which I am looking and that I am here working among the Eskimo. The glamour certainly has not entirely worn off yet."[51] There was never a shortage of work or adventure that might otherwise be construed as "masculine" for women missionaries. Unmarried women often travelled considerable distances from their stations and, like Beeching, sometimes did so "unchaperoned." In the spring of 1896, the *Canadian Church Magazine and Mission News* recorded that Caledonia's "lady" missionaries "have sometimes pretty trying times of it, for they go up and down the rivers in small boats, teaching and nursing at their various stopping places, which are not always of the smoothest as regards either water or land."[52] They experienced the multifaceted demands of mission work and enjoyed freedoms that went well beyond gender norms of the day. Through their work, they also developed long-lasting and close friendships with other women missionaries.

## Female Friendships

The community of Anglican missionary women in the north was not large. Distance may have divided these women but a spirit of neighbourliness and sometimes even intimacy were part of their mutual experience. Beyond the patriarchal "mission family," new forms of surrogate families developed in the north. In order to overcome the feeling of isolation most women regularly corresponded with friends and relatives at home while forming close bonds with other women in the field.[53] These friendships were valuable and sometimes crucial, especially at times of crisis or

Bessie Quirt with the first group of Inuvialuit girls at Shingle Point (Tapqaq), fall 1929. *Standing, left to right:* Lucy, Toki, Dlorac, Agnes, Ruth, Millie, and Madeline. *Kneeling with Bessie Quirt:* Emily, Mary, and Mabel.

loneliness. In her work entitled, *Independent Women: Work and Community for Single Women 1850-1920*, Martha Vicinus explores relationships between Victorian professional unmarried women. Her focus is entirely on single women who worked in institutions such as deaconess houses, boarding schools, or convents. Vicinus argues that, in public, many women were typical "upper-class ladies of severe manners and distinct demeanour. But privately their society permitted, and they experienced, a wide range of emotional behavior with intimate friends. The very distance and self-control demanded of them in public rebounded to make moments of intimacy more precious; friendships bore the entire weight of the emotions."[54]

Again, it is important to emphasize that Vicinus focuses on single women and their female friendship networks. The pattern she observed is also apparent with single women missionaries in the north, and to some degree her conclusions pertain to married women as well. One could argue that at times missionary wives behaved like single women and developed similar relationships. The intensity of the work and the isolation frequently led to close friendships. Husbands were often away for months at a time, so women had to rely on each other. Their positions as missionaries imposed fairly rigid behavioural expectations, but when they were with their friends they could act much more freely.

Through her long tenure in the Yukon, Selina Bompas came to know many women missionaries intimately. For example, when Bompas was visiting Britain in 1885, she corresponded with Sarah French, who was at the time planning to leave for northern Canada to marry the Reverend T.H. Canham, then stationed at Fort McPherson. French was from Galway County, Ireland, and had agreed to marry at the age of forty. Bompas wrote to her sister-in-law about French: "Miss French (Mr. C's fiancee) seems a very sweet girl I have had several letters from her & had to tell her about all her outfit and advise her about many things."[55] She and Bompas travelled back to Canada together in the spring of 1885. Apparently, they were detained in Winnipeg for one year because of the second Riel Rebellion. This friendship began with Bompas offering advice on life in the north and lasted through travel and living together in Winnipeg, until the Canhams's retirement. Another close friendship was formed with Susan Mellett, originally from Ireland, where she had taught in the Ragged Schools. In 1893, at the age of 23, she signed up as a missionary and was met at Forty Mile (Ch'ëdäh Dëk), her first station, by Bishop Bompas.[56] Several times throughout her career she recalled that first meeting with Bishop Bompas and claimed to never forget his disappointment at seeing that she was the only worker sent to the north by the Church Missionary Society for the year. He was always hoping for an increase in the mission staff, but all Bishop Bompas found that year was what Mellett described as a "little person."[57] Her remark may well have been more of a reflection on Bishop

Bompas's expectations and perceptions of women. He did not appear to be a promoter of women missionaries, unlike his contemporary, Bishop William Ridley.

Mellett lived with the Bompas family and taught school at Forty Mile and later at Rampart House (Jiindé Tsik). According to her diary, Selina Bompas immediately appreciated Mellett: "Our household goes on very peacefully and happily. Miss Millett [sic] is a real blessing to us. She is a thorough Irish girl and a good churchwoman. She gets on well with everybody. The children are devoted to her, and she keeps them in first-rate order. One comfort is that she has good health and is not troubled with nerves. She bears the cold manfully, and was only a little startled lately when her blanket at night was fringed with icicles from her breath freezing."[58] Interestingly, Bompas chose the term "manfully" to describe Mellett's endurance of the cold. This implied that Mellett had a certain grit which may not have been in the possession of "proverbial daisies." Bompas and Mellett spent many hours together learning the Tukudh language.

In 1898, Bishop Bompas officiated at the marriage of Mellett and the Reverend R.J. Bowen, who arrived in the Yukon in 1895. Mellett and her new husband moved to Dawson (Tr'ochek) and then to Whitehorse, (Kwanlin) where Selina Bompas became a regular house guest. There the Bompas-Mellett friendship continued.[59] In May 1901, when Bompas became ill with pneumonia, she recorded in her diary that she had "been most tenderly and lovingly nursed and cared for. Mrs. Bowen came from Whitehorse and stayed a fortnight."[60] When a missionary became ill or was about to deliver a child, it was not uncommon for co-workers to nurse them if they were within travelling distance.[61] When she lived at Forty Mile, for example, Bompas corresponded with and frequently visited Ada Naylor. In the case of the birth of Naylor's second child, however, Bompas wrote to apologize for not responding immediately: "It must seem very unkind and unfriendly of me to have sent you no word of congratulation on your new treasure as also on your speedy restoration to convalescence, of which the Bishop [Bompas] tells me. Believe me, I did rejoice in your happiness, and congratulate you most sincerely as also the "Herr Papa" on the rapid increase of his nursery."[62] Bompas went on to say that she had simply been too busy to write, but that she was very eager to hear the details of the birth: "When you can spare time I would much like to hear a few particulars of No. 2. Whether he is full size and vigorous looking like Edgar, and any other items you can spare me concerning Baby or Edgar and *last not least* yourself will be lovingly welcome."[63] In this case, Bompas failed to visit Naylor during the delivery of her child but perhaps the reassurance that she was not far away may have been comforting. A few months later, Ada Naylor invited Bompas to a patriotic concert at Whitehorse. Though she wanted to attend, Bompas had to decline but wrote that she looked forward to seeing the new baby and telling her friend all the "Forty Mile news and gossip."[64]

Even after leaving the Yukon in 1906, Bompas corresponded with her former colleagues. Writing to the Stringers in 1910 she told of a visit with the Naylors: "Mr. Naylor has been reading to me as I sit under that oak and maple trees of his beautiful garden at Frelighsburg [in Québec] where I spent a very pleasant fortnight last July. His eldest son Edgar was born at Forty Mile just twelve years since."[65] She enjoyed hearing the daily news of life in the Yukon, but she also wrote to encourage the Stringers in their work. At one point in 1909, when Bishop Stringer was on circuit in the Mackenzie (Deh Cho) River area and had not been in contact with his wife, Bompas wrote a letter of assurance: "I think you have good reason for anxiety but not for alarm, his long absence can all be explained." She ended by advising her to "keep up yr. character" and, if she had not already, she must try to get a copy of *Anne of Green Gables* and "read it at once."[66]

In the same way that married women offered support to each other, unmarried missionary women also turned to each other for companionship and support. At Shingle Point, for example, Bessie Quirt recognized that other workers in the mission field looked up to her. Flossie Hirst, who nursed at Pangnirtung after working at Shingle Point, became very close to Quirt. Quirt related to her diary that she felt an intense loyalty and spiritual responsibility toward Hirst:

*Left to right:* Minnie Wilson, Charlotte Selina Bompas, Bishop W.C. Bompas, Gertrude, Reverend Isaac O. Stringer, Alex J. Stringer, and Sarah A. Stringer.

Last week she was feeling all right physically but got a depressed and lonesome streak on. However she's been quite herself since I went and slept with her on Wednesday night. She seemed to enjoy so much having me back to cuddle her up again. My Flossie darlin she has caused me a lot of worry and unhappiness but I am glad my love for her has cost me something. I feel almost frightened knowing upon what a pinnacle she places me and how she looks to me for her example and tries to live to please me. Oh that I may never lead her even a step off the path her master would have her tread.[67]

The demands of missionary life often shifted boundaries of gender, yet women missionaries did not cease to respond to one another as women. The evidence suggests that these relationships exhibited emotional and physical bonding. The isolation and strain of missionary work encouraged such closeness. In her study of nineteenth-century gender relations in Victorian America, Caroll Smith-Rosenberg emphasizes the prevalence of intimate friendships between women. She concludes that, within the confines of family and close friends, a woman's world developed, a world that

Florence Hirst and Bessie Quirt skating at Shingle Point (Tapqaq) in the winter of 1932. Women missionaries were active in the outdoors, frequently skating, hiking, and boating.

was characterized by what she calls a "generic and unself-conscious pattern of single-sex or homosocial networks. These supportive networks were institutionalized in social conventions or rituals that accompanied virtually every important event in a woman's life, from birth to death ... Within such a world of emotional richness and complexity, devotion to and love of other women became a plausible and socially accepted form of human interaction."[68] Rarely, however, is there this same intensity expressed between male missionaries in the northern field. Men travelled and worked together, but the surviving records do not reveal discussions of similar intimacies.[69]

Monica Storrs, who became well known in the Peace River region of northern British Columbia in the late 1920s, shared an intense friendship with Adeline Harmer, who joined her in 1931. Storrs was described by historian W.L. Morton as a "church woman through and through." Born in London in 1888 to the Reverend and Mrs. John Storrs, she was educated at the Francis Holland Church of England School for Girls in London. When her father was appointed Dean of Rochester in 1913, she began her active career in church work. After his death in 1928, she started a new life as a missionary.[70] Storrs worked in the Diocese of Caledonia as a Fellowship of the Maple Leaf Sunday school teacher and scout and guide leader for two years, before she returned to England to bring Harmer back with her. Harmer was a long-time friend and the daughter of the Bishop of Rochester. Storrs reflected in her diary how it felt to be with Harmer: "It was almost a joy being at Peace Coupe again, the place where I had been so anxious last September and was now so perfectly hopeful and happy with Adeline."[71] She and Harmer immediately began building a home in which they intended to share a bedroom. Although much of the building was contracted, Harmer and Storrs found themselves doing some of the physical labour. "On Sunday," Harmer quipped in their diary, "we became perfect ladies shaking off the chrysalis of filthy dark blue overalls."[72] For a fleeting and perhaps unconscious moment Harmer seemed to adopt a new gendered space for herself and Storrs.

Like Storrs and Harmer, Edith Beeching and Christine Carleton also shared a close friendship. Writing to the Church Missionary Society, the Reverend Albert Hall observed that "Miss Beeching and Miss Carleton are much attached to one another, veritable sisters, and they now live together in the girls home." Carleton herself commented on how well she and Miss Beeching got along: "Miss Beeching and I are truly happy together – we each have our distinct work although I live in the Girls home – living together is such a pleasant arrangement."[73]

At Metlakatla, an intense friendship developed between Jane Ridley and Margaret West. Bishop Ridley often commented on how close they were. They often spent as much as two hours a day reading Tsimshian together and, when Jane Ridley was forced to return to England for one year, West went with her as her nurse. When Jane Ridley died a year after their return in December 1896, West expressed her grief: "What her loss is to me I cannot tell. She was more than guide and friend and I do trust that her loving words and example may fit me for the work our master has set out here. It is difficult to write much more now."[74]

Despite the loss of her close friend, West continued with her work and developed similar friendships. Bishop Ridley observed that "Miss West mothers the young fellow workers and the new ones already have given their love and trust to her as she did to her who has just died."[75] Like Quirt, West was placed on the pedestal of the feminine ideal, but it was not a site either inhabited permanently. They did not, as Denise Riley would put it, "make a final home in that classification." Years later, in 1931, after West died at Metlakatla, it was noted that she and Rose Davies (who had arrived in Metlakatla in 1896) had worked in "harmonious and loving agreement." West and Davies were partners in supervising the Ridley Home, and, claimed the *North British Columbia News*, would be "inscribed on the Roll of Honour, of the Pioneer Missionaries of Caledonia."[76] The network of female companionship was often tight and long-lasting. The women in the Yukon and Arctic kept in close contact with one another and appeared to have a strong sense of collective identity and a shared past. Missionary women in the north during the 1930s frequently referred fondly to the first generation of missionaries and the origins of the Anglican Church in the region. The list of pioneers was well known. On her way to Shingle Point

Monica Storrs bringing in the kindling near her home in Fort St. John, January 1949.

in 1932, Adelaide Butler stopped at Winnipeg to visit the Stringers. She described her visit by saying that she "was in society and I enjoyed myself."[77] She thought Mrs. Stringer was "very motherly" because she insisted that Butler should take a long rest before leaving on her journey.[78] Stringer corresponded with women who went north well into the 1930s. The Anglican community was small and the women who entered it shared experiences which bound them together. The unique setting and conditions of their work heightened the intensity of their friendships and produced a certain camaraderie that has too often been overlooked or attributed only to men.

The experiences of both male and female missionaries in northern Canada reveal that gender boundaries were fluid. Masculine and feminine stereotypes broke down with the demands of mission work. Despite the fact that the image of missionary women was closely tied to Victorian domesticity, in reality women exercised freedoms in the field that they could not have at home. And once they had completed their tenures, female missionaries continued to stretch the boundaries of gender conventions. British and Canadian women, including Selina Bompas, Sarah Stringer, Elizabeth Wilgress, Ida Collins, Bessie Quirt, Louise Topping, and many others, were called on to give public lectures on their lives in the north.[79] In the summer of 1904 Deaconess Elizabeth Wilgress addressed the Napanee woman's auxiliary and was offered $25 for her efforts. She was said to have "delighted everyone," with her mission tales.[80]

In her obituary, it was noted that Deaconess Ida Collins was well known for her speaking talents. Born in Maidstone, Essex County, Ontario, in 1863 Collins attended classes at the deaconess house and graduated in 1899. After serving in Alberta residential schools for six years, and as a deaconess for two years in Ingersoll, Ontario, she went to the Yukon in 1909 and stayed for four years. According to the *Canadian Churchman*, which described her as a veteran missionary to the Yukon, she was a popular speaker: "Miss Collins was greatly gifted as a speaker and was much sought to give addresses before meetings of the Woman's Auxiliary and other Church groups."[81] Similarly, during her furlough in 1938-9, Louise Topping spent most of the year travelling and lecturing throughout her home province of New Brunswick, telling audiences about her experiences as a missionary in the north.[82]

The image of missionary women as feminine role models for Aboriginal women denied the reality of a life of potential adventure and pleasure. These aspects of life in the north were sometimes justified to those who might question women's adventurous spirits as a response to a religious calling. Within the context of religion, women could go beyond traditional roles. In his memoirs, Bishop Archibald L. Fleming praised Prue Hockin, a missionary nurse who had been in the north for twenty-five years: "In my opinion it is not too much to say that she is the epitome of what a white woman in the Arctic ought to be – efficient, self reliant, generous of nature, good humoured and with an ever increasing devotion to the Lord."[83] By the mid-twentieth century, the description of the type of women wanted in the north had changed from the time of William Duncan, who had expected women missionaries to teach Aboriginal girls how to make bread, to reflect the reality that had long been obvious.

Pangnirtung, early 1930s. *Left to right:* Grace Reeves, E. Prudence Hockin, Gwen Keary, and two young Inuit women.

# 4

# "Oh, To Be in England": Making a Home Away from Home

> We can only speak of the things we carried with us, and the
> things we took away. My father, of course, was bringing the Word
> of God – which fortunately weighs nothing at all.
>
> – Barbara Kingsolver, *The Poisonwood Bible*

At every level of experience, from acquiring basic necessities of food, clothing, and shelter to ritual celebrations and travel, the northern environments influenced the lives of missionaries. As newcomers, they constantly re-constructed their worlds of experience, knowledge, and understanding. The responses to their new circumstances were highlighted in their diaries and letters. Specific patterns of expression, for example, became associated with arrivals and departures as liminal moments. A departure from a northern station became known as "going outside." "Outside" represented civilization. The "inside worlds" in the north were frequently imagined in antipodal terms, with boundaries drawn by the signs and discourse of a superior "outside" world. While in part they intentionally reinvented Britain, or southern Canada, in the north, they unselfconsciously reinvented themselves. This chapter will argue two points. First, the missionaries under consideration tried to structure time and space in the north, and secondly, through those experiences they were themselves changed.

Scholars tend to treat the process of colonization as a one-way relationship, with colonizers thrusting their cultural baggage on unsuspecting subjects. For example, in an intriguing portrait of British women in colonial Nigeria, Helen Callaway explores strategies adopted to impose what she calls "imperial culture." While acknowledging differences from colony to colony she suggests that colonists in Nigeria attempted to establish both informal and formal rules signified in part through a variety of rituals: "the case might be argued that imperial culture exercised its power not so much through physical coercion, which was relatively minimal though always a threat, but through its cognitive dimension: its comprehensive symbolic order which constituted permissible thinking and action and prevented alternative worlds from emerging."[1] What Callaway fails to consider at any length, however, is the propensity for White women to be transformed by their experiences.

Missionaries in Canada's north also tried to impose a symbolic order both on themselves and on Aboriginal peoples. This included introducing rituals and material objects that symbolized many aspects of their own culture. In northern Canada, however, all missionaries relied heavily on the alternative world of Aboriginal local knowledge. They adapted to new seasonal rhythms and modified their rituals to northern conditions. The boundary between cultures frequently shifted. Missionaries did not simply impose one world on another. It was much more syncretic. And when missionaries went out on furlough or after they had moved away from the north, they were no longer the same people. No matter how they viewed their work or race and gender relations before they arrived in the north – and there were variations in expectations and perceptions – their experiences changed them substantially.

Travelling to and from mission stations invariably inspired missionaries to reflect on what they had experienced as much as on what they had accomplished. They were instructed to prepare written reports to their parent committees after arriving in the field, but even before their arrival they usually had made extensive comments in letters or diaries about their adventures en route. They became, in a sense, unofficial travel writers. The travel writing genre has recently attracted scholarly attention, especially from those interested in gender and imperialism.[2] During the latter half of the nineteenth century, travel writing became a popular literary form. Reflection and writing were especially encouraged by evangelicals. One of the most influential analyses of travel writing is undoubtedly the work by Mary Louise Pratt, entitled, *Imperial Eyes: Travel Writing and Transculturation*. Pratt discusses how travel writing reproduced particular sites of colonization in European language and values by constructing images for readers in the metropolis. She argues that the "European improving eye" viewed the landscape as empty, yet full of potential. This was very similar to the way that many missionaries regarded Aboriginal peoples, as empty spiritually and culturally, but full of potential. Travel writers, explorers, and missionaries frequently overlooked the meanings that the landscape held for Indigenous peoples. "From the point of view of the inhabitants of course," states Pratt, "these same spaces are lived as intensely humanized, saturated with local history and meaning, where plants, creatures, and geographical formation, have names, uses, symbolic functions, histories, places in indigenous knowledge formations."[3] Influenced by Pratt's work, Karen M. Morin studies varying "contact zones" between British women travellers and Aboriginal peoples in the American West, in the late nineteenth century. Morin argues that the texts represent an entire "range of socio-spatial relationships of domination, subordination and resistance." Traveller's observations depended upon how closely they came to know, or whether they had actually spoken to the Ute, Sioux, and Yosemite whom they wrote about.[4]

Like Morin's travellers, women missionaries in northern Canada reacted to their new environments in a number of ways. For many, the emptiness of the land was a recurring theme. Others responded to their northern landscape with comparisons of the world from which they came. Some women adopted both strategies to write about their experiences. In these cases, written landscape portraits were cast in terms that reflected the writers' own background and descriptions were meant to resonate with British and Canadian readers. As Albert Memmi has observed, colonizers tended to glorify the mother country, with its "positive values, good climate, harmonious landscape, social discipline, and exquisite liberty, beauty, morality and logic."[5] In Memmi's view, colonials had their gaze "constantly fixed" on the mother country, and the longer they were away the more they romanticized it.[6] Romanticized images of Britain stood out in sharp contrast to depictions of northern Canada as uncharted and uncivilized.

**Travelling to, from, and within the "Inside"**
On her first journey to the north, and with little knowledge of northern history, Selina Bompas spoke of the "solitary waste" of the land that she saw around her in the Diocese of Athabasca. Just as Monica Storrs would do fifty years later, she drew an analogy between Aboriginal peoples and gypsies: "If all the populations between London and Constantinople were to disappear except a few tents of Indian or gipsy encampments, and were all the cities or towns obliterated except a few log huts on the site of the chief capitals – such is the solitary waste of this land."[7]

Monica Storrs displayed similar sensibilities. She thought and wrote about England incessantly and confessed, in candid terms, to being "fatally English." She believed, like Bompas, that the north was untouched. In his introduction to her edited diaries W.L. Morton employed a telling quotation from Storrs with reference to land she purchased in the Peace River area: "Quite as wonderful as inheriting the walls and traditions of centuries is to acquire a bit of nameless, untouched bush and start everything from the very bottom." She was thrilled with the acquisition of her property, but, like other missionaries she saw the landscape as vast, empty, and virgin. The towns which had been populated by settlers failed to appeal to her. She described Calgary as "rather an awful town, so glaringly hideous and awful in every part." The town that she lived closest to, Fort St. John, appealed to her even less: "if only where the beastly little town of Fort St. John is we could just plant Rochester instead."[8] To Storrs, Rochester epitomized a cultural locale of real significance with its castle dating back to the Norman conquest, or its imposing Anglican Cathedral, a constant reminder of a Christian past.

Even after they had adjusted to their new surroundings, some missionaries continued to think about Britain in nostalgic terms. As Bompas settled, she soon began to appreciate the landscape. After moving from Fort Simpson (Líídli Kuë) to Athabasca in August 1876, she was struck by the beauty of Lake Athabasca, which she described as "picturesque, with small islands dotted on its surface, reminding me somewhat of the coast of Argyleshire."[9] She could not resist her apparent fixation with Britain nor did images of home abate with time. In the fall of 1881, with winter setting in, she confided that she pined desperately for an English summer:

> I think of it sometimes with a kind of yearning to smell a sweet violet, or a cabbage rose to look again at geraniums, fuchsias, myrtles and the rich wealth of colouring in an English flower garden; to see some lovely oaks and elms to see the lilacs enriched in their colour with the golden laburnum. I know not how I shall bear the rapture of all this, anymore than I could bear to hear a symphony of Mozart or Haydn, or a song of Beethoven or Schubert; these all seem to belong to another state of existence to which I can hardly fancy I ever belonged.[10]

In Bompas's memory, certain sights and sounds of Europe were magnified. She thought of beautiful summer flowers and classical music as part of her past life, an existence she believed to be more civilized than the one she was presently leading. Bompas, like others, was prone to describe the local scenery in pastoral images, drawn from a fanciful sense of what she had left behind. She was comforted in her northern setting by remembering England. Flowers and spring were especial reminders of home.

Florence Hirst, originally from Yorkshire, lived in the north for eight years when she too confided that she was dreaming of a spring in England. In April 1937 Hirst was working as the matron at the Pangnirtung hospital, on Baffin Island, when she described the approaching spring:

> The seeds in the window box are just beginning to show green – and all nature seems gay. I come into my room in the morning and look around and count the flower-seeds as they start to grow ... and with a great sense of well being I think "Oh to be in England now that April is here"! With the warm sunshine pouring through the window and the green shoots it isn't hard to imagine that England is not far away. It is only when one's gaze travels off through the window to the snow covered hills that one realizes that spring is here in name only.[11]

Remembrance of the home country was a typical representational motif for missionaries in the north, especially for those from Britain. Britain, or more precisely the imagined level of civilization that Britain had achieved, served as a powerful backdrop for missionaries in the north. Many Canadian missionaries, like the British, described the landscape as empty and rugged. They did not, however, write as longingly of their home environments.

In describing the empty landscape some Canadian women, unlike the British, spiritualized their environment. In *Women's Orients: English Women and the Middle East, 1718-1918*, historian Billie Melman shows how missionaries and tourists feminized landscapes and biblical scenes. She concludes that women had to devise new techniques for expressing themselves: "Women's work for women is one thing. Writing about it is another. Both are compatible with evangelical gender ideology and the policy of the metropolitan missions. But describing landscapes, relating the story of a journey, this is something altogether different. It involves a redefinition between the pilgrim and the historic places and a space traditionally perceived as public and identified as male. Of course ... evangelical gender ideology emphasized the negotiability of domestic and public spheres. And vital religion made women's travel more acceptable than ever before."[12] Melman argues that women travellers went beyond traditional gender roles and participated in a narrative process inspired by their travel and religious experiences. In some cases this was reflected in a marriage between evangelism and travel writing. Women could express their enthusiasm for travel by focusing on descriptions of holy places. Similarly in Canada's north, women sometimes portrayed the landscape in terms that expressed their religious views.

Miss Ridgeway, for example, saw the hand of God in the natural landscape. Originally from Saskatchewan, she worked at the Chooutla School at Carcross (Natashaheeni) in the late 1920s. Like other missionary women she was overworked, responsible for nursing, teaching, and caring for children in the evenings. However, she did take time to reflect on the meaning of her new environment. In her first letter to the woman's auxiliary she described the land around her, which she saw as one of "huge placid lakes and mighty rushing rivers. I have heard disappointed prospectors (gold seekers) calling it "the land God forgot," owing to its vast silences and huge snow and ice fields, but to my mind one feels infinitely nearer to the great Creator and Maker of the Universe when one looks with wonder and amazement on the works of His Hands – especially when one gazes spellbound on the radiance of the gorgeous displays of Northern lights seen in this territory, with their radiating hues and varied shapes and curious crackling sounds."[13] Ridgeway saw the land as "placid" and sublime. Another who spiritualized the landscape was nurse-missionary Minnie Hackett, who was stationed at Aklavik from 1926 to 1930. In a letter to the woman's auxiliary she described her life in the north:

Many people are under the impression that we must get lonely and depressed being so far from the civilized world, but it is not so. Sometimes

I go into the bush when all is still and quiet and God seems very near. You know the words of my favourite hymn – one of John Greenlief [sic] Whittier's poetical ones

I know not where his islands lift
Their founded palms in air
I only know I cannot drift
Beyond his love and care[14]

Outdoor living and hiking in the bushes prompted Hackett to feel close to nature and by extension close to God. Another Canadian woman, Gertrude Thorne, felt the same overwhelming presence of God in her surroundings in northern British Columbia's Nass River (K'alii Aksim Lisims) valley. Thorne was married to the Reverend Oliver Thorne, who was sent to Aiyansh by the Canadian mission society in 1921. Gertrude Thorne was from McConnell, Manitoba, and appears not only to have adapted comfortably to her new setting but also to have found religious meaning in the landscape. She frequently visited a nearby well to bring water back to her home. In her outings she claimed to feel drawn closer to God:

I have gone many a time in morning cool or noon-day heat for a pail of fresh drinking water. The spring lies near the path at the foot. Stopping to dip from the shallow well, though all unlike, yet I am reminded of another well in a far land and feel that for me any moment may bring to light inestimable treasure, not indeed the ancient relics, but the hidden wisdom. Was it not to a woman at a well that Christ spoke so freely of His life and purpose? ... And are not the waters of my spring as irrefutably His as the well of Palestine and as true a symbol of the living water? And coming back upon the winding ascent I have stopped along the outmost ledge to send a message of good will to our valley. It is worth stopping a few minutes to look at. Some of our poetically inclined writers have spoken of the plains of our great land as the "smile of God." If wide prairie and sunlit field could be to them as the smile of God, cannot my cliff in the southern mountains with its changing lights and shadows, its dazzling scintillations and veiled reticences, suggestive of mysteries withheld, be to me as the eyes of God? And who shall be able to look daily into the eyes of God without being both humbled and exalted by the moment of communion?[15]

While visiting her particular well and viewing the landscape around her, Thorne felt an intense closeness to God. These emotions helped her to derive joy from her daily tasks.

Ridgeway, Hackett, and Thorne all felt an overwhelming closeness to

God in the landscapes of the Canadian north, and Ridgeway even went as far as to claim a connection between the presence of the Lord and the aurora borealis. Yet, significantly, none of these women wrote about the land as being occupied by Aboriginal peoples. It was portrayed as a spiritual landscape by some, and by others as empty and uncivilized. Generally women's relationship with the landscape demonstrated that they had little knowledge about local history and Aboriginal traditions. But, unlike travellers or tourists who responded in similar ways and drew on parallel experiences in the metropolis, missionary women were sent to the north to live and work, not just to observe and move on.[16] Thus they were forced to come to terms with their settings and to reflect on the way that Aboriginal peoples lived.

How did women missionaries perceive their new lives in the north and what does this tell us about gender, religion, and mission? Historians and literary scholars who have analyzed gender and travel writing have found differences between men's and women's texts. Sara Mills, for example, identifies an obsession with nature as a convention in women's travel writing, and argues that it was more common to see emphasis on flowers and nature than on descriptions of people.[17] In her view men were more likely to express themselves in the masculine discourse associated with empire and adventure largely because they were conditioned to do so. Similarly, Linda S. Bergmann, who has studied women's Arctic narratives, concludes that throughout the nineteenth century the discourse of conquest and hardy adventure contributed to the American and European belief that "nature in the far north" was a "masculine arena."[18] Overall, northern missionary women did not generally revel in the glories and adventure of travel to the same extent as the men discussed earlier, who drew on the contemporary association with muscular Christianity. They did however discuss outdoor life and, unlike the women studied by Mills, they occasionally provided accounts of individuals met in Aboriginal camps. They, in fact, focused on domesticity but not entirely to the exclusion of outdoor living. While they were travelling, they slept in Aboriginal camps and ate and socialized with the residents. These close relations could have compelled women to reconsider their perceptions of the landscape as empty.

On her way from Herschel Island (Qikiqtaruk) to Peel River in the spring of 1898, for example, Sarah Stringer informed the newsletter of the woman's auxiliary, *Letter Leaflet*, that she and her husband had stopped at a camp to rest before pushing on. "When we reached here," Stringer wrote, "we were quite played out, and our faces were, and are, red and sore with the sun and wind, and I was glad to get to an Eskimo Camp, where there was a warm stove and a warm welcome."[19] They were welcomed by the people and indeed relied on their hospitality. "Kunnuh," one of the family members that the Stringers stayed with, was their guide. He was described as an "encouraging native," anxious to learn about the Bible and to sing hymns.[20] They travelled at night and slept during the day: "we had sunlight all night, so we might say there was no night. But it is impossible to travel in the day time as the snow is so soft and the dogs find it hard work." Like missionaries all over the world, they had to be flexible to adapt to many everyday circumstances from severe climate to much longer summer days.

Like Stringer, Catherine Hoare, stationed at Aklavik, described her travel experiences. She journeyed about 650 kilometres in the winter of 1921 and, as she put it, "it is not at all like travelling in civilization." Hoare travelled from camp to camp visiting patients and was prompted to comment on the amount of supplies one had to pack before going on the trail. She included in her list "your bed, your food, and the necessary pots and kettles to cook it in. And not only that, but you must carry enough extra food, to be able to invite the Eskimo to eat with you. Then of course, there is the dog food also." With a sense of adventure she described the tips and turns one might be likely to take when travelling by dog sled: "It is quite thrilling wondering what is likely to happen to you next. You'll be busy watching that you don't get your head knocked off while dashing under a fallen tree, when, all of a sudden your dogs disappear, and next minute you find yourself toboggan and all, on top of them, down on a creek or

Sarah Stringer journeying from Dawson to Fort McPherson (Tetlit'zheh) with guide William Blindgoose and pack dogs.

river twelve or fifteen feet [five metres] below." At the end of a day's travel she was thrilled to see the light of a camp where she always felt welcome. Like Stringer, she found that the Inuit were very hospitable to their visitors: "You must have the experience yourself, to be able to realize just how welcome that light looks. There is never any question as to whether you will be received. In fact you do not need to ask permission. You simply enter and make yourself at home. They kindly poke up the fire for you to warm yourself and cook your supper. Then they clear a space for your bed, beside theirs on the floor."[21]

It should be pointed out that spotting camps along trails was not coincidental, as Aboriginal guides proved knowledgeable, competent, and absolutely necessary for long journeys. Both Stringer and Hoare relied on Aboriginal guides for orientation on the trails and for warmth and hospitality at camp stops. There is very little evidence of Aboriginal resistance to Anglican missionaries in the north. Generally, it appears that mutual hospitality was shared. This is not to say that the message of Christianity was greeted with the same amount of enthusiasm but, as outsiders, the missionaries appeared to have aroused a great deal of interest.

Nevertheless, travelling in the north was not easy, and there were complaints. Writing to her sisters, who were visiting Algiers at the time, Winifred Marsh was quite disheartened at her travel experience. She had just been on holiday in southern Canada where she enjoyed what she felt was civilized company. This made the contrast of travelling back to the north even more striking: "It's quite hard for me to settle in again, life is so crude & such a mighty contrast to what I've been used to lately, especially in Canada, where I gained entries into many beautiful families & homes."[22] The sense of novelty that accompanied visiting Canadian families soon wore off once the hardships of northern travel became routine:

> You cannot imagine how rough the trip from Le Pas to Churchill was. Ugh. However God took care of me & brought me safely through. How would you like to travel for 19 hours with only stops for a drink of deer hairy tea on a sled. We reached a shack at 11.30 p.m. had to kindle a fire, cook some food & finally crawl cold & shivering into an ice cold deer skin bag. Fortunately the night wasn't long, because we were up at 4.0 and away to do another 18 hour day. The native led us through terribly rough sea ice – just miles of great jags and piles of ice. Often the dogs bounded 6-8 ft beneath and I was balancing above the precipice on the sled.[23]

Marsh gradually adjusted to her home at Eskimo Point (Arviat) and the rhythms of life in the western Arctic. Many years later, she published a book of her watercolours, which displayed her impressions of the north and included sketches of flowers and wildlife. In the introduction Marsh justified her painting: "All the words in the world could never have expressed for me the secret of the charm of that land."[24] Marsh obviously adapted to the landscape and, in a sense, sought to appropriate its "secrets" and "charms" in her paintings.

Women took the good with the bad when it came to northern travel. They were prepared for some discomforts and, if they were not too "delicately reared," they could see humour in certain situations. Deaconess Elizabeth Wilgress, a school teacher on her way to Hay River (Kátl'odéech) expressed her mixed views of northern travel when she wrote to the woman's auxiliary to update them on her progress:

> It is just a week since we began our journey from Athabasca Landing, and two weeks since we left Edmonton (and I might say civilization!) and took to camp life. Camp life is a curious mixture; it is at times most romantic and full of interest, as when we drove through beautiful parkland, the ground covered with wild flowers, or across a lovely valley, with a charming little gravelly creek running through it and camped at night on a bed of violets. And then again it becomes monotonous and even unpleasant, as when the harness broke in pulling us out of a deep mud hole and left us sitting in the wagon while the horses ran off in a fright. However even the trying parts have their compensations.

Luckily, Wilgress was well supplied with a combination of gaiters, long gloves, a green veil and aromatic vinegar to ward off the mosquitoes. She did not hesitate to comment on the ship's crew, most of whom were Aboriginal peoples: "We have about 12 Indians and half-breeds in our crew, and six white men, all told. The guide is a very tall, fine looking half-breed Cree. Very few of them speak English, and it is very odd to hear the guide shouting his orders in Cree, or listen to the men chattering to each other as they rest." Perhaps Wilgress anticipated an encounter which involved the use of English, rather than Cree. Despite several mishaps on the way, Wilgress admitted to enjoying "very much living in the fresh air."[25]

Some women clearly could not endure the discomfort of either travelling or living in the north. Mosquitoes and extreme temperatures drew comments from many. Elizabeth Field, stationed at Hazelton (Gitenmaks), in the interior of British Columbia's Caledonia diocese, felt rather uncomfortable with both seasons, complaining that "Our summer has been very trying – so hot at times and a great deal of rain; but I am sorry it is over. I dread the thought of winter, which is usually so long and cold, and the isolation very trying."[26] Long, cold, and dark winters were certainly part of the unique experience of northern life, especially for those in the Arctic.

The extent to which missionaries depended on Aboriginal peoples is underrated in the correspondence, but travelling and living in the north particularly in remote areas would have been impossible without Aboriginal guides and hunters.[27] Missionary women were usually chaperoned by other missionaries or Hudson's Bay Company servants, but boats travelling into the interior of British Columbia or to the far north always employed local guides. Photographs of travellers with Aboriginal guides and packers are common in collections of early twentieth-century missionary archival materials. And while many at times described the "solitary waste" of the land, at other times missionaries relied entirely on what Pratt calls "indigenous knowledge formations."

Missionaries relied on Aboriginal peoples in ways that they themselves often underestimated. Dependence on Aboriginal peoples for food and other provisions was extensive. Sarah Stringer found that, when she and her husband were stationed at Herschel Island, most food and clothing was supplied from the surrounding area: "We slept in bunks covered with deerskin; we dressed in clothes made of caribou hide and trimmed with wolverine fur; we lived on caribou, moose, mountain sheep, seal, duck, goose and the occasional dry groceries that I bought once a year on a shopping trip to Fort McPherson."[28] Many essential goods could not have been harvested by the Stringers.

Missionaries initially expressed revulsion for the sight and smell of bear and caribou meat. But, they usually had to adapt to them. Adelaide Butler was willing to wear Aboriginal-made clothing but, as she put it, "I draw the line at eating the same kind of food."[29] Selina Bompas articulated her changed perspective in the fall of 1874: "I used to watch the Indians in our boat with such amaze and disgust – eating a piece of bread with a lump of moose deer fat like lard! I believe I could now do the same with great satisfaction."[30] Food could also become, for the first time in the lives of these missionaries, a source of concern. Bompas recorded several occasions when Aboriginal women came to her door with meat just as the mission house ran out of provisions. Bompas, Butler, and others worried about food shortages and found themselves eating what may at one time have repulsed them. Butler once remarked that even the Inuvialuit could find it hard to live off the land: "there is certainly not any food to be obtained about here, and then people say we should be able to live off the country! Even the Natives themselves cannot do that, along the coast here anyway, and most of them have gone into the delta for the winter."[31] Similarly, Charlotte Canham described the winter of 1895-6 as a time of great scarcity. According to Canham the hunt had been unsuccessful that year "so that at times we had very little meat for ourselves or dogs."[32] Missionaries regularly mentioned and often fretted over food and supplies.

On occasion, the more intrepid attempted to obtain their own food. The Reverend Frederick Thorman of the Diocese of Caledonia at Telegraph

Creek arrived from Britain in 1917, after having served two years at the war front as a padre. He was returning to the station he had left in 1915, this time with his wife. In describing their arrival he suggested that she was "considerably younger" than himself and added that he was looking forward to her help in the mission house: "The culinary arrangements at the mission will no doubt improve. I was my own cook for two years, and I at least can remember all about it. Under her supervision the windows will have curtains and there will be other dinky little drapings about the house to make the place like home."[33] If this was all the evidence available about Elsie Thorman, one might assume that she was confined to the domestic sphere. But in fact, four years after her arrival there was a revealing letter in the *North British Columbia News* about a hunting expedition she, her husband, and son had taken. In March 1920, they left their mission home and travelled about sixteen kilometres into the bush where they set up camp. The first full day of this expedition saw the Reverend, gun over his shoulder, go further into the bush on snowshoes. Elsie Thorman stayed behind, kept the fire burning, and worked at the camp: "I gathered brush all morning to raise the bed further from the snow, cut down more wood for the fire, and shot squirrels for their skins to line Rob's moccasins – leaving their bodies after skinning for the dogs." After the first few days, her husband shot two moose and began to haul the meat back to the

Sarah Stringer mixing bannock in camp en route up the Porcupine River, 1924.

camp, where Elsie Thorman cut and dried it on poles and packaged it in sacks. This took about eight days and,when finished, they returned home by dog sled:

> We reached the mission cabin at about 12 o'clock – healthily tired, hungry but very happy – feeling better in mind and body and ready again for work and the many difficulties missionaries have to face. I know we both enjoyed our hunt and Holiday and so did Rob. And that is the kind of life the Indian leads half the time and he is happier out in camp than in his log cabin and far more healthy.[34]

Thorman's conclusion is rather surprising since usually, when the Tlingit went to their spring camps, missionaries could not reach them. They were away from the villages and inaccessible yet Thorman had the sensitivity to portray camp life as happier and healthy.

Like food, clothing also became an area for negotiation between Aboriginal peoples and missionaries. For Bessie Quirt, the approach of her first Arctic winter was seen as a mixed blessing as recorded in the fall of 1929: "We're rather dreading the period of darkness and the coldness of the winter, but even at that we're almost anxious to see what it will be like."[35] She was well prepared since Susie, wife of the Inuit catechist Thomas Umaok, had prepared an "ategee," or outdoor coat, for the cold winter days. At first Quirt was uncomfortable: "it feels so dreadfully long and sloppy – I feel precisely as though I were out in my bed-room slippers and night dress – I suppose I'll get used to it like everything else."[36] Her ambivalence eventually did give way to acceptance. Winifred Petchey Marsh also relied on local Inuit knowledge. In 1937 after the birth of her first child she realized that he would need a pair of winter boots: "An Eskimo woman, Nellie, kindly made him finely sewn, waterproof, white sealskin boots, which I kept clean by washing in soapy water and hanging up to dry. But they always became stiff. So Nellie taught me how to chew the shoes to soften and reshape them."[37] Like Marsh, Sarah Stringer also had a woman sew outdoor apparel: "I have my dressmaker engaged for the week (a Husky woman making a new fur suit for me and my baby also)."[38] Photographs of White women wearing Aboriginal made clothing were often sent home and quite regularly used for recruiting purposes. In 1914, when Stringer visited England on a promotional tour, she modeled an Inuit parka.[39]

Selina Bompas urged that women be adaptable and willing to learn from Aboriginal peoples. She warned that one should listen and not be resentful "when your Indian girls offer to fill your moccasins with straw when suffering from cold feet, because it is a fact which many have found out for themselves that a little hay in the shoes is warmer than knitted socks or corked soles."[40] She also cautioned that women be aware that in very cold weather the most important parts of the body to keep warm were the hands and feet. To avoid potentially deadly frostbite, both had to be carefully protected: "For your hands nothing but mittens will do for you in winter, no gloves would keep your fingers from freezing, but any Indian woman would turn you out a pair of mittens, as neatly made as any white man can accomplish, beaded most tastefully and edged with fur."[41]

Bompas learned about adaptability the hard way. On her first trip to northern Canada, she had been warned to dress warmly while travelling: "I had come provided with the thickest of serge dresses, as none of my friends had realized the possibility of anything but frost and cold in these northern regions."[42] She found the summer heat rather oppressive and enjoyed taking dips in either rivers or lakes at any opportunity. She learned, however, that this behaviour was not well received: "The weather has been and still is oppressive 91 in the shade some days Miss M & I only keep ourselves by frequent bathes in the Lake the water is so delicious – but the dear Indians are somewhat shocked and scandalized – they never would dream of such a thing as washing all over! & it is whispered that our bathing has driven away the fish."[43]

Travelling to their stations or going out on furlough also provided the occasion to contrast environments. The word "civilization" was usually raised in this context. For example, when Mrs. Canham, who had been stationed at Rampart House (Jiindé Tsik), went on furlough in the spring

Bishop Isaac and Sarah Stringer in London, England, in 1914. Here Sarah models an Inuit parka for her audience.

of 1896 she was awestruck on arrival at San Francisco. "I cannot attempt to describe our feelings," she wrote, "at finding ourselves once more in civilization, it felt like coming into a new world and made us feel very much behind the times in everything."[44] While for Wilgress, Edmonton was perceived as the end of civilization, Canham believed her return to civilization was marked by her arrival at San Francisco. Sarah Stringer concurred:

> It was November when we reached San Francisco and as I walked down the gangplank I could feel stares of the women on the dockside boring clean through me. It was a little while before I divined the reason: I had left Toronto five years ago when big sleeves and wide skirts were in fashion. Now all the dresses went straight up and down and I looked like a quaint creature from the past, which in many ways I suppose I was. For the first time I realized how long we had been away from civilization![45]

Concerned about their appearance, Stringer and Canham saw changed clothing fashions as the marker of their hiatus. Yet these concerns were not expressed when women were in the north; as female missionaries they rarely commented on their appearance or clothing except in preparing for winter. Rather than a concern with fashion, they flaunted their disregard for clothing as a form of liberation. Was it only in "civilization" that women felt compelled to appear in the latest fashions? Perhaps the slippage in gender boundaries was suggested as much as a freedom from fashion/commodity. From her perspective in Pangnirtung in the early 1930s, Prue Hockin claimed not to miss shopping: "It doesn't look much like Xmas but I guess it is because there are no Xmas shop windows. It is sort of a relief not to have to shop."[46] Adelaide Butler boasted about her freedom from changing tastes in fashion: "One doesn't have to worry about fashions up here."[47] Monica Storrs seemed to have had endless fun with various wardrobes. Storrs admitted that she and her Peace River companions hardly looked like religious women:

> I'm afraid we look more like Cossacks than holy Spinsters, but that can't very well be avoided and anyway we are all three practically identical as church Cossacks. We wear fur caps with ear flaps (mine is cyprus lamb), short brown canvas coats lined with sheepskin, two pairs of mitts – the inside wool and outside horse or moose hide, brown corduroy breeches, two pairs of woolen stockings fastened with thongs of the same undressed hide which fastens round and round the ankles and twists in anywhere – rather like the shepherds in a mystery play at home.[48]

Storrs delighted in describing what may have seemed for home audiences to be slightly outrageous. As the Depression wore on, she and the other

Anglican women workers in the Peace River started wearing uniforms. Clothes had become too expensive and uniforms were certainly more functional. Like other missionary women, Storrs appeared to enjoy not having to conform to fashion constraints. In this respect, the north represented freedom for women church workers. When they returned to the south, however, a consciousness of traditional femininity may have reasserted itself, as is suggested when Canham and later Stringer arrived at San Francisco.

### Symbols of the "Old World" in the North

Like travel, relocation and settlement prompted specific responses based on gender constructions. In her study of German women travellers in nineteenth-century North America, L.K. Worley identifies a highly suggestive tension in women's travel literature. She asserts that women travellers challenged the ideal of Victorian femininity by going off to see the world, yet they also felt a need to create familiar domestic spaces in their new locales.[49] Like European travellers all over the world, missionary women brought as much of their old lives as they could either squeeze into their suitcases, have mailed, or shipped. They decorated their interiors to reflect what they remembered. Of course decorating interiors with objects from home was common among practically all new immigrants to Canada. According to historical geographer John J. Mannion, who studies Irish settlement patterns in eastern Canada, material culture can be transplanted either with the migrating group or can be "reproduced from memory in the new environment."[50] Missionaries in northern Canada did both. We must distinguish, however, between the immigrant's impulse to decorate interiors with familiar objects and some missionaries' desire to assert authority. At first glance the materials transported from Britain to the north suggest that missionaries were like immigrants seeking to create comfort zones or cozy nostalgic corners. Some possessions transported by missionaries did just that. But they also brought many objects to introduce Christianity. Jean and John Comaroff forcefully assert that missionaries in South Africa manipulated domestic space to allow them to "impose their values on local domestic arrangements." They point to a deliberate effort to teach the Tswana that domestic space with "new furnishings" and "new architecture," had a specific order, that "'sleeping,' and 'sitting' and cooking and dining each required a discrete place and set of 'things.'"[51] These domestic rituals laid out "the geometry of cleanliness and godliness," and also reflected the "essential inequalities of gender, status, and power."[52] The Comaroffs interpret material objects as signs of missionary efforts to colonize consciousness. They suggest that furnishings were not merely transported for the sake of comfort and familiarity, and have no doubt that material objects were consciously displayed to promote Christian domesticity: "Charity for the English middle classes, might begin at home. For colonial evangelists, however, it began by giving heathens the very idea of home."[53] British domesticity and the use of social space are also examined by Alison Blunt, who takes as her subject the prescriptive literature produced to teach British women in India how to run their households. She argues that domesticity and imperialism were intertwined and that British women were advised to run their households as though they were miniature versions of the empire.[54]

Similarly, in the north, mission homes linked gender, religion, and efforts to assert cultural hegemony. Women in particular governed a material culture to promote the conversion process; objects were displayed that could be used to teach Christianity and inspire national loyalty. Evangelical womanliness emphasized the centrality of the domestic sphere. Women missionaries acted as role models of domesticity, which meant representing their authority through the ideal hearth and home. At the same time, however, mission homes were public spaces serving as examples of cleanliness and order. This is not to say that each object taken from southern Canada or Britain was deliberately chosen to change the consciousness of northern Aboriginal peoples. However, objects such as clocks, China dishes, flags, and school bells had cultural meanings in and of themselves.

In *The Ginger Tree*, Oswald Wynd, born in Tokyo of Scottish missionaries, portrays an unmarried woman missionary in early twentieth-century Japan. The novel's protagonist is invited to the missionary's home, where she is surprised by the interior:

Miss Bassett-Hill's house is Japanese style ... and stuffed with furniture from England. Thick carpets are laid over the matting though you still take off your shoes in the entrance, and I couldn't believe her drawing room when I saw it, desks, book-cases, a plush covered sofa and chairs all crowded in, and all seeming very insecure on the soft flooring underneath. A high bookcase trembled every time I moved in my chair and I had the feeling flimsy walls were going to topple in on us under the weight of framed portraits, Miss Bassett-Hill apparently needing to bring all these reminders of her ancestors with her to the wilds of the Orient. There was not one thing in that room beyond basic design and woodwork which hinted at Japan, even the sliding paper doors glazed to suggest french windows.[55]

Wynd nicely captures the oddity and humour of an unsuspecting character being faced with an unexpected interior. Like the fictional Miss Bassett-Hill, by 1892, Selina Bompas also had many of her own furnishings. As she recorded in a letter sent to England, she surrounded herself with all the comforts of home:

I have my own furniture round me which came quite safely, my chairs and little tables and carpet and mats, all the dear home treasures of pictures and photographs, with my bookshelves which are quite full, so you may think of me as very snug and comfortable, although with only sloping rafters. I sit at my window and look at the beautiful Yukon flowing by so stately and yet swiftly, and the Eastern mountains which I tell myself lie towards Salisbury.[56]

Bompas had made herself secure in the north with possessions which reminded her of England. She appreciated the beauty of the Yukon River, the glory of northern wildflowers, and the aurora borealis, yet her gaze was unquestionably "constantly fixed" on her homeland. While comparisons can be drawn with other newcomers who transplanted material culture, something more is suggested. Mission houses were striking contrasts to the so-called Aboriginal "huts," "hovels," and "camps," disparaged by many of the missionaries in northern Canada, or the homes of either Indigenous Japanese or South African Tswana. Lines between a sense of security or comfort and one of superiority could be easily crossed.

Missionary correspondence suggests that most women presented their interiors in a style that signified the familiar. When Bessie Quirt arrived at Shingle Point (Tapqaq) in the fall of 1929 her first reaction was disappointment. The mission house had long been abandoned and was in a

The interior of Sarah and Reverend Isaac Stringer's home at Herschel Island (Qikiqtaruk), 1897. The pictures on the wall, the hutch, and the chairs reflect the elaborate material culture that was part of the mission enterprise.

mess: "It was indeed not a pleasant reception coming to a cold and dirty house which had been closed for some time. But things were handy and we soon had a meal ready. It was a dismal enough prospect and one couldn't help wondering how we'd live there over winter."[57] Just two months later Quirt elatedly and proudly described her new surroundings: "Yesterday I got my pictures put up in our bedroom and it looks more homelike and put Betty's and Reita's photo in frames, and hung them in our corner. What a lovely corner it is! The old dish out of the mission house makes a good foundation covered with chintz. Then my book ends, candle, candy jar, pen tray, photos and little pictures make a nice looking dish of it and our photos mottoes and pictures on the wall above make a memory haunt of it. The two wicker chairs and cushions complete "our corner" and here we love to sit to read and write at night after the work is done and the girls all off – and we eat our meals amid these same pleasant surroundings."[58]

Monica Storrs also brought her treasures to the north. When visitors called at the farmhouse where Storrs spent her first two winters, they could be entertained by gramophone recordings, including Beethoven's Fifth Symphony, brought from England. When not listening to records Storrs read Barrett-Browning or poetry aloud from the *Oxford Book of Verse* to her housemate.[59]

Reading English literature or dreaming of an English spring helped some missionary women feel at home. Their closest contacts with the "outside" world, however, were the arrival of ships and letters from friends and relatives at home. Dockings were always greeted with enthusiasm. Missionaries were never sure of exact port dates, but excitement mounted from the moment incoming vessels were spotted. In the fall of 1935, Florence Hirst described a frenetic scene brought on by the docking in Pangnirtung of the RMS *Nascopie*. Early one morning, she noticed people running around outside and immediately ran upstairs. "My object in running upstairs was partly to catch the first glimpse of civilization after a whole year, but mostly to put up the flag. We hoist the flag up through the upstairs window. As I looked through this window I saw all the flags in town going up, such activity."[60] For Hirst, ship time brought excitement and expectations signified by patriotism and tempered by fear: "It is one thing to expect the boat – but when expectations are finally realized the feeling is altogether awful. It is both joyous and frightening – joyous because we wonder what news is contained in our mail after such a long silence."[61] Yet the joy of receiving news from home and periodically new workers or visitors even for Hirst far outweighed the fear of bad news.

Selina Bompas waited desperately for letters as well. In the winter of 1875, William Bompas returned to Fort Simpson in February with letters that had come in on the Hudson's Bay Company sledge: "The company's sledge meant an extra mail and it had brought letters – dear precious English letters for which I had so longed and prayed and wept for eight months past. I do not think that ever in my life I felt such a thrill of joy and gladness as when William poured them upon my lap."[62]

"Civilizing," or making their new environments appear more like their old, was very important for some missionaries. While particular aims, from comfort to overcoming feelings of homesickness to demonstrating cultural superiority, no doubt played a part, objects used to celebrate Christian holidays and other social occasions deliberately introduced a new symbolic order, particularly such holidays as Easter and Christmas. Providing Sunday services was only part of the duty of Anglican missionaries. Easter, Christmas, and other commemorations were usually presented elaborately at mission houses to emphasize the power of Christianity and empire. Missionaries went all out for festive occasions.

In reporting to the mission press concerning the condition of Inuit women on Blackhead Island in the Arctic, the missionary J.W. Bilby lamented the lack of community festivities. His article, directed at an audience of young Anglicans, portrayed Inuit women as hard-working. He described their daily tasks, and then asked: "How would you like to be an Eskimo I hear you say very decidedly, 'Not at all,' especially as these people do not have birthdays, or feast-days or holidays like yourselves. Many of them do not know how old they are. Some of them know what Christmas is, chiefly through the things sent out from England, which the missionaries give them at Christmas time, and, of course tell them of the Saviour of the world ... Now while you are enjoying your good things in England you will not forget, I am sure, what I have told you about the Eskimo women, and you will pray that all the people may learn more about our Saviour and his birthday."[63] For Bilby, introducing European culture could instill a sense of history, principally symbolized by the birth of Christ.

Missionaries frequently expressed their concern with culture by commemoration. From flying the flag for the Queen's birthday to celebrating Christmas, they were determined to mark special occasions. Certainly they were not the only newcomers to do so. Sarah Stringer noted in the spring of 1898, for example, that whalers aboard a ship anchored off Herschel Island had decorated themselves in orange and green so "the natives thought they would try the same and several of them were wearing ribbons of green on their furs," to mark St. Patrick's Day.[64] Stringer also noted that she and her husband had made a special effort to celebrate Christmas in 1897 in a distinctive way because it was the Aboriginal peoples' "first celebration of Christmas day and they all seemed as if it was a Merry Christmas."[65] According to Stringer, about 100 people attended.

Elaborate festivities accompanied the arrival of Easter and Christmas at mission stations. Narratives of Christmas concerts and plays are notably extensive in the missionary literature. Planning for these celebrations was mostly done by women. They cooked, prepared gifts, and organized and directed plays and concerts. Adelaide Butler recalled the children at Shingle Point being delighted during Easter 1935 when they saw how she had decorated the main dining area with cutouts of spring flowers and Easter baskets: "There were many exclamations of delight especially from the new children when they saw the new pictures and the Easter frieze, and then began to work up the holiday spirit."[66] But she was sometimes disappointed. Mission station Christmas parties with gift-giving and feasting had become a well-established custom in the north. One Christmas, Butler recalled how diligently she prepared for their Christmas play, but was greatly disappointed when the Aboriginal peoples who had arrived for Christmas packed up quickly after the holiday and departed:

> Mr. S. [the minister] was planning extra services while the people were here, but they all packed up and went off home the day after the native feast – they said they had not enough dog food but I have since heard that they all went over to Herschel Island for a New Year's jollification – the H.B. trader's wife gave a party for them, and there was lots of fun and dancing. That is how much they think of the mission. They got here in time for the concert and the distribution of gifts, and stayed just long enough to have a good blow out, and get what I had for them, but they are just as human as anyone else and go where they can get something. That sounds very cynical, doesn't it, but I do like the natives, many of them better than the white people, but they are so poor these days that I really don't blame them for getting all they can as the white people have exploited them in the past and the H.B. company are still doing so.[67]

Butler's comments suggest several things. They indicate the high hopes, however misplaced, given to festivities as a means of introducing Christian culture. At residential schools, like the one at Shingle Point, Christmas was discussed and prepared for by the matrons and staff with great eagerness. As well, Butler reiterated her belief that the Aboriginal peoples had not lived up to her expectations, that they too often seemed unappreciative. Yet she did not blame them. She was cynical about the relationships between the Aboriginal peoples and institutions that were alien to them, be they the Hudson's Bay Company or even the Anglican Church.

Missionaries brought materials to help celebrate European holidays. Whether it was Union Jacks to fly on the Queen's birthday and on the arrival of ships, or items needed for Easter decorations and the staging of Christmas plays, the missionaries were prepared. In celebrating Coronation Eve with a patriotic concert, or in distributing European clothing as gifts, missionaries attempted to "improve" the social landscape.[68] The north became a theatre for empire and the Aboriginal peoples became the audiences, participants, and actors as well.

Over time, rhetoric about the glory of British civilization, or the greatness of empire, appears to have declined, undoubtedly because of a generational shift in the mission staff and the fact that many missionaries after the First World War came from Canada. Imperialist discourse did not entirely disappear, however; in 1939, just after the notorious abdication of Edward VIII and the coronation of George VI, a revealing ceremony was held at Aiyansh in the Nass River valley. According to the *North British Columbia News* this raised a good deal of excitement in the village, with many Nisga'a participating in the ceremony:

> The proclamation was read by the Chief of the village council Mr. Robert Skadeen; the flag was lowered then raised; a bugle sounded before the proclamation was read, while shots from a revolver gave the salute. We had our Church service then rang the bell, and raised the Union Jack and shouted "God Save the King." In the afternoon we were surprised to hear a tumult, it was the women and children on parade dressed in tribal regalia to celebrate the occasion. King George has on the Nass river, as loyal a people as may be found within the empire.[69]

A photograph accompanied this article, which captured the Nisga'a on parade carrying a flag. The rhetoric of a "glorious empire" was less strident, but there was still symbolic ceremony connected to the idea of empire. This description also suggests that Nisga'a women and children organized the parade, which implies that they wanted to mark the coronation themselves and were not persuaded to take part in the ceremony by the missionary. As well, they wore their own "tribal regalia."

Symbolic objects were undoubtedly important to the missionary experience. The "cargo cult," as anthropologists have aptly named the process of removing specific materials from one culture for specific purposes in another, would have been absolutely useless to missionaries had Aboriginal peoples not been inclined to respond. Aboriginal peoples usually travelled at their convenience and celebrated within the context of their own symbolic worlds, yet they appear to have responded positively to the Christmas and Easter food and gifts or "loaves and fishes." Ultimately, staging Christian or even patriotic celebrations in the north depended on Aboriginal co-operation. And, further, by introducing new material objects in the north they no doubt were starting to create desire for consumption and ownership.

The interfaces between religion, colonization, and gender are especially clear when one analyzes the symbolism of the domestic sphere, and the specific rituals and anticipation of Christian celebrations in northern Canada. Missionaries may have held preconceived ideas about how they would order what they thought of as the "new world," but as time went on they often had to modify their expectations. They had to adapt to new rhythms and rely on Aboriginal peoples, not only to participate in their festivities but also to share their local knowledge. Life in the north often meant learning new habits of dress and travel and coping with long winters. Missionaries had to become sensitive to local conditions, particularly to seasonal rhythms. These rhythms were well articulated by Florence Hirst in a statement that revealed rare insight:

> Human beings have been born and human beings have died, travellers have travelled – and returned, natives have come in to camp and natives have gone out of camp, the hunting season has been discussed a hundred times, the seal question, the caribou question, the fur question, the native question has arisen and subsided, but still we go on and we realize that in spite of everything Human beings are born and human beings die, travellers still travel, komotiks [sic] and dog teams still go and come – and the various phases are still brought up daily regarding Arctic life & living & that there is nothing new under the sun.[70]

Northern missionaries often discussed births, deaths, travellers, hunting, fishing, and as Hirst put it, the "native question." They, too, became travellers and depended on the advice and comfort provided by Aboriginal guides. As much as missionaries were liaisons or emissaries of their culture, Aboriginal peoples were holders of their cultural knowledge and their guides to another set of practices.

Missionaries were always between two cultures. When they were in the north they decorated their interiors with ornaments from their home cultures, were entertained by European authors and musicians, and celebrated Christian traditions by arranging concerts and holiday festivities. When they went on furlough, they were invited to give guest lectures on their experiences and were portrayed as experts on northern traditions and cultures. They displayed either material or photographic evidence of northern life, and demonstrated crafts to the "outside" world; yet, when they were "inside," they showed little appreciation for them. They did not surround themselves with Aboriginal cultural artifacts, but did send Aboriginal crafts home.[71] The ironic position that missionaries found themselves in is probably best represented by Selina Bompas. After years of yearning for Britain, once she had retired from and left the Yukon, she claimed that she missed it desperately.

Physical and social realities were created by the missionaries in the north. Space, including landscape and social relations, was reshaped by missionaries and Aboriginal peoples, as Doreen Massey argues: "as a result of the fact that it is conceptualized as created out of social relations, space is by its very nature full of power and symbolism, a complex web of relations of domination and subordination, of solidarity and co-operation."[72] Symbolism, power and co-operation were in a constant state of negotiation and renegotiation on the northern mission frontier. Aboriginal peoples and missionaries were both changed by the encounter. Missionary women changed as a result of their lived experiences. Their encounters and travels forced them to reformulate old ideas. They found that, while they tried to hold onto vestiges of their old lives, they had to reshape their identities in their new environments. And yet, while many spent time in the north imagining what they had left behind – when they finally went "home" they reminisced about and missed their days as missionaries.

# 5
# Motherhood and Morality

## Mothers of the Empire

Methinks I see beside the camp fire sitting
Many an Empire Mother at her knitting,
Take heart! The bonds of friendship draw us close –
Soon we shall be one family – who knows?

The Mothers of the Empire are mothers of us all,
From humble cot or palace they hear Britannia's call.
On Baffin's icy margin or Africa's sultry shores,
They hear the call to duty and answer it by scores.

See them trooping to the standard, hear them answer to the cry
Across the far-flung frontiers (Theirs not to reason why).
The hand that rocks the cradle is the hand that rocks the world,
And it waves above each infant head a Union Jack unfurled.

(chorus)
They are the Mothers of the Empire,
The sisters of the free –
Hands across the sea;
Girls of the Bulldog breed!
From New Zealand and Australia, Ceylon and Wai-hai-Wei,
Bermuda, Malta and Bangkok,
Chips of the Old Grand Block[1]

While this little song, written in the 1940s, mimicked the age of "high imperialism," the connection between motherhood and empire began in the early years of mission work in the north and carried on through to the 1940s. Throughout these years the image of missionary women as "mothers" was remarked on continually. Women were described as mothers of the church, mothers of the children in residential schools, and mothers of junior clergy. By contrast, non-Christian Aboriginal peoples were constantly compared to children, so that the motherhood analogy was especially apt in the eyes of the missionaries and Church authorities who used it. Christianity, motherhood, and morality were inextricably linked.

Historians and mission scholars have long recognized the existence of the discourse of maternity in the mission fields of Asia, India, and Africa. Jane Hunter, who has written on missionary women in China, suggests in her work on the "exportation of domesticity" that maternity or "the inter-action between 'the home and the world' [is] a fertile ground for both further empirical and theoretical inquiry."[2] Margaret Jolly has considered the connection between maternity and empire in a pair of intriguing case studies taken from the lives of two colonizing women in the South Pacific. Jolly argues that gender had a major influence in colonial encounters, the experiences of White women having been shaped by the fact that they related to Aboriginal women differently from men: "The symbolic consti-tution of the relationship between colonizing women and colonized women in the familial mode as that between mother and daughter was a poignant but strategic expression of the tension between superordination and identification, between detachment and agonized intimacy, between other and self."[3] Women could relate to each other because of their com-mon experiences as women. The rules of behaviour in colonial settings encouraged detachment rather than intimacy between races, yet the mother-daughter relationship introduced a parallel norm while maintaining some detachment.

Implicit in the motherhood image was the understanding that women were guardians of morality. In her study of matrons and self-prescribed rescue workers in the American west, Peggy Pascoe identifies certain pat-terns in what she calls a search for women's "moral authority." She stresses three distinct characteristics: "its origins in a 'women's culture' rooted most firmly among white middle-class women, its use of the female values of that culture to strengthen the social authority of women, and its assumption that those values applied (or should apply) to women of eth-nic minority groups as well as to white women."[4]

As historian Anna Davin has shown, the link between empire, mother-hood, and race was constantly reinforced in early twentieth century Eng-land.[5] Motherhood rhetoric was employed to encourage women to take an active role in populating both England and the empire. Increased birthrates and a focus on children's health would contribute, women were assured, to the prosperity of the nation and the empire. Motherhood, as Barbara Caine concurs, was powerful.[6] Women were encouraged to increase their role within the domestic sphere, and then, to move, with "religious zeal and fervour," beyond their homes and even beyond their nation.[7] As a result, domesticity and maternalism were perceived as both binding and liberat-ing for women: although at first they might seem to be limiting ideologies, they could also be used as deliberate strategic identities to extend women's influence.

A maternal identity was especially strategic in the north. It allowed women more freedom to practise their ministry than they would have had in either southern Canadian dioceses or in England. Like Pascoe's rescue home matrons in the American west, women missionaries saw themselves as the purveyors of a Christian womanhood which, once introduced, would appeal to all. As in other mission settings, metaphors of maternity were frequent in the diaries, letters, and articles produced in the northern mission field. Women missionaries developed mother-daughter relations with young Aboriginal women who stayed in mission houses, and they attempted to mother Aboriginal children, but there is very little evidence that they felt sisterly solidarity with Aboriginal women their own age.

The idea that missionary wives could be symbolic mothers to the church or to those who attended the church obviously was remarkably consistent over time. The image of motherhood was pervasive in popular missionary literature. Such womanhood was expressed in a number of ways intricately linked to the missionary's self-perception and identity, particularly women's identity as mothers. Parent societies sometimes called women "Mothers of the Church" and missionary women, in turn, described themselves as mothers of Aboriginal children. Male missionaries and outside observers contributed to motherhood images that supported those constructed by the women missionaries themselves. When the Reverend William Collison was preparing to marry and leave for his first mission station in 1873, he was told that the Church Missionary Society parent committee approved of his wife Marion Goodwin because she would be a "true mother to the infant church at Metlakatla."[8] At the death of Mrs. Ridley, Bishop Ridley claimed that the Tsimshian saw themselves as orphaned.[9] And when Stella Du Vernet, wife of the second Bishop of Caledonia, died in 1929 she was described as a "real mother to the clergy, and indeed to the hundreds of young men who were trying to establish themselves in this new land."[10]

Motherhood became an essential part of the identity of missionary women and, to a significant degree, it justified their work. Moreover, notions of being a "mother" to Aboriginal peoples gave women a feeling of both physical safety and superiority in the field. The image lent a sense of status and freedom and created boundaries of maternal authority that gave women missionaries a feeling of self worth and responsibility. Ironically, this identity could imply extended roles for women because it represented both a position of authority and protection. This authority derived from the imagined superior status of some White Christian women missionaries. The discourse of motherhood points to many of the ironies inherent in the northern mission experience. Motherhood became a dominant discourse used in a context that had been constructed as masculine. Furthermore, the rhetoric of motherhood could have implied a very limiting role, but instead it provided women with opportunities to expand their functions in the multifaceted work at and beyond the mission stations. And the motherhood image was most strategic and ironic for those women who were not biological mothers themselves, women who had turned to mission work as an alternative to traditional roles. These women transcended expectations regarding gender, but relied on traditional rhetoric to construct their identities.

In their diaries and letters, missionary women positioned themselves as mothers, sometimes with tragic implications from these identities. The metaphors of motherhood and family were relied on to organize a sustained structural intrusion into the lives of northern Aboriginal peoples. The identity allowed women to give shape to their lives, to construct a persona that they thought justified their work. This reformulation of the self meant that – sometimes for the first time – women identified themselves as mothers and as White.

## Children and Mothers of the Empire

Kathleen Martin went into the field in 1916 quite conscious of the fact that she would be on her own as the only Anglican missionary in Fort Selkirk. She had been encouraged by a minister in Vancouver to contact Bishop Stringer about working in the north. A trained teacher, Martin claimed to always feel "drawn to the work amongst the Indians." She had no missionary training, but had taught Sunday school in Vancouver for a number of years. When Bishop Stringer responded to her inquiry he confessed to being short-staffed and in need of a man for the Carcross (Natashaheeni) school: "The Reverend W.T. Townsend who now teaches the school has volunteered as Chaplain for the front, and his name has gone in with my approval. I had thought of having a man, but it is possible that a lady teacher might do."[11] As it turned out, Martin was sent to Selkirk where there was an occasional Aboriginal catechist, Jonathon Wood, but no other missionary nearby. Bishop Stringer described Selkirk, north of Whitehorse (Kwanlin), as a "rather lonely place," but assured Martin that there were two White women, probably traders' wives, in the village. Except for occasional trips to the "outside," Martin stayed in the Selkirk area until the early 1950s.

Like other women, Martin delighted in mothering the children in her village. At a point when she felt discouraged and wondered about the value of her work, she claimed to be cheered up by a visit from Peter McGinty, Chief of the Selkirk Band (now Selkirk First Nation – Pelly Crossing). McGinty wanted to know how long Martin would be staying. He apparently wanted her to continue her work, as did others in the village. "I really did intend going out in the summer to stay," reported Martin to Bishop Stringer, "but the Indians won't even consider it. I scold them, order them around, spank their youngsters, and do all sorts of queer and unheard of things, but still they seem to want me to stay."[12] And when she went to Vancouver in 1928 she wrote to Bishop Stringer to tell him that she was very anxious to return: "I miss the children very much, no one seems to need a 'white mother' here."[13] She obviously reveled in her status as a mother to Aborigianal children and identified herself as a "White mother." As a single woman Martin was redefining motherhood, and was certainly very conscious of her Whiteness.

Like Martin, Selina Bompas cared for several Aboriginal children at various mission homes throughout the Yukon and identified herself as "Mama Bompas."[14] She grew attached to the children, especially the babies. Her first was an infant named Jennie. When Jennie died in 1877, Bompas remarked that she had "from the first viewed the Indian children as my especial charge." She identified Jennie as a "motherless child," brought to her during the Christmas season of 1875.[15] In caring for children she gained from their company. Bompas disclosed her emotional need for Jennie as she nursed her: "The dear babe is still very delicate and has needed constant watching and care ever since she came to me a year ago. Still, she has been a great blessing and comfort to me, and I know not what I should have done on some of these long dreary nights without her little hand patting my face, and her bright little face cheering many an anxious hour."[16] Bompas was always pleased to have new children in her home, but at times they prompted bittersweet longings for former charges: "It was very merciful of God to let me have charge of another little Indian child. It was very painful at first, as she is just the age of my little Lucy the year we went to Fort Norman [Tulit'á], and one seemed living over the past again, and at times almost forgot the interval of deep sorrow."[17] Mary also reminded Bompas of Lucy's "quaint Indian ways," suggesting once again Bompas's tendency to construct racial difference. Yet she undoubtedly gained a sense of accomplishment through looking after children. In 1900 the Bompases moved to Cariboo Crossing in the southern Yukon, where Bishop Bompas planned to open two new missions, and they decided not to adopt any more children. Selina confessed great sadness, stating that she had grown so fond of caring for them that she "had lost an object in life."[18]

Florence Hirst claimed similar feelings looking after Inuit children in Pangnirtung. In the winter of 1936 she described how she felt about a tiny infant girl:

> Betty is now 6 lbs 6 oz [3 kg] and is the darlingist [sic] little thing I ever saw. I was never so happy in my life before because since this other baby, Rhoda, came in, she has demanded so much of Prue [Hockin]'s attention that Prue has turned Betty right over to me – I feed her – bath her dress her – scold her and love her – She is the sweetest softest most cuddlesome little thing. A real Eskimo – covered with blue spots and brown skin. I think she smiled at me yesterday.[19]

Three days later, as Hirst related: "I don't think I was ever so happy in my life before as I am with the sole care of this little motherless mite, Oh she is a pet. Fat and sleepy, and soft and cuddlesome! I just love her with all my being."[20] Betty stayed at the hospital for her first three months and improved steadily. Hirst lamented the day when she would have to go home but Betty died in her sleep unexpectedly. Hirst wrote in her diary:

> She passed away in her sleep ... with a faint smile on her face, and her little hand up above her head, just as Prue left her. It must have been her heart, which is not unlikely when one realizes just what background she had.
>
> For days I have been completely lost, having no baby to feed and play with, bath and dress. She has been with us for three months, and now has been called to join her mother – It is a blessing since she had no mother, we never could see what the future for her was to be. The dear Lord solved that problem for us in his dear wonderful way.[21]

Hirst's description bears the marks of Christian grandiloquence, and seems to assume that the Inuit might not care for a motherless infant; it suggests once again that racial barriers were constructed to suit circumstances. She probably knew quite well that had she not been there, members of the community would have nurtured the child. Yet, Hirst undoubtedly cared deeply for the children, so much so that she volunteered to paint the children's ward with murals of igloos, kayaks, and polar bears, meant to provoke

"Mama Bompas" with one of the many children she came into contact with during her mission in the north.

a familiar environment for the young patients. Hockin and Hirst both achieved a sense of purpose through mothering "motherless mites." Like Bompas, they were saddened when children to whom they had grown attached returned home. When Rhoda, the infant that Hockin had cared for left the hospital, Hirst claimed that "It well nigh broke our hearts, for we felt that we were more to the child than her own mother – we had cared for her since she was 7 weeks old, and she was now one year."[22]

Like mission homes and hospitals, northern schools also provided a setting for missionaries to conceive of themselves as mothers. Teaching children took place in varied settings and depending on both the location and population, a school could be either in the mission home, a separate building designated as an Indian Day School, or in a residential school. In general, the missionaries tried to establish an educational setting at each station. The earliest schools seemed concerned with projecting a positive, though culturally specific, family life. The image of a happy family was important. In describing life at the residential school in Hay River (Kátl'odéech), for example, Reverend Thomas Marsh described the attributes of Miss Orr, a school teacher. According to Marsh, Orr was "mothering the little children in every way, seeing that they are kept clean and their clothes mended, that the sick are brought to Mrs. Marsh or me, as the case may be and seeing to all the other cares that a family of twenty-two or twenty-three children must bring."[23]

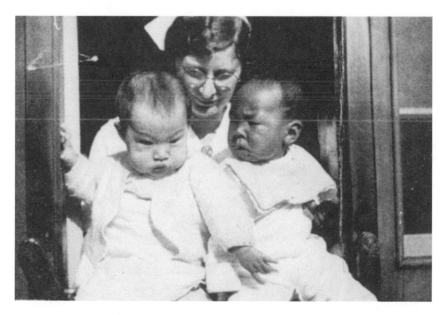

Prudence Hockin with two of her infant charges at Pangnirtung. Like Florence Hirst, she too enjoyed caring for children.

A short time after this was written, journalist Agnes Deans Cameron arrived for a brief stay at the Hay River school before returning home to relate her adventures in the north. In her work entitled, *The New North: An Account of a Woman's 1908 Journey through Canada to the Arctic,* Cameron wrote that Hay River was the "most attractive" mission in the north, and that her impression of the Anglican School was "of earnest and sweethearted women bringing mother-love to the waifs of the wilderness, letting their light shine where few there are to see it."[24]

One of the primary aims of the mission schools was to teach children about Christianity from as early an age as possible. A clear articulation of this goal is found in the Queen Charlotte Island (Haida Gwaii) missionary William Hogan's colourful prescription for creating Christians: "I believe the great secret of success, in all missions is in getting hold of the young of both sexes & training them from six years old till fifteen & implanting the bible teaching doctrinarily deep in their hearts."[25]

At Metlakatla this was attempted over time by several missionary women from England. In 1898, for example, Mildmay-trained Church Missionary Society missionary Alice Tyte wrote to the parent society about her experiences but apologized for not having more time to discuss her work: "I know that you will understand that with a family of twenty five one has a heartful, headful and handful, with very little leisure time to sit quietly and write even to our dear ones and the many loving and sympathetic friends in the homeland."[26] For Tyte, as for many others, the image of family life was important for her self-perception as a mother figure.

A description of children taken away from their real mothers and sent to residential schools challenges the image of missionary women as mothers. What is painfully obvious is that missionaries involved in Aboriginal schooling held persistent attitudes and perceptions that what they were doing was justified. Otherwise they could not have participated in the process. Two very striking accounts written by Selina Bompas in 1908 and Ethel Catt in 1928 suggest the torment of Aboriginal schooling. As missionaries, Bompas and Catt tried to show how children became accustomed to their new environment; yet their resistance and painful struggle at being trapped in school seems more obvious. Writing for a juvenile audience, Bompas described a typical first-year experience:

> The first year of school is often very irksome to an Indian child. He will be merry as a grig at times, but if he catches sight of his father or any friend going hunting, the hunger for freedom comes upon him. He will start to run after the hunter, and if caught and sent back to school, he will cry and yell until the whole camp is roused, and tearful sympathizing mothers rush in to know who is dealing this harshly with their darling. The girls are equally resentful of restraint, and look upon a closed

door or window as their natural enemy. These spasmodic fits of intolerance of confinement cease after a year or so; but we have to remember that fresh air is an Indian's most needed element; he was born and bred in the woods, and has early been used to such extremes of temperature as would make a white child shudder.[27]

In Bompas's experience, children resented the constraints of school because of where and how they were "born and bred." She went on to describe how a little girl, Frisky, escaped from her bedroom window and ran away because she felt like picking berries.

In a similar vein, Ethel Catt wrote of three children whom Bishop Stringer had sent from Herschel Island (Qikiqtaruk) to attend the school at Hay River. Catt was told to shepherd them and other children from surrounding mission stations from Fort Chipewyan down to Hay River. She began with three siblings George, John, and Mary ranging in age from five to nine years old. They could not speak English and were apparently very frightened. Before they left, John would occasionally disappear, have to be found, and dragged or carried back to the mission. George sat on the bottom of the gangplank and refused to go on the boat. He had to be carried on. Once aboard he locked himself in the washroom. Finally, as Catt was putting the children to bed the first night aboard the ship all three began to cry. As Catt wrote: "I tried talking, singing, coaxing, but nothing would do & of course they did not know a word I said." They finally made it to Hay River, and Catt concluded that, despite the efforts of these three "creatures" to resist being harnessed in, they had "fallen into school ways beautifully and will make fine men and women."[28] Scenes like this were repeated time and time again across the north as children were taken to residential schools. In 1928, Miss Ridgeway at Carcross school recognized the problem as well. In her report to the woman's auxiliary she claimed that she was overwhelmed with work: "I have 36 children to teach – from those who do not know one word of English and scream at the oppressiveness of a roof over their heads for the first time to seniors in Grade Six."[29]

There seems to be little disagreement about the impact from residential schools on Aboriginal children left, in Kenneth Coates's phrase, "betwixt and between" two cultures, unable to cope fully in either the White or their Aboriginal world.[30] Former students experienced traumatic disruption in childhood and adolescent development. Worse still, school missionaries alienated them from their traditional languages and practices. In spite of an obvious discordance between children's needs and the school environment, missionaries persisted in the belief that they were improving Aboriginal children and that such schooling would make them, as Catt put it, "fine men and women."

Missionaries in northern villages were instructed by their bishops to be on the lookout for children to attend schools. If parents refused to send their children there was very little that could be done. And many Aboriginal parents did resist. Some students returning from schools for the summer spoke of the terrible experiences in the schools, and, as a result, parents sometimes refused to let them return. Missionaries denied the rumours and defended the schools. In the scramble to "civilize and Christianize" Aboriginal children, the awareness of these emotions and responses seems to have been neglected. Rather than have Aboriginal mothers raise their own children, "mothers of the empire" became surrogates in residential schools run by the Anglican Church from Hay River on Great Slave Lake to the Chooutla School at Carcross, Yukon.

In these schools, the metaphor of maternity persisted well into the 1930s. Toronto-born deaconess Mabel Jones declared her feeling of pride when eight children were confirmed at the Shingle Point School where she worked: "This beautifully solemn Service always stirs one to the depths, but perhaps this Service had special meaning for us in that those who were confirmed, with one exception, were our boys and girls whom we had the privilege and responsibility of mothering for several years at school. We felt something of the awe mixed with joy of real parents when their children stand forth and publicly make Christ their choice."[31] Mothering "motherless mites" became for many women a way to justify their work in the north. They were convinced that their benevolence was necessary, and that they could best secure their positions by reformulating themselves as mothers. While it is most tempting to be critical of these efforts, it must also be said that the women's responses to the children appeared to be based on close, intimate bonds.

### Mothers of the Empire Remake Marriage and Motherhood

A recurring theme in missionary literature focused on how Aboriginal children were raised. British and Canadian missionaries most often saw themselves as superior mothers and they devalued Aboriginal women's maternal skills. The most common complaint missionaries expressed was that Aboriginal mothers were weak disciplinarians. Typical of this complaint was an article entitled "Indian Girls and Women," which appeared in the *North British Columbia News*. Here, Aboriginal women were said to be lax with their children: "Unselfish she slaves for her husband and her children, without thinking of herself at all. Not that she attempts to train the children in ways of obedience, for the child pleases itself entirely, its will is never crossed. The children please themselves whether they attend school or no the parent never compels."[32] Similarly, Sarah Stringer in an address to the women of Winnipeg's Canadian Club in November 1931 claimed that Inuit parents "never punish a child when they ask them to do something they do not persist in having them do it, the parents ask them why no, but they do not insist."[33] Parents, but most usually mothers, were thought to be weak and passive with their children.

By contrast, children in mission schools were disciplined and regimented. The plan for female children to attend residential and Indian day schools was for them to learn how to manage households and raise children. Girls and boys were taught how to speak, read, and write English and girls had an extra emphasis on household management.[34] In the same letter in which the Reverend William Hogan insisted that biblical knowledge be implanted "deep in the hearts" of Aboriginal children, he also commented on the value of teaching girls domestic duties. He admired the teacher, Miss Dickinson, and the way she "trains them so that they may be able to take care of their own houses in days to come & prepares them in all household duties."[35]

At the Girls School at Metlakatla, according to the Reverend Keen, a rigid routine was followed by the students. The girls usually started school at the age of ten and would stay until they reached sixteen or seventeen. Their routines at the home were very clock-oriented. "It is now 4:30 p.m. and they have work to do before tea," Keen stated. "A large basket full of stockings is brought in and distributed and these the girls proceed to mend. At other times of the day we might have seen them washing their clothes, or scrubbing the floors, or cooking or learning dress-making." The Reverend Keen believed the girls would "become true Christians" and, equally important, good housewives under the guidance of women teachers.[36]

Sarah Stringer at the Dawson Hostel with girls who are on their way to the Chooutla School at Carcross (Natashaheeni). *Left to right:* Jane, Elizabeth, Bella, Sarah, and Alice.

Preparation for marriage and a life of household labour was the objective and as the matron of the Ridley home for "white and half-breed" children at Metlakatla claimed: "The girls do cooking, sewing, dressmaking, laundry and household work. The boys take their share of the housework, clean the boots and knives, saw and chop the wood, and in the spring and summer do some gardening."[37] According to Margaret West, the pupils began their day at 6:00 a.m. and until 7:30 a.m. did a number of designated chores. They then met in a large playroom "for united prayers and praise to God, who has, for the time being, permitted us to be one family and we often pray that the lessons we learn together at these morning meetings may sink deeply into our hearts and bring forth fruit into our lives."[38] West wanted the Ridley House to function like a family home. Clearly, institutional life did not at all correspond to family life, but the family ideal remained a constant ideological gloss and moral model.

The preparation for marriage undertaken by girls in the schools and homes established by the church had a certain irony. Young girls were being prepared for marriage by women missionaries, many of whom were unmarried themselves and may in fact have been attracted to the mission field because it appeared to offer freedom from prescribed roles in their own societies. Missionaries hoped Aboriginal girls would marry, and apparently this desire had some influence. Florence Edenshaw, a Haida woman from Masset on the Queen Charlotte Islands (Haida Gwaii), remembered as a child playacting weddings. She recalled vividly the parts played by her playmates:

Once Phoebee, Emma [Matthews], Douglas and I decided to play wedding in the woods. "You want to marry Douglas?" "No." They ask another one. "No." They were all shy. "Who's going to marry Douglas?" No one said anything. "Florence you marry him." "OK." We got somebody's veil to take to the woods. Phoebe and Emma put flowers at the front of the veil. They worked at it for quite a while and then they put flowers on their hats that they made out of skunk cabbage leaves, and they made bouquets. All the bridesmaids followed me down to the village. I don't remember if we pretended to have a feast or not. I must have been ten or eleven.[39]

Pretending to have a wedding was probably a common form of play for many children in North America in the first decade of the twentieth century. But as Margaret Blackman has observed, it is significant that Edenshaw and her friends were not pretending to be at a potlatch, nor were they modelling the traditional winter dance. They were acting out a Christian ceremony. Church santioned marriages were important markers of cultural change and mission success.

A Tagish-Tlingit Elder, Angela Sidney, remembered in the 1970s a conversation with an Anglican missionary, Mrs. Watson, who taught school in

Carcross, Yukon. Julie Cruikshank recorded Angela Sidney's memory of the conversation that took place in 1916:

> "I understand that you are married."
> I said "Yes."
> "Did he give you a ring?"
> "Yes, he gave me one – his own ring – one time when we went to cache."
> "Are you married in church?"
> I said, "NO."
> "Well, you know what?" she said. "You're not supposed to be like that. You've got to get married in church!"
> Well, I told her I didn't mind, but my husband wouldn't want it – not to get married in church.
> Mrs. Watson waited for George Sidney to come home from work that evening:
> "I understand you're married," she told George.
> "Yes, Angela Johns."
> "Well, you know you've got to get married."
> "We are already married, Indian way. It's just as good, isn't it?"
> "That's not good enough," she told him. "You've got to marry her white man way. I raised that kid!" she told him.[40]

She convinced George that a Christian ceremony was necessary but her involvement did not stop there. As Angela recalled, she brought her a cream-coloured linen suit, white shoes, a hat, and a string of pearls: "She told me everything I should wear." Watson had her way and the Sidneys were married – again. Angela Sidney's story of Watson's insistence on a Christian marriage is illustrative of how intensely involved missionary women could become in Aboriginal women's lives. Yet, Angela Sidney did not recall the story with bitterness. In fact, at the beginning of the conversation she said "Oh, she was so kind, she loved me up and everything."

Both Edenshaw and Sidney give testimony to the persistence of the missionary's desire to assure that the young girls they came into contact with were married. And marriage was not enough; their relationships had to be sanctified by Christian marital ceremonies.

One reason missionaries encouraged Aboriginal girls to marry was because they hoped that, once family life was established, Aboriginal peoples would end their seasonal migrations and settle permanently in villages. When an Aboriginal girl married, a feeling of accomplishment and satisfaction was expressed. Reporting to the *The New Era* in 1908, Elizabeth Wilgress sent a photograph and a description of a young girl named May Kai who married at Hay River: "We are very glad to see her married though she is only sixteen. Her husband is the son of the headman of the village."[41]

On another occasion Sarah LeRoy, also at Hay River, wrote to the *Letter Leaflet* about how pleased she was when one of her former students married: "You will be interested to hear that Laura is married. You know she left the school last July. She wrote me a letter saying she was busy in her new home. We are always glad to hear of the girls being married, as they are open to many temptations in their free life."[42] This seems a typical response. It was generally agreed that Aboriginal girls who had been influenced by the Anglican Church and schools would make good wives, but single Aboriginal women would face evil temptations. Their "morality" was guarded by their "surrogate mothers." Yet some missionaries, like Kathleen Martin, realized that the options for Aboriginal women were limited. She confessed to Bishop Stringer that it was "a pity to have the girls marry so young and yet it is the only way for them if they remain in camp."[43] The implication was that if they remained single and stayed at Selkirk they might become pregnant.

Concern about chastity or the "many temptations" of young Aboriginal women stemmed in part from the arrival of White settlers. White men working in construction camps in northern British Columbia or mining for gold in the Yukon caused missionaries great fear and anxiety. As threats to the aim of Christian missions, the behaviour of White men was carefully scrutinized and often criticized. Some settlers represented the evils of White society and potential disruption of the harmony that missionaries were trying to achieve. If White miners would not attend church or show any outward signs of living Christian lives, how could missionaries be critical of Aboriginal peoples? How could missionaries continue to claim that they represented a world where everyone was civilized and worshipped Christ, when the miners so openly defied this claim? As Whites began to come to the north in larger numbers, especially after the turn of the century, this problem became more apparent.

Selina Bompas was one of the first missionary women to speak out. She was gravely concerned about the impact of gold miners in Forty Mile Creek, the winter headquarters for many newly arrived miners. In the May 1895 edition of the *Canadian Church Magazine and Mission News*, Bompas expressed her fear that miners would have a bad influence on Aboriginal women. While she conceded that some miners were quite respectable, others of a "very different type" caused her grave concern:

> And thus our Indians, being brought into contact with the white man, fall in only too easily with his taste for luxury, love of gambling, coarse, vile language, and for the miserable and ruthless degradation of women. Our American citizen would scorn to marry an Indian; indeed, by an iniquitous law of his country, he is forbidden to do so. But the higher law of God he can set aside and ignore. The sweet, oval face and laughing eyes

of our Indian girl pleases him; he knows that she can be made as deft with her hands, as tidy and orderly, as skillful with her needle as any white woman. She is sadly, deplorably vain, poor child, and a gay shawl or two, a pair of gold earrings, will sorely tempt her, as the bag of flour has tempted her father to wink at the transaction.[44]

Bompas saw herself as a moral guardian over unsuspecting Aboriginal women, fearing the "inclinations" of White men. Her statement showed her contempt for White men who ignored Christianity.

Veteran missionary Bishop William Ridley made the same fears known. Referring to gold-seekers and Aboriginal peoples near the northern British Columbia town of Atlin, he claimed that "These children of the forest grow into fine types of humanity until Americanized by contact with lustful whites who disgrace their nominal Christianity and degrade the Barbarians."[45] Elizabeth Soal at Hazelton (Gitenmaks) in north central British Columbia wrote to the *North British Columbia News* in 1916, when Hazelton was home for about 200 White newcomers: "One very sad feature of the work here, is the very adverse influence of so many of the white men in their neglect of the Sabbath and holy things. As a result the attendance of the Indians at divine service has been reduced very considerably, but we still have great hopes for the future, for by the Grace of God we are doing our best to teach the children the way of truth and thus we sow in hope and trust in *Him* for the increase."[46] Kathleen Martin had similar anxieties. In Selkirk she was known to, as she asserted, "have it out" with White men who ignored the Sabbath.[47]

Despite the fear of White men's moral danger, there seems to have been very little resistance to mixed-race marriage. This lack of concern reaffirms the aspiration of missionaries to see Aboriginal women married. Missionaries frequently commented on the marriage of former female students or of acquaintances to White men in non-judgmental terms. Selina Bompas was very pleased to report on a woman by the name of Julia Sims, who had been adopted as a young girl by the Reverend Sims and looked after in her older years for a short period by herself. According to Bompas, Julia was "uncivilized" and "hopelessly bad and possessed of every evil propensity." Bompas insisted, however, that: "God's grace prevailed at last, and man's extremity is God's opportunity. Julia is now the wife of a white man, Mr. Horsefall, a very pleasing and respectable man. They were married about eighteen months ago by Bishop Reeve, have one little daughter, and appear to be contented and happy as possible, and Mr. Horsefall said to me when calling on us at Moseyed a few weeks ago since, 'a man could not have a better wife.'"[48] The same accepting attitude was exhibited by Kathleen Martin at Selkirk when in 1921 her Aboriginal maid, Alice, married a White man. The Stringers were in the village for a short visit and at that time Stringer performed the marriage: "My Indian maid Alice, was married on Tuesday evening to one of the white men here and they went off in a launch on Wednesday for a honey-moon trip up the McMillan River."[49]

In some cases Aboriginal women's marriages to White men went unopposed because it was hoped they would contribute to assimilation. Lay worker, C.F. Johnson, who had laboured in the mission field for twenty years and was supervisor of the Dawson Hostel for Half-Breed Children, reported on a marriage which took place between a hostel resident and a White trading post manager: "We have just had word of the marriage of one of our girls to the manager of a small trading post in the far north. She was a very capable young woman and will make a real home for the man she married. Her last six months at St. Paul's Hostel were spent in the kitchen where she received a training which will now be of inestimable value." Johnson speculated that with many more White men coming "into the country," there would be more mixed-race marriages: "The process of assimilation is going on around us, slowly but surely, so that in the course of time there will be no native problem."[50] Whether or not assimilation was a shared goal among missionaries, it was quite obvious that missionary women in particular felt responsible for the moral development or sexual control of Aboriginal girls, as reflected in their desire to see them married in Christian ceremonies and settled.

Training Aboriginal girls as domestic servants was considered an acceptable alternative to sending them back to their families. Mary Mellish, a teacher in Moosehide (Éhä Dädhëchan Kek'ét), reported to *The New Era* in 1905 that she had a six-year-old girl living with her whom she was training: "She is not at all pretty but is smart, and in time will make a good servant; there is such an improvement in her already."[51] In the same year it was reported in the *Letter Leaflet* that three young women from the Chooutla school at Carcross had been employed as domestic servants in Whitehorse. One worked for Sarah Stringer.[52] In 1923 the same paper mentioned Gladys Roberts, who was graduating from the Carcross school:

> Our other graduate is Gladys Roberts, who has been in school for the last twelve years and has done very well in her class room work. She has been trained for domestic service, and will we hope, have a good influence wherever she goes. She is returning to Moosehide, near Dawson, to her parents, but hopes, after spending a short time at home, to take a place of service in Dawson, and earn her own living.[53]

Other young women returned to their villages and worked as aides in the smaller schools. In a report from Rampart House (Jiindé Tsik) and Old

Crow, the Reverend McCullum mentioned that he was being aided in the school work by Magi Daniel and Eunuch Ben, "two graduates of the Carcross Residential School."[54] However, from the missionary's perspective, choices for young Aboriginal women were limited. Missionaries did not offer a variety of options for young women's independence and that was certainly never their stated objective. Their goal was to introduce Christian womanhood and to protect and nurture the morality of Aboriginal women on an increasingly changing frontier.

## Motherhood as Independence

One of the most significant changes that occured in the northern mission field after the First World War was that more single women were recruited and they were given more autonomy. This fundamental shift was marked by a new willingness to send women to stations not already occupied by male missionaries. When the Church Missionary Society began to send unmarried women into the field in the late nineteenth century, they always did so to stations where male clergy were established. Once stationed, women might go to smaller posts or canneries for a few days or even an entire season. But unmarried women were urged to travel in teams of two. There is no evidence to suggest that danger or fear of sexual scandal were of concern, although this may have been why women were generally not sent to stations by themselves. After 1920 the Canadian mission society was almost entirely responsible for this region and they were not as reluctant to allow women to work single-handedly in the field.[55]

Until 1936, for example, no permanent White missionary had served the village of Old Crow, a settlement in the northernmost part of the Yukon. In 1936 Bishop Geddes announced that Mildred McCabe would take over the work. Ignoring the previous work done by the Aboriginal catechist, Geddes described in a letter to his friends the work that McCabe would do:

> We were fortunate in getting a very suitable person to begin this difficult task, and Miss Mildred McCabe traveled with me to Fort Yukon at the beginning of June and then on up to Old Crow to open up this new work. Miss McCabe is admirably suited I think for this isolated post. She is a fully qualified Nurse and is also a graduate of the Deanery training house in Toronto. She served for four years on the staff of our hospital at Aklavik and was in fact a member of the staff at the same time as my wife. She has also 2 years experience working among the Indians at Fort George on the east side of the Hudson's Bay, so that she knows the far north with its difficulties of isolation and also knows the Indian peoples and is very fond of them so I think that if anyone can make a success of this new venture that one is Miss McCabe.[56]

As Bishop Geddes declared, McCabe was highly qualified for the new work. While he recognized that she would be isolated, he was not concerned that McCabe was single and alone at the mission station. Sexual danger was not a consideration. Bishop Geddes offered a detailed list of the work she was expected to perform: "In addition to being the resident nurse of the district Miss McCabe is also to teach school if time permits, and also do missionary and evangelistic work for which she is well qualified."[57]

Eight years before McCabe was appointed to this position, she had written a letter to the *The Living Message* in which she expressed her admiration for women who worked in the mission field without men. She was speaking specifically of Isabel Gibson and Ethel Catt. Catt worked as a missionary in Peru before accepting a post in northern Canada. Gibson was a nurse from St. Catharines, Ontario, and had lived in the north for ten years. According to McCabe, throughout the winter of 1927 Catt performed all the mission work in Fort Chipewyan: "I can't recall whether I told you in my last letter about Chipewau [sic] where Mrs. Gibson and Miss Catt met us. They have a nice Church, School and Mission House. Miss Catt stayed in the Mission *alone* last winter. Here she taught school, Sunday School, and took the Church Services on Sunday, and also took the Burial service several times. Rev. and Mrs. Gibson are there now, and when Mr. Gibson is away Mrs.

All Saints Church, Aklavik, 1926.

Gibson takes the services. I think she is a brave woman."[58] McCabe thought that Gibson was brave because she could step into her husband's shoes and take the service when necessary. She undoubtedly felt Catt was also brave, too, since she made a point of emphasizing that Catt stayed alone one winter in Chipewyan.

Similarly, Bertha Shearman was described by her husband as brave. In May 1930, she travelled between Kitkatla and Prince Rupert (a distance of about 130 kilometres) with several Aboriginal men. Shearman had been at Kitkatla, a village of about 250 Aboriginal persons at the time, for about a year, where her husband noted she was a faithful worker with nursing skills that endeared her to the local Tsimshian. However, at times, patients had to be sent to Prince Rupert. Shearman described such a case in the *North British Columbia News*:

> On May 16 one of my right hand helpers at Church, was taken ill but I was not made aware of the fact for four days when messengers fetched me. My wife went with me and we saw at once that he required the doctor's attention. They refused to take him to Prince Rupert and my wife attended him three and four times daily making suitable invalid nourishment from our own store, as his people had been feeding him on seaweed and corn beef. I also paid him daily visits. He, at last, said he would go to Rupert, if I would go with him. This would mean closing down the school so my wife said she would go. They got ready and left about noon in a rough sea. After a journey of about 7 ½ hours, and encountering an enormous whale, besides a large number of great drifting logs, they reached Rupert safely, and carried the patient to hospital my wife remaining with him until 10 o'clock that night. The doctor operated and my wife returned first thing the next day. She was most brave in going alone (80 miles) with Indian men, but these works of mercy are well worth the trouble.[59]

Shearman described his wife as a brave woman for having travelled with Aboriginal men in much the same way that McCabe attributed bravery to Mrs. Gibson. Shearman saw his wife's action as being inspired by Christian mercy, placing it within the context of a calling or, as biographer Arabella Stuart Wilson called it, "Christian heroism."[60] Women missionaries were described as brave heroines, although these representations of bravery or heroism differed from those of men. If a man had been in the same position as Mrs. Shearman he would not have been considered especially brave. Women and men might perform the same work in the mission field, yet considerations of gender meant that their work would be described very differently. Whether male missionaries felt that they were placing women missionaries in physical danger when they left them alone and the extent to which women missionaries feared being without a non-Aboriginal male cannot be determined. While it may have been considered, the sexual risk to missionary women is not discussed in the writings available, but there may be sexual implications underlying this labelling of women as brave.

Constructions of identity based on bravery, heroism, and motherhood provided women with more freedom to act on their own without the immediate direction of male missionaries. It became increasingly common for women to work on their own in mission stations. There had been times in the past, as with Mrs. Ridley in the winter of 1884, that women stayed alone in mission stations, but this was often a result of circumstances, not deliberate planning. Male missionaries might have been on circuit or delayed in their travels when women took over services and performed other work. There were also other occasions when missionary women travelled as a solitary woman, but accompanied by at least a guide. Entirely alone, however, was something that in fact they rarely were. They were working in villages with Aboriginal residents, usually in close proximity to other White or mixed-race families perhaps involved in the fur trade.

The church's acceptance of unmarried women in the field was not entirely new, but their numbers had increased considerably since 1918. Their persona and presence had, in the intervening years, been shaped by a discourse of maternal power. Winifred Neville represented this new type. When she resigned from her nursing duties in 1952, after having been sponsored by the woman's auxiliary at Hay River since 1929, a praiseworthy article entitled "Mother" appeared in *Arctic News*. The author described how Neville had gained this status among the Deh Cho Dene: "'Gomma' is the name which was given to Miss Winifred Neville by the people among whom she worked as a nurse for so many years. She is justly proud of this name, for it was not lightly given, but spoken with reverence and devotion. 'Gomma' means 'Mother' in the language of the people who gave it and surely this speaks to us of love bestowed and felt."[61] Neville was portrayed as a mother to the Dene children of Hay River as well as the entire community:

> To live for twenty-three years in isolation among Indians with no missionary to turn to or call upon; no teacher to help you; to be both nurse and doctor with only a small building to work in; the responsibility of chores, wood-cutting, gardening, painting, carpentry, etc., and greatest of all the task of trying to reach souls for Christ the Saviour. This was what this modern saint brought to Mackenzie River, the record of which we and the whole Church are rightly proud.[62]

In Neville's case, motherhood took on a new meaning. She was not only a lone missionary capable of caring for children when the need arose but, in the eyes of the church, her presence as a White woman missionary was secure. As a mother, she was not only protector but protected.

A few months before the article on Neville appeared, a short note on Hay River referred to her as one who, for many years, had "held the fort at Hay River not only as a nurse but as a teacher, minister (insofar as she may) and general adviser and counselor to the Indian people as well as the white population."[63] The church avoided open discussion of the fact that women in the north often acted as ministers. Although not ordained, Neville and many others, especially after 1920, performed virtually the same duties. It would not be until 1976 that the Anglican Church in Canada permitted ordination of women.

The language used to describe Neville's life and work reflected a gradual shift that began in the early twentieth century but, in the Canadian mission field, became more common after the First World War. Concepts of heroism were evident in nineteenth-century mission biographies and women were frequently included in those male hagiographies as wives. But, once women went to mission stations by themselves, a new language of "Christian heroism" began to emerge. Women's actions in the field began to be described as equal in stature to those of men. They were not presented as radical or even as feminists, as were the "new women" of the day: rather, they were seen as ordinary women performing extraordinary tasks as demanded by their circumstances. The heroic identity which emerged along with the safety of the maternal metaphor combined to justify and sustain women in work that had previously been performed largely by missionary wives.[64]

# 6
# Contesting Control while Encouraging Zeal

Today everybody calls her Juju. *Juju* is grandmother in the
language of her people, the Gwich'in. She is *juju* to Inuvik, where
she lives in the long-term-care facility of the town hospital. And
she is *juju* to people of four generations of the North, from Old
Crow to Fort McPherson, Aklavik to Yellowknife – four generations
to whom she ministered and taught and well, mothered.
Whatever I could do, I could do it for the church.

Whatever little I know, I pass it on to my people.
Sarah Simon

– "Sarah's Story: 99 Years in the North," *Globe and Mail*,
22 March 2000

Each missionary who went into the northern field did so with specific
goals and practical means in mind. Their objective was to win converts,
and they were often deeply influenced by stories of dramatic conversions
in other mission settings well before they began their work. Missionary
perceptions of their successes and failures provide important evidence concerning how religious experiences were constructed for all persons in the
mission field. Most missionaries eventually realized that Aboriginal peoples responded to certain aspects of the mission that they found valuable
from their own world view and that they took from Christianity what
appealed to them. As a result, missionary strategies had to be modified and
their expectations tempered.

The reception of Christianity in Aboriginal communities took place
through a cultural interface that is difficult for historians to interpret. To
many, Christ represented one more spiritual deity. Giving up other customs for conversion to Christianity seemed not only contrary to tradition
but unnecessary. Historians and anthropologists have offered several
explanations for conversion, which range from the desire for more status
and enjoyment of the ceremonies, to dissatisfaction with old ways and
the belief that Christianity would empower the colonized subject. Just as
the desire of some Aboriginal peoples to please missionaries was a reason
for conversion, so too were factors such as fear of the new order and fear
of hell.[1] Some may have converted for a combination of reasons. Often, it
was marginal and demoralized individuals who experienced conversion

first: those who felt alienated, such as orphans or slaves, may have found Christianity appealing. For the purpose of gaining more status, chiefs may also have found Christianity attractive.[2] It is important to acknowledge the diversity of Aboriginal responses to Christianity. Kerry Abel, for example, argues that the Dene "accepted some aspects of the mission teachings in the nineteenth century" but, not surprisingly, retained many of their own cultural traditions. The distinctions that Christians made between the sacred and the secular had little resonance with the Dene, whose spirituality encompassed the natural world. As Abel argues, missionaries at least until the late nineteenth century failed to change Dene life: "Life on the land, flexible marriage partners, and continuing respect for individual decision making were still part of Dene life."[3] Nonetheless, missionaries continued to attempt to remake the Dene and other First Nations in the belief that their Eurocentric world view would ultimately prevail.

Studies of missions in other Canadian settings suggest similar conclusions with respect to conversion. Italian immigrants in early twentieth-century Toronto, for example, were willing to attend Methodist meetings held in their neighbourhood but, according to Enrico Carlson Cumbo, this did not guarantee a commitment to their denomination. Women took advantage of free sewing utensils, purchased fabric at reasonable rates, and used Church nurseries, but that did not mean obligation: "Missionaries acknowledged that Italian women used these functions for purely practical ends. If frequenting the missions meant having to listen occasionally to sermons and, less likely, attending religious services, they did so in the recognition that one could always be *in* but not necessarily *of* the congregation."[4] What concerns me about northern missions are missionary perceptions of how their message was received.

Evangelical missionaries in the north frequently expressed frustration over their inability to meet their aim of imparting Christianity or of moving potential adherents beyond being "in but not necessarily of." Conversion seemed not merely slow but altogether negligible. This complaint may have reflected unrealistic expectations and preconceptions. Parent committees warned that conversion would be slow, yet hopes ran high among missionaries that they could convert quickly by simply revealing Christian truth. They did not anticipate the resilience of Aboriginal cultures nor the possibility that Aboriginal peoples might incorporate Christian beliefs and practices into their existing belief systems.

**Heroic Christians**

Some missionaries coped with frustrations and disappointments by glorifying successes. They constructed simplistic narratives about their own and the church's history in their region. Like missionary-written memoirs, church newspapers could go even farther in myth-making and adulation of missionaries depicted as "wilderness saints."[5] Hyperbolic descriptions of how missionaries carried out dramatic struggles against "heathen darkness" were commonplace. Jean and John Comaroff have placed such writing in the context of Victorian and Edwardian sensibilities: "theirs was an epic quest, their emerging sense of 'biography' as a 'moral career' providing a model of and for heroic history – their own as well as that of the heathen lands that would become colonies of God and the British monarch."[6] If the work was not romantic or truly effective, it could be presented as such.

One feature of this writing was its insistence on promoting converted Aboriginal peoples as stellar role models with attributes that mirrored missionaries' own hopes. Idealized portraits of Aboriginal Christians were deemed a positive sign of progress and potential. Aboriginal Christians were portrayed in obituaries and letters directed to the parent committees and sent to church newspapers. They were cast typically as converts who gained such heroic status in the eyes of the missionaries that they were invested with the attributes of sublime beings. These descriptions were meant to convince readers that progress was being made and to reassure missionaries that success was possible.[7]

One woman who was described as a great Christian was Sarah Legaic. Born in 1855, Legaic was the daughter of Tsimshian chief Paul Legaic. Her obituary, which appeared in the *North British Columbia News* in 1914, describes Legaic as a very active Christian who taught in the day school at Metlakatla, assisted Bishop Ridley in translations, and continued until her death to work loyally for the woman's auxiliary. The obituary, prepared by the Reverend Gurd, was written in elegant and consciously rhetorical terms: "On November the fifth last, there passed away a notable Indian woman named 'Sarah Legaic,' we might have said Indian lady, because in her actions, demeanour, and intercourse with others, she exhibited those elements which belong to one of nature's ladies." Legaic was more than a woman; she was a lady. In the Reverend Gurd's mind, "ladies" behaved in a certain fashion that would have been deemed proper by upper-middle class society. He saw Legaic as a superior Christian: "A leader in all social undertakings which had for their objects the betterment of natives. Those who know the general traits of the Indian character will most appreciate her superior manner of life. The meaning of the word Legaic is 'mountain' and she exhibited in a marked degree the high and noble ideals which her name and rank indicated." No doubt Legaic was an active Christian Tsimshian. But a reading of this obituary shows how the author perceived Aboriginal peoples as a homogenous culture. Legaic was portrayed as an exception to her race; she did not hold the "general traits of the Indian character."[8]

Julia McDonald's obituary echoed similar sentiments. She was the wife of the Yukon's first missionary, Archdeacon Robert McDonald. Julia was from

Peel River, where she met and married McDonald. They travelled among the Gwich'in Dene and she helped him to translate the Bible into Tukudh. When she died in July 1938, *Northern Lights* recognized her contributions, but did so in relation to her husband and in contrast to her race: "It was in this work of translation that Mrs. McDonald was able to render the greatest assistance to her husband. Not only her knowledge of the Indian language but also her knowledge of the people, their customs, and the country in which they lived, as well as being possessed of more than the average intelligence of her race, made her a most valuable help meet."[9] Like Legaic, McDonald was presented as a superior example from a lesser norm. She enjoyed special elevation as an Aboriginal Christian.

Others, especially Aboriginal catechists or school teachers, were often placed on a pedestal by missionaries. They became symbols of Christianity's potential in the north and a positive sign of the Church's success. This was particularly true for the Edenshaw family, who lived in Masset on the Queen Charlotte Islands (Haida Gwaii). Anthropologist Margaret Blackman's biography of Florence Edenshaw Davidson recounts the Edenshaw family history and provides insight into how Christianity influenced them. Florence Edenshaw was born in 1896, two years after the death of her grandfather, Haida Chief Albert Edenshaw. Blackman cites one Church Missionary Society missionary's account of the Edenshaw family that

Mrs. Julia McDonald, with her children Mary, Neil, and Hugh. Julia McDonald was married to the Reverend Robert McDonald and worked with him to translate the Bible into Tukudh.

describes them as highly respected by both the Haida and missionaries alike. In glowing terms, missionary Charles Harrison wrote of his admiration for Albert Edenshaw and his family:

> I had the privilege of baptising him and his wife and of receiving them into the church. They were afterwards confirmed by Bishop Ridley and became communicants. When baptized he received the name Albert Edward, the Christian name of the late King Edward. [Edenshaw's] eldest son, George Cowhoe, was the first native teacher on these Islands, and I also had the privilege of baptizing him, his wife and family. He [Edenshaw] had only two sons and the other is so well known that he needs no recommendation from me. His name is Henry Edenshaw. I baptised him also. After his brother's death he succeeded him in his chieftainship and also became the teacher of the Masset Indian school, which position he filled remarkably well for several years. He is now franchised and entitled to all the privileges of the white man, and no better business man could be met with on this entire coast ....
>
> I have no hesitation in saying that it is principally due to his [Edenshaw's] manlike ways, his influence, and example that the Haidas [sic] have taken so readily to the ways and customs of the whites, and that at the present moment they are one of the most advanced and lawabiding races on the coast.[10]

Neither the prominence of the Edenshaw family nor their devoutness is disputed here. But the hyperbole used to describe the idealized attributes of this family, with conventional references to race, suggests a similar pattern in perceptions of Aboriginal Christians. Converts held the promise of spreading Christianity. As a result of the influence of the Edenshaws, Harrison suggests, the Haida had taken to the "ways and customs of the whites." It seems that respect accorded to Aboriginal Christians depended on mimicry, on their behaving like White people. Just as non-Christian Aboriginal peoples were portrayed in a derogatory way, Christian Aboriginal peoples were seen from the context of a value system that had a consummate purpose. Missionaries in northern British Columbia consistently pointed to the Edenshaws as examples of the most upstanding Christians.

The impact of Christian missions was undoubtedly visible to Florence Edenshaw's generation. She remembered, for example, the experience of female puberty seclusion which she went through at age thirteen in 1909. Her sisters, who were just three and six years younger, did not go through it because according to Florence Edenshaw "we became like white people then."[11] Like Legaic and McDonald, Edenshaw was a dedicated Christian. She was very conscious of her Christian beliefs, which, according to Blackman, had been emphasized in her upbringing:

The home Florence grew up in was a Christian home. Her mother sang hymns as she worked, not Haida songs, and her father began his daily carving with prayer. Florence's uncle, Henry Edenshaw, who exerted a great influence on his sister's children, was the missionary's assistant, Sunday School teacher, translator of the bible into Haida and, in the words of every missionary who ever worked with him, a "model Christian." Florence and her sisters were baptized and confirmed into the Anglican Church, were taken to Sunday school each week by their parents, and were married in the church. At age fifteen Florence joined the Woman's Auxiliary of the church and has been an active member ever since.[12]

Florence Edenshaw obviously contributed to the life of the church in Masset. And yet as a "true Christian," she had not relinquished all the beliefs and practices of the Haida. She still believed in reincarnation and, like the rest of her family, participated in the potlatch. She retained her Haida language. While missionaries respected Aboriginal Christians who developed close relationships with the church, they tried to give the impression that the converts had abandoned their cultures. The real impact of the Anglican Church was concealed. It was one thing to boast about their successes, but quite another to ignore the fact that some Aboriginal peoples blended Christianity with their own customs. Unfortunately for the historian, biographies like Florence Edenshaw's are rare. Certainly, her family blended Christianity with their traditional culture.

### "For fear of disturbing the faith they have"
Despite the optimistic nature of descriptions of Christian Aboriginal peoples, the fact was that the number of converts to Christianity was not substantial in the early years. The Stringers had worked at Herschel Island (Qikiqtaruk) for nearly five years before they had their first convert and, by the time they left for another post, they had baptized only "a few individuals." The Reverend Stringer was openly frustrated: "of the results very little can be said. I am afraid there are many stony-ground hearers. Many seem willing to learn, and will listen attentively and assent to what is told them, still there are the same evils and superstitions as before that tend to counteract all missionary effort. But we must work on and hope and pray, even there be no harvest for a time."[13] Stringer visited Herschel Island in 1909 and was delighted by the increased number of those wanting to marry and be baptized: "For many years this, my former field of work was discouraging, but I believe steady though slow progress was made each year. How thankful I was to see what was in some sense the first fruits of many years of work."[14] In private and public correspondence, Stringer demonstrated the kind of dogged patience he demanded of others. Generally, however, missionaries were conscious of and frustrated by the fact

that those who had converted to Christianity seemed always on the verge of slipping back to their so-called heathen ways; it would be more accurate to say that the converts had never completely abandoned their traditional lifeways. Though they rarely assumed that Aboriginal peoples had completely converted, Europeans and Canadians did not appreciate or fully understand that syncretism was the most they could expect.

While the objective was complete conversion, conversion was no guarantee that Aboriginal peoples had relinquished their traditions or "improved." No single word better exemplifies the method of missions than "improvement." Normally, however, the term was used to portray non-Christian Aboriginal peoples. Yet, it also referred to Aboriginal peoples who had been baptized and were still said to be in need of improvement, as they persisted with their traditional customs. Missionary belief in improvement was relentless. All previous behaviours were to be given up, as was implied in a statement by Sarah LeRoy at Hay River (Kátl'odéech) in 1916:

> I wish I could send you a picture of the scene before me. This window overlooks the village where the Indian children are to be seen at play, little girls in long dresses, and little boys in long trousers. Just now I saw three women with lighted pipes start off for the woods with their axes and now they are returning, each one with a heavy load of firewood strapped on her back while the men have spent the evening playing a

Reverend Harry Sherman Shepherd, Bishop Archibald Lang Fleming, and Reverend Thomas Umaok with the first confirmation class at Shingle Point (Tapqaq), June 1934.

drum and gambling with squares of tobacco or some small article. They are so like children. They are all Christian Indians but have not yet given up many of their heathen customs. Improvements in their homes and outward appearances can be noticed each year, and we will continue to pray that God will soon win them to himself and that it will be a continued joy to them to serve him.[15]

While LeRoy paternalistically labelled Aboriginal peoples "so like children" and heathen, she ironically comes close in her assessment to what Christianity might have meant for Aboriginal cultures in the north. In this case she was describing Deh Cho peoples. LeRoy maintained that, although they were Christian, they still, to her regret, had not relinquished their traditions. Improvement was not enough for some missionaries, as they wished to have all customs eradicated entirely. The Reverend Frederick P. Thorman was of this mind. In the summer of 1919, he went down the Liard River to visit several communities and claimed to be pleased with the results but expressed real anxiety about the living conditions of those among whom he travelled:

My summer trip down to the Liard Post was a great success. I held many services. I also vaccinated over one hundred Indians against small-pox. They are very wild Indians, and, a great deal of witch-craft (often involving human sacrifices) is practised. Polygamy, too, is very frequent. Many of them have received Christian instruction, but even this is sadly mixed with their old barbaric beliefs. On this occasion I baptized no one, but I promised to return next year to further instruct them in the Christian faith. It is essential that they first relinquish all their pagan beliefs, ideas, and practices before baptism, and this they seemed loath to do at the outset.[16]

Neither LeRoy nor Thorman could be content with any blend of Christian and Aboriginal practices and beliefs. In each case, improvement was necessary; however, Thorman was obviously far more agitated. He could not tolerate any sign of what he called "barbaric beliefs." Like many other missionaries, LeRoy and Thorman failed to understand that to most Aboriginal peoples complete acceptance of Christianity was unappealing and incompatible with their spiritual beliefs. Yet this did not mean that Christianity was rejected. Instead, some Aboriginal peoples accepted some parts of Christian practice and adapted them to existing cultures. Thorman made direct contact with Aboriginal peoples, not by baptizing, but by vaccinating them. Such a practical aspect of mission work appealed to those he met.

Early in her career as a missionary at Fort Selkirk, Kathleen Martin realized that it was best not to discourage suggestions of Christianity among the northern Tutchone. At one point, she recorded her concern over a dance that took place after the death of a man in the village. Death feasts were customary but usually offensive to missionaries. Martin, however, did not seem to be quite as opposed as other missionaries, accepting the fact that Christianity had made a limited impact:

> I do not think that they mean wrong as they are so anxious for me to say a prayer for them when they were ill, but these other teachings that have come down through generations have still got the strongest hold. They calmly inform me at times that Jesus told them this or that, and they believe so firmly what they say that although I reason with them I would not dream of contradicting them for fear of disturbing the faith that they have got.[17]

These Aboriginal people accepted parts of Christianity and talked to Martin about Jesus, but they did not do so to the exclusion of their own beliefs. While some missionaries were frustrated with the continuation of Aboriginal traditions, others were flexible enough to allow for both local cultural custom and Christian discussion. Martin, for example, was pleased with what she perceived as the Tutchone grasping some Christian concepts. Women like her who lived permanently in the community were closer to the people and generally demonstrated more patience or a deeper under-standing of the syncretic nature of Christian mission. Martin's familiarity with individual families certainly placed her in a different position than itinerants like the Reverend Thorman. Known in northern missionary cir-cles to be well liked by the Tutchone, Martin expressed a level of comfort in her work.

Like Martin, British missionary Adelaide Butler recognized that some of the Christian Inuit maintained their practices. Thomas Umaok, the first Canadian Inuit deacon, worked at Shingle Point (Tapqaq) when Adelaide Butler was there in the mid-1930s and she averred that Umaok had not entirely given up his prior beliefs: "Thomas and Susie, our native Catechist and his wife, still retain some of their old heathenish superstitions, and they have an idea that there is a 'hoodoo' on the house they have moved into."[18] Butler does not doubt Umaok's Christianity, but she is conscious of his ways that she considers to be heathen.

If the success of Anglican missions in the north is to be measured by the number of converts who did not maintain any of their traditions, this story would be one of grim failure. While missionaries emphasized their success stories, they also had to acknowledge tensions, even in the sustainability of conversion. Concern with success, moderate success, or failure to have Christianity accepted by their audiences is significant because it reflects how missionaries saw themselves and their work. Like Bishop Stringer, many believed that the "stony ground hearers" would eventually convert. This belief sustained the missionaries. Terrence L. Craig argues that "belief was the foundation of these people's lives: To preserve themselves they had to preserve belief not only in their divine cause but that the divine cause was being achieved."[19] Even small gains could be construed as success, as Kathleen Martin claimed: "I would not dream of contradicting them for fear of disturbing the faith that they have." Faith sustained missionaries but limited their recognition of the syncretic nature of the mission process.

### Romance or Drudgery?

Although mission work may have been constructed for home audiences as "romantic," and missionaries cast as "Christian heroes," the reality was far different. Missionaries' experiences transformed some of their initial expectations and forced them to address the substantial difficulties they faced. Their correspondence implies that their work was far from romantic at times. Yet, even in their darkest moments, they clung to an image of themselves as noble servants.

The romantic view of northern mission work was tempered markedly by the monotony and routine of daily tasks. Sometimes the spiritual purposes of mission work had to give way to the practical. For some, the burden of mundane chores combined with the environmental conditions amounted to drudgery. In an article prepared for *Aiyansh Notes*, the Reverend J.B. McCullagh admitted that "the mere act of living and dwelling in these back woods stations constitutes a good half of the work required, and, except one can regard it as a work done for the master, it is liable to generate the idea of drudgery and fill the mind with discontent."[20] The same sense of disenchantment was expressed by Miss F. Copeland when she described the Collison family for *Aiyansh Notes* in 1911. She found the Collisons "happy" in their home and work, but fighting an ever-present risk of melancholy: "Yes 'happy' in spite of the many trials and difficulties of work amongst the Nishgas, in spite of real fights against the powers of darkness, in spite of much humdrum drudgery, in spite of the biting cold Nass winds and abundance of rain, rain, rain."[21] The upkeep of mission stations and strains of daily routine prompted many to describe mission work in these terms.

In writing to the Church Missionary Society about her engagement to the Reverend W.H. Collison's son, Bertha Davies described her experiences of nearly three years in the field. Born in Buckfastleigh, England, Davies arrived at Metlakatla to work as a trained nurse and missionary with the Church Missionary Society in 1897. She felt her chores befit a "working woman": "What makes the work very heavy is that all the house work has to be done by the children & of course they have to be taught to do it & superintended all the time – One feels that a working woman would do it just as well certainly there is no romance about the work but one does see a great improvement in some of the children."[22] In response the committee congratulated her on her upcoming marriage and contended that her work, while far from glamorous, was nonetheless uplifting: "It is not as you say romantic but it is far better. The performance of everyday commonplace duties for Christ's sake, the exhibition of Christian love and of patience, the example of devotion and humility are marked by our dear Master's eye and their regard here and now may be beyond all expectation."[23] They closed by wishing her continued good service as Collison's wife. As a basic Christian tenet, the Church Missionary Society believed that commonplace, humble work was God's work. In the context of a religious calling daily tasks were important.

Nonetheless even sublime drudgery had its limits. Just a few months before this, Bertha's sister Rose had sent a similar letter:

> After nearly three years experience as a nurse here I think I might be allowed to say that I do not think a missionary nurse is necessary. Twice during the time I was at the hospital we had 6 or 7 patients at the same time: occasionally there were 3 or 4 but most frequently only one & weeks would pass without anyone. To attend to the spiritual needs of these patients there were no less than 3 missionaries the Dr. his wife and myself. With regard to the ordinary nursing I can only repeat that I do not consider this required a missionary at the rate of 100 a year I consider a working woman who will act as servant to the hospital & do the little nursing there is to do, all that is needed.[24]

As a result of her letter Davies was transferred to the Ridley children's home.

This was not to be the end of the complaints. Alice Edwards, who arrived at Metlakatla in 1898, returned to London five years later with a list of concerns. Her description of the working conditions prompted a letter from Miss Gollock, then in charge of women missionaries. Gollock expressed concern that women missionaries were not adhering to the religious training of the young children under their care in the children's homes. She was pointed and frank and demanded answers to specific questions. Even though four women missionaries served at the station, in her view little time had been spent on inculcating Christianity:

> Do you concur with the account that Miss Edwards gives that otherwise these four ladies have no opportunities for engaging in any outside missionary work? Will you also kindly tell us how far you feel with her that owing to the difficult nature of the girls, the spiritual response even from those who have been resident for some years is painfully small, their

example and influence on the younger ones being far from what we all desire? How far do these children yield to loving care and sympathy and how far only to the sterner discipline of actual punishment? We really are most anxious to know the real facts of the case. Please help me. Miss Edwards seems to feel that you and Miss West, Miss Soal and herself are mainly engaged in the rough sort of work which a country-born matron might do, and have scarcely any opportunity for doing personal and spiritual work amongst the girls. We shall be glad to know what Bible classes are held by the missionaries in the Homes, and what opportunities are afforded for meeting for prayer among the girls. We are fully aware that you are all working with unsparing devotion but are you clear that it is on true missionary lines as to spiritual work?[25]

Gollock pointed to problems that existed throughout the north. If work with Aboriginal children was the key to a future Christian society, how could this be done by those bogged down by routine chores? To what extent was spiritual work emphasized? Unfortunately a response to Gollock cannot be found. The Davies sisters and Alice Edwards agreed that their talents were being wasted. What they saw as the mundane aspects of mission life, the plight of "working women," kept them from their higher calling. One can surmise that their concerns were inspired by the fact that women were often expected to be responsible for the domestic chores. And class prejudices may have lurked behind some of these concerns. Spiritual work was limited at times by the practical demands of orphanages, boarding houses, schools, and nursing stations. It seems that there were times when the mission station seemed hardly the place for spiritual reflection, or even basic gospel teaching. Gollock's questions challenged the very foundations that missionaries were trying to establish. Yet, the missionaries themselves probably wondered sometimes how spiritual their work really was.

When missionary women expressed impatience or doubts concerning their effectiveness, they sometimes yearned for renewal, rather than dwelled on failure. Bessie Quirt revealingly confided that her life at Shingle Point needed spiritual rejuvenation: "I feel I've been living the life of a spiritual pauper since I came here, but it is so much better now. I do need grace and more grace and Christ like love to live this life as I would live it, and witness as I should."[26] After an intensive period of loneliness Charlotte Selina Bompas confided in her diary that she had to fight despair: "My loneliness sometimes seems very great. I tell myself to work harder or not to brood or despond. I want to live a higher more spiritual life and then I shall not feel so lonely."[27] Despite Bompas's determination to overcome despondency, she was frustrated by the apparent ineffectiveness of her work, confiding that "one is often depressed concerning the mission work, the disappointments are so great, and there is so much that is painful and unsatisfactory to contend with."[28] On the other hand, signs of progress prompted relief and gratitude: "there have been a few little chinks of light amid the general darkness for which one feels glad and thankful."[29] Throughout these and many other accounts metaphors of darkness and light were employed repeatedly, which takes us some distance in understanding missionaries' religious fervour and determination. Sarah LeRoy, at Hay River (Kátl'odéech), expressed a common attitude: "The fight against the evil one has been hard, but still the joys of service have overbalanced the discouragements and disappointments."[30]

Although disheartened by monotonous routine or slow gains, missionaries always hoped that something could be served by the practical example they set. Gertrude Thorne at Aiyansh, wrote of the "hewing of wood and the drawing of water," as an act of worship and spoke of the landscape as humbling, as the menial tasks of life in it demanded.[31] Striving for strength through humility was a common principle shared by most Anglican missionaries. In the face of the many setbacks and disappointments encountered, this force allowed the church to continue to function. In describing her work at Alert Bay ('Yalis) in 1898, Christine Carleton gloried in her sense of humble dignity: "It is wonderful the joy and peace God gives one in doing the most menial and humble thing and we do have some very humble things to do sometimes and sometimes things that one naturally dislikes but the feeling all goes as one realizes it is done for the master's sake."[32] Whether her angst could be so easily soothed is hard to determine. Obviously for Bertha Davies and Alice Edwards it was not. Nonetheless a devout attitude had to be nurtured in the mission field if it was to be borne at all. Evangelicals were especially inclined to turn practical work into religious duty.

For Elizabeth Wilgress at Hay River, the prescription to success was proper behaviour and respect for others: "The Red Indian is instinctively and closely observant. He notices trifles which we never see. And if the missionary, who has come to teach him, is betrayed into impatience or anger, unfairness or any other un-Christlike action the Indian silently observes and judges. On the other hand, if the teacher, upheld by our prayers, and in the power of Christ, leads a consistent holy life though he should never preach a single sermon, yet his influence carries a weight far and near, which can never be measured."[33] Wilgress was less concerned with sermons and scriptures but, like Thorne, she believed in sublime humility. For those truly called by God, a modest approach would serve well in the field. Patience and humility were necessary missionary characteristics.

Wilgress was concerned that missionaries be careful not to betray the "observant" Aboriginal peoples. She still saw the diverse peoples as a single racial entity but, like Martin, she urged caution so as not to discourage entirely those who showed any interest. For missionaries it became clear over time that their images had to be reconstructed if the church was to have any impact. The idea of conversion led so often to frustration when the hopes of eradicating local traditions were not met. Reflecting on their work led some missionaries to feel utter discouragement, while others were moved to write in glowing terms about their accomplishments and to feature prominently certain Aboriginal Christians. And, yet there were others who were willing to accept any sign of understanding of Christ's message as hope and believed that if they acted as "models of g/race" their behaviour and beliefs would be mimicked.

Missionaries in the north reacted differently to their work. At times they felt very unhappy and frustrated, but hopeful. In fact, they were always hopeful. Initially they expected to eradicate all signs of cultural and spiritual beliefs. When they found that there were Aboriginal peoples who could be held up as fine examples of Christianity they were anxious to celebrate them. And then they overlooked the fact that they had exaggerated the negative attributes of non-Christian Aboriginal peoples. Nonetheless, new approaches had to be adopted in order to find ways into Aboriginal cultures. The most successful new strategies and Anglican institutions in northern Canada between the late nineteenth century and the early 1940s were arguably the woman's auxiliary and the Church Army. The woman's auxiliary and the Church Army represent two institutions that appear to have appealed to Aboriginal cultural traditions. Both were imported and reshaped in northern settings. While neither were part of the initial strategy of the northern mission, each was in part responsible for remaking the northern Anglican church. Neither one of these institutions was part of the formal structure of the Church Missionary Society and both were initiated based on perceived needs in the mission field rather than on instructions from either London or Toronto. Another outstanding feature was the propensity for White missionaries to want to control their operations, whilst at the same time feeling a desire to assure that Aboriginal peoples participate in and at times lead the movements. In other words, they represent a contest for control over Christianity.

## Sowing Seeds of Sisterhood

The woman's auxiliary of the Canadian Anglican mission society operated on two levels. It provided women in southern Canadian parishes with a sense of power and the feeling that they were working toward a global Christian mission and, at the parochial level in the north, it gave missionary women a specific instrument for drawing Aboriginal women into their circle. Missionary women viewed woman's auxiliary meetings as a way to incorporate their teaching with work that was already familiar and comfortable for Aboriginal women. Auxiliary meetings with Aboriginal and mission women initially were likely to focus on making crafts for fundraising purposes. Aboriginal women had long been responsible for the preparation of clothing and were accustomed to preparing hides and sewing in groups, so that the activities were not alien, even though the mission women generally provided meeting space. Had Aboriginal women not been comfortable, they might not have attended these meetings.

The opportunity to meet together was empowering for women. In her study of Carrier-Sekani peoples from British Columbia's northern interior, Jo-Anne Fiske demonstrates how such women's organizations as mothers unions, which had been active there, inadvertently helped to cement a feeling of sisterhood among Carrier women. Fiske focuses on the impact of economic and social disruption experienced by Carrier peoples from the early twentieth century to the 1950s. Carrier women seemed to adjust better than men because of their ability to rely on one another, especially in groups. Fiske argues that "as women adjusted to Catholicism and state intervention they were able to use church-sponsored auxiliaries to influence community affairs.[34] Bridget Moran, in her biography of the prominent Carrier woman, Mary John, entitled *Stoney Creek Woman*, suggests that women who came together on the Stoney Creek reserve in the 1970s to knit or sew became politically active when a community crisis arose.[35] The original intent of Christian women's organizations was not to politicize Aboriginal women, but over time some groups nevertheless found themselves involved in local issues.[36]

The origins of the parochial Anglican Church woman's auxiliaries varied from place to place across northern Canada. Clergy in the north were generally enthusiastic about having woman's auxiliary branches in their dioceses; yet, until the early twentieth century, they showed little interest in their development. When Bishops Ridley and Bompas were not travelling, they were busy with either translations or administrative work. The national woman's auxiliary contributed financially to northern missions and continually recommended the creation of local branches. Auxiliary work was associated with southern White women and it was not until more White women settled in the north that branches were established. Though established on the basis of southern concerns, the northern woman's auxiliary quickly assumed a character of its own.

In the Diocese of the Yukon, the woman's auxiliary was dominated in its early years by White women.[37] Throughout the gold rush and post-boom period, White newcomers were numerous enough to call for a women's organization. The woman's auxiliary responded to this demand. In 1904 branches were established in Whitehorse (Kwanlin), Carcross (Natashaheeni), and Dawson (Tr'ochek). Their motto, "For who hath despised the day of small things," was suggested by Bishop Bompas, who believed that small things, such as cold or isolation, had to be overlooked to keep faith with the larger vision of mission. In reference to the origins of the Carcross branch, Selina Bompas, first president of the Yukon Territory Woman's Auxiliary,[38] recalled that for the Carcross women simply finding a time to meet posed a challenge: "Our meetings were held at eight o'clock p.m. They had to be at that late hour, as most of us were working members, and neither the stationmaster's wife, nor the telegraph operator, nor the postmaster's sister, nor the lady of the customhouse officer, who all did their own work, could contrive to make any earlier hour convenient, or even feasible. Still less could our dear school teachers vacate their field of operations."[39] Meetings were scheduled around the routines of working women, all of whom were White. Despite this, Bompas wanted northern auxiliary members to remember that, not long ago, Dawson was the site of an Aboriginal peoples camp near the mouth of the Klondike River. In typical Bompas fashion, she went on to lecture the women:

> The poor Indians are nearly swamped by the white man. You have invaded their territory, cut down their forests, thereby driving away their moose and caribou, and depriving them of their very means of subsistence. Yet the evil is not unmixed with good. The banner of the Cross is now, thank God, unfurled among you, and now sick Indians are welcomed and lovingly tended in your hospitals. The children are taught freely in your school here, as proof that the hearts of the white women have loving thoughts and intentions for others besides themselves; that they do not live only for the gold dust of the Klondike or the nuggets of discovery, but take active and prayerful interest in the Leper's children of India, and the Chippewa Indian boy in the Shingwauk Home of Sault Ste. Marie, and the sweet girl missionary, Miss Wade, sent out to China.[40]

She tempered her recognition that Europeans had invaded Aboriginal territory with the hope that White women would now work for people Bompas describes as "the poor Indians." Bompas warned auxiliary members to keep the organization's goals and objectives in mind. She saw the auxiliary as an institution that might relieve northern gentlewomen from monotonous routines and provide a sense of collective purpose as well as an image of missionary work in other colonies. She wanted them to read the auxiliary's *New Era* to keep informed of church work as a global mission. Bompas wanted auxiliary participants to feel integrated, part of a larger movement, working toward the same Christian purpose. While she ignored the role of Aboriginal women, annual reports suggest that they gradually became involved.

The woman's auxiliary in southern Canada was established to aid missionary work, concentrating on parishes well beyond local borders. Yukon's auxiliary, on the other hand, was in a missionary diocese and thus, as Sarah Stringer, president from 1906 to 1931, reported: "it is considered that we are doing missionary work if we help the parishes and missions in the Diocese."[41] In other words, northern chapters worked for themselves. In some Yukon parishes, the junior branches focused on Aboriginal children. In the annual reports for 1910, Carcross, Whitehorse, and Dawson all claimed to have active junior auxiliaries. Ida Collins, matron of the Carcross Residential School, reported that the children in her group had taken pledges to support untainted leper children in Honan, a kindergarten in Nagoya, Japan; a hospital in Lytton, BC; and the education of missionary's children. To raise funds, they sold girls' bead work, boys' scrap books, locally grown vegetables, and muskrat skins.[42] The junior auxiliaries were supervised by White women and, in theory, served to educate Aboriginal children about missionary work abroad as well as in their own diocese. The junior auxiliary branch at Carcross in 1921 claimed a membership of twenty-six. That year, four members left school to return to their villages and, according to the supervisor, it was hoped that they would become "missionaries to their own people."

The minutes of the annual meetings indicate that, in most cases, Aboriginal and White branches were separate in the Yukon. For example, Margaret Johnson, who prepared the Carcross junior auxiliary report for 1915, made a point of distinguishing her group: "This is an Indian Branch of the Junior Woman's Auxiliary. All the members except three – the Johnson children – are Indians. All the money earned by work has been earned by the Indian children, the white children's contributions being given in the collections."[43] Aboriginal children, whose efforts as Christians were magnified in the eyes of the missionaries, produced and sold wood-carvings and bead work.

Apart from the children's auxiliaries, attempts were made to include Aboriginal women in the creation of their own branches. At Moosehide (Éhä Dädhëchan Kek'ét), a village near Dawson, Selina Totty started an "Indian Branch" in August 1910. "We are not able to report great things of our W.A. Branch at Moosehide," she reported to the annual meeting, "but we are glad to be able to say that the members, who are all Indians try to take an interest in the good work." She went on to say that a group of five women were attending meetings regularly, where they used "Indian hymns and as far as possible Indian prayers."[44] She hoped that the women would soon be "able to undertake some useful work for God in connection with the other Branches of the W.A."[45] In 1913 the membership had increased to twelve and a sale of work was planned.[46] But, in 1915 disaster struck because, as Totty claimed, "six members have become unfaithful."[47] This setback, however, did not represent the end of the branch, which was revived the following year. The Reverend Totty began these meetings with prayers and, to the delight of the Aboriginal women, served tea during the gathering. At one such meeting, it was noted that one of the women called out to the Reverend Totty when she saw the teapot coming, "good man, good man."[48] The following year, the Moosehide branch combined with the Dawson woman's auxiliary for a sale of their work and earned $43.75. Totty reported that an executive had been elected, with Eliza Isaac as president and Sarah Harper as vice-president. Other offices were filled by Selina Totty.[49]

"Indian branches" were few and far between. Most branches, such as the Dorcas Society, were made up of White women who believed they were working "for" Aboriginal women. Established in the winter of 1916, the Dorcas Society's basic aims were to clothe, feed, and help provide for those in need. Their most substantial endeavour was to distribute huge bales of clothing from the south. After its first year, the Dawson Dorcas branch boasted the following: "Bales were sent to Rampart Indians weighing 162 lbs., containing men's overcoats, suits, underwear, socks and boots, women's and children's clothes, and footwear. Bishop Stringer distributed amongst the Peel River Indians a generous supply of clothing of every description, including overcoats, complete suits of clothes, underwear, overalls, pajamas, socks, stockings, boots and shoes, for men, women and children. One bale went to the Indians at Mayo and some poverty stricken Indians at Moosehide were given clothes."[50] Perceptions of impoverished Aboriginal peoples drove the Dorcas work. The Dorcas women in the group

Dawson woman's auxiliary. *Back, left to right:* Miss Carlson, Mrs. McCarter, Mrs. Galpin, Mrs. Mills, Mrs. Townsend, Miss Vale, Mrs. Chapineau, Miss McAdam, Miss Tilling, Mrs. Johnson, Mrs. Totty, Mrs. A.E. Lee. *Front:* Mrs. Shirley, Mrs. Osborne, Mrs. McFarland, Mrs. Stringer, Mrs. Hickling, and Mrs. Hawksley.

wanted to see Aboriginal peoples properly dressed in European style clothing even if the garments were cast-offs from the south. Their perceptions of Christian charity were cast in terms of an imperial discourse which saw Aboriginal peoples as impoverished and backward.

During the 1920s the Yukon's woman's auxiliary membership grew. However, its work shifted away from foreign missions to focus more on the local diocese. The auxiliary continued to support overseas mission work but did not take on new foreign pledges. In Sarah Stringer's last presidential address, given at the diocesan annual meeting in 1931, she noted that the auxiliary had "become more comprehensive than ever. We include social service and religious education. In our Social Service work more Hospital visiting is done as well as Welcome and welfare work."[51] Although Selina Bompas had warned the auxiliary not to become too secular, by the 1920s, secular work was increasing. However, evangelical Anglicans in the north had always combined religion with education and health care, so this was not a fundamental change. The practical aspects of life remained central for them.

Part of the growth Stringer noted in 1931 included the creation of a new branch in Old Crow. The attendance of two Aboriginal women, Mrs. Kendi, and Julia McDonald, both from Old Crow, drew a great deal of attention at the 1931 annual meeting in Dawson. Julia McDonald was the wife of the first Anglican missionary of the Yukon, Robert McDonald and Mrs. Kendi was the wife of Julius Kendi, one of a handful of ordained Aboriginal deacons, whose parish, Old Crow, was the furthest northern village in the diocese. Mrs. Kendi started a women's auxiliary branch at Old Crow. When Imogene McCullum visited Old Crow in 1930 she found the beginnings of a woman's auxiliary with thirty-five members, a substantial number considering that there were only about 200 Aboriginal people in the village.[52] In her presidential address Stringer reported on McCullum's visit:

> In 1930 one of our vice-presidents made a visit to one of the outlying missions in our Diocese – Mrs. McCullum accompanied her husband, the Reverend A.C. McCullum, to Old Crow. She found that Mrs. Kendi, wife of the Reverend Julius Kendi, had already started a branch of the W.A. amongst the Indian women. However, they needed the direct guidance which Mrs. McCullum was able to give them and they started again with renewed energy and devotion.[53]

In a subsequent report McCullum praised the work of the Old Crow auxiliary, adding, "I cannot adequately express to you my feelings as I saw these folks gathered together and realized the task before me in trying to give them a message of help and service, to have them realize their share and responsibility in the 'Work of the Master.'"[54] McCullum displayed the usual cultural presumptions when she saw herself providing guidance to the efforts of the woman's auxiliary in Old Crow as if Vuntut Gwitchin women could not organize themselves without it.[55] Aboriginal branches were rare in the Yukon, perhaps because there was tension about direction.

This tension certainly was evident to Laura Beatrice Berton, a Dawson school teacher who moved from her Toronto home in 1907. She joined the woman's auxiliary and became well acquainted with Sarah Stringer, who lived in Dawson at the time. In her memoirs, Berton recalled the Stringers with great admiration, noting that the family often had Aboriginal visitors: "There always seemed to be a line of Indian sleighs parked in front of Bishop's House whenever I passed. Mrs. Stringer called them 'the roses around my door.'" Berton suggested that they came to discuss problems with the bishop and that Sarah Stringer always treated them with respect and warmth: "I soon discovered that Mrs. Stringer was a woman of great latent strength. Nothing ruffled her. Whether she was talking to the Indians, crossing the Rat River Divide, or shaking hands with the King and Queen (and she was presented on five different occasions) she never lost her inner serenity which marked her every action. She treated duchesses and savages with equal respect."[56] Stringer was often described as a homey and motherly person and appears to have been popular.

Like other Dawson settlers, Berton quickly became aware of the rigid hierarchy of the town which emerged after the gold rush. Although aware that Aboriginal peoples were marginalized, she spoke of them as did others of her time and place, as savages. Apart from her impressions of Stringer, Berton recorded a moment in the history of woman's auxiliary meetings that could be interpreted as tragic. Yet the incident reveals the missionary's liminal position with respect to race relations. Stringer and Berton were at a tea held by the auxiliary in Dawson in the early 1930s. Berton recounted Stringer's behaviour in detail:

> I remember when she quite unconsciously caused a tremendous flurry among the ladies of the Woman's Auxiliary, because at one of the woman's auxiliary teas she sat Mrs. Julius Kendi, an Indian woman from Mayo, at her right. Mrs. Stringer who never gave a thought to protocol, placed Mrs. Kendi there because she felt the native woman might be nervous unless she sat close to someone she knew. The other ladies were terribly upset, but if it had occurred to Mrs. Stringer that Mrs. Kendi was seated at the place of honour, I am certain she would have made no change.[57]

Stringer had disrupted conventional protocol by inviting Kendi to sit beside her at the tea. Fortunately, Stringer was sensitive to the possibility that Kendi would feel isolated.

The attitudes of newly arrived White women in the north beg comparison with women who resettled the American west. According to historian

Glenda Riley, women in the westward movement came with predisposed images of themselves as moral missionaries: "As moral missionaries embarking on a crusade to the West in general and to American Indians in particular, women had prejudice toward Indians firmly in mind before they even set foot on the westward trail. To heighten and enhance their own powers to civilize, women generally were ready to be assailed and shocked by the primitivism of the natives they would soon confront."[58] Over time, after the gold rush, the boundaries of race in Dawson and Whitehorse became drawn very tightly to the point where Aboriginal peoples were denied residency rights and missionaries sometimes found themselves in the middle of disputes between Aboriginal peoples and settlers. The incident with the Dawson woman's auxiliary was that the women were gathered to further the cause of mission and Kendi had in some respects become a missionary to her people; but as an "Indian woman," she was perceived by the other auxiliary members as unfit to sit beside Sarah Stringer. This attitude may go beyond mere social norms and, instead, be a reflection of the tensions within the broader Dawson society.

In more isolated locations where Aboriginal women dominated demographically, the tensions were not as severe. Pangnirtung, on Baffin Island in the eastern Arctic, provides an interesting contrast. The first woman's auxiliary meetings in Pangnirtung were recorded by Florence Hirst, who launched a branch with Prue Hockin in the winter of 1935. Hirst was very enthusiastic, considering it an ideal setting for Inuit women and children to work with her and Hockin. She described the first meeting as a success: "The evening was a happy one and we were much elated when Cunie informed us later the Saudlo had told her that the women were all agreed on the fact that it was the best party they had ever had and it was far ahead of their dances. The W.A. is one of my chief joys, for it is a means of becoming more intimately acquainted with the mothers and the babies, (we still have a large percentage of active juniors) than in any other way."[59] Hirst was pleased because she felt that she could come to know Inuit women better through the meetings.

The auxiliary in Pangnirtung grew rapidly. A year later, Hirst boasted that they planned to increase their contributions: "Our W.A. meetings held on Thursday nights are a great joy to us. Where we were able to send out $38 last year, we hope to be able to send out $50 this. Of course we may not achieve this objective. But there is nothing like aiming high, is there?" Hirst also reported that she looked forward to a time when Aboriginal women could work on woman's auxiliary projects in their camps: "In time we hope to be able to have materials to equip the various camps and place a woman in charge, then let them hold their own W.A. meetings in their own little camps, whilst at the same time being able to feel that they too have a part in the glorious organization, and have the privilege and opportunity of forming in fellow-ship with all the other members of the W.A."[60] It seemed as if any small-scale success held enormous promise, almost without limit. In the same journal entry Hirst revealed her dream of a sisterhood of workers across Canada: "The Pangnirtung W.A. has received several messages by radio from various W.A.'s in civilization much to the great joy of our own members. It has helped them to realize that their 'white' sisters in civilization have actually 'taken them in' as it were."

Hirst's idea that White sisters in "civilization" had taken in or welcomed Aboriginal women to the auxiliary is telling. She saw it as a unifying organization for all women, regardless of location or race. And yet her reference to "women in civilization" who had taken in women who lived in what she perceived to be less civilized conditions indicates the persistence of her colonizer's view.

In the fall of 1937, membership in the auxiliary at Pangnirtung had grown to the point where there was scarcely room to hold the meetings at the hospital house. During the summer of 1938, a large outdoor picnic was attended by 150 women. Hirst reported "great excitement – The women so thoroughly enjoy everything. This is one day in the year when it would seem as though the men almost wish they could be women."[61] This too seems a telling observation.[62] In the Canadian north, the feeling of connection to a larger organization beyond their villages may well have been meaningful to Inuit women and, for Hirst at least, it implied a sisterhood.

On her visit to the Arctic in the winter of 1942, Elizabeth Fleming wrote a short memoir of her impressions. This unpublished manuscript is replete with details of her visits to northern communities, including Pangnirtung. She was very impressed with its woman's auxiliary branch. At one meeting she attended, twenty-three Inuit women, fifteen children, and seven White women were present. According to Fleming, all were enthusiastic:

As I looked around I was tremendously impressed by the immaculate appearance of this group of women and their babies. I felt that in raising them up to such a high standard Nurse Hockin and her associates had accomplished a triumph for it is not easy to desire or to achieve personal cleanliness when living in a tent or igloo. I was also impressed at seeing the W.A.'s member's badge, a silver Winchester Cross, pinned on every parka bosom. But most of all I was impressed by the dignity and reverence with which these simple, Eskimo women conducted the service in their own tongue.

As I listened I tried to picture in my mind their weekly meetings held on Friday evenings as each group travelled far and wide. Of course the Pangnirtung branch gathered each Friday at the hospital but the others would be at the floe-edge hunting seal or inland hunting caribou. What a strengthening and sustaining feeling of fellowship to know that at that same hour in other tents and igloos scattered across that land of endless snow, their sisters in faith were also sewing and singing hymns and studying their portion of the scripture. And the W.A. member's prayer which these dear primitive women utter so from the heart binds them in fellowship to all the thousands of W.A. members of the Anglican Communion who repeat that same prayer in English in the great "outside."

... It is to the wonderful spirit and loving Christian leadership of Nurse Hockin and the others that these women owe their emancipation. The Missionary can evangelize but it is hard for a man to enter with understanding into the life of an Eskimo woman.[63]

Fleming's view was similar to Hirst's. She believed that a Christian sisterhood had been formed at Pangnirtung between the Inuit and White women. She still spoke in colonialist terms but her intent was to suggest the establishment of a comfortable environment where a common boundary was possible. She went a little further, saying that the woman's auxiliary was a separate sphere where women could relate to each other as women, a space that could not be entered by male missionaries. She suggested that the woman's auxiliary could also represent emancipation for women.

Uncommon as it is to see references to women's emancipation or the broader women's movement in the auxiliary correspondence, missionaries at times seemed conscious of gender as a political force. For example, in 1916, Stella Du Vernet, wife of the Bishop of Caledonia, suggested at the diocese auxiliary's annual meeting that they should pray for prohibition and suffrage: "In view of the proximity of the referenda on prohibition and suffrage in British Columbia," recorded the *Letter Leaflet* in November 1916, "the president impressed on all members of the woman's auxiliary the importance of using their influence and prayers on behalf of these two movements. Although women like Du Vernet and Fleming were well aware of the women's movement," the extent to which auxiliary meetings might have discussed women's status in society is not discernible.

Like the other women missionaries in the north, Winifred Marsh in the early 1940s organized a woman's auxiliary branch at her station at Eskimo Point (Arviat). She started the Little Helpers, which included infants and children up to the age of 10. In a letter to her friends back home, she described the organization and outlined what she hoped to achieve:

I have started a woman's instruction Class. In Canada we have the little helpers, the Babies Branch of the Woman's Auxiliary of the Church of England, a purely missionary organization is [sic] very powerful and strong. The Little Helpers embraces also the Font-Roll – so I have launched out on this idea. The mothers come once a week & I give them an idea in a simple talk, something they can teach their little ones. In order to help them to remember and possibly, years hence when they are away from the mission help and contacts I give each mother a stamp which she sticks in her own album. The great hindrance to the work here is the apathy of women, who when they go away from the Post often relapse & live as pagans. The men contact us more during the year – but the women are isolated & keen young Christians come under the rather awful domination of old pagan mothers "In Law."[64]

Like others, Marsh believed that it was important to teach children about Christianity from a very young age, yet she also expressed concern that her impact on the women of Eskimo Point (Arviat) was temporary. She believed that even Christian Inuit could easily slip back into "pagan" ways once away from the mission station. She seemed to underestimate the syncretic nature of the reception of Christianity. Yet she remained optimistic, hopeful that Canada's powerful woman's auxiliary would have an influence in the Arctic. Her optimism was not misplaced. There were Aboriginal women who gained substantially from their experiences with the woman's auxiliary and, like McDonald and Kendi, spread the word among their own people.

One such evangelist was Sarah Simon, a Gwich'in Métis from Fort McPherson. During the years 1923 and 1929 Simon travelled to Hay River and Aklavik and learned more about the woman's auxiliary. While at Hay River, her name appeared on the woman's auxiliary minutes as an assistant. At the meetings she heard about the work done by women to spread Christianity.[65] Simon recalled that "in 1926 I went to Hay River & learned more about the woman's auxiliary from Miss Sowden more about W.A. works & listen carefully when they have meetings so I thought if I go back to my people I will try my best to tell them what woman's auxiliary must mean to them & what they must do." The meetings at Hay River included discussions about women in China and India and foreign mission work. One meeting ended with the thought that "we can not all be missionaries and go to the foreign lands but we can all be missionaries at home by working and praying."[66] Such messages reflected the idea that the members of the auxiliary were home missionaries spreading Christianity within their own communities. At Simon's last meeting in Hay River she was presented with a gift of appreciation for her work. The minutes noted that she had "worked very faithfully for the woman's auxiliary & will be missed very much."

Between 1929 and 1937, Simon was the woman's auxiliary president in Fort McPherson. Few Aboriginal women held this role and none for so long. In 1940, she was awarded a life membership in the Arctic Diocese of the woman's auxiliary, an honour, as it was put, that no other Aboriginal woman shared. At the diocese's annual meeting in 1941, Simon presented her interpretation of the first auxiliary meetings in Fort McPherson. She had vivid memories of the first meeting when she acted as interpreter: "first open with hymn and closed with prayer. the next week we got together. with thread needles thimble. 3 yrds. of print from Mrs. Firth. Each one gave little pieces. so we started quilt. we one made a month later. we sold that too Wm. Firth for 10.00 we made 14 quilts in June 1919 we had a sale. I don"t know how much we made but I know Mrs. Reid gave it to Bishop Lucas."[67] During a visit in 1949 to Fort McPherson, Archdeacon D.B. Marsh, Winifred's husband, reported that Simon conducted the woman's auxiliary meetings "just [as] if she had been trained to the job."[68] From her experiences in Hay River, Simon became adept at attracting members and holding meetings.

Sarah Simon promised that she would learn about the woman's auxiliary and bring it back to her people to teach them what they must do. As the annual reports for the Arctic Diocese throughout the 1930s and 1940s indicate, she did just that. In 1933, for example, Marguerite Latham recorded her impressions of Simon after a visit to Fort McPherson:

> I wished many of the W.A. leaders could have been present to see the "fruits" of those who have gone on, those who have laboured in and around McPherson in the years gone by, former Missionaries' wives. The Church at McPherson constantly reminds one of all those who have been there in the past, it is warm and cosy and comfortable. It was a treat to be in it with our Indian friends. Sarah Simon had arrived at the Fort several weeks before Christmas to prepare the children for their concert. She has also directed and managed the decorating of the Church, which looked very much as our own Churches do outside at Christmas. I was surprised and so happy that since there was no lady Missionary there, Sarah had been led to give of her love and thought and time to make the annual gathering of her people at Christmas as happy as possible, and to keep it fittingly. I think we ought to feel very grateful to Sarah for her voluntary help. She loves the work and gives her best, speaks and understands English splendidly, and is such a bright, keen witness for Christ.[69]

Simon, like other Aboriginal Christians, characterized the relationship between Anglican church missionaries and the Aboriginal peoples of the north. This cultural hybridity was evident in the ordination of Aboriginal deacons, who, until recently, were always men.

### Aboriginal Ministry

One of the objectives of the Church Missionary Society was that once Christianity was introduced and a church established, missionaries sent to the area would spread the word elsewhere, and Aboriginal catechists would guide the church. The founders of the Church Missionary Society, especially Henry Venn, believed strongly in Aboriginal ministry. By the late nineteenth century the Church Missionary Society expressed concern that Aboriginal ministry was not taking root in northern Canada. For example, in 1901 Baring-Gould, secretary of the Church Missionary Society, wrote to Bishop Ridley to suggest that he readjust his staff and free up a missionary. He wanted Bishop Ridley to understand that, as he put it, "the paramount claims of the teeming masses of India, Africa and China" would now take priority. He drew to Bishop Ridley's attention the fact that there were "urgent gaps," and that the committee had recommended that, where the "heathen were sparse," missionaries be pulled out. "You will, I feel sure," Baring-Gould declared, "sympathize with us in not allowing European missionaries to remain in charge of districts where no heathen are within reach; where the missionary is practically a pastor."[70] The real purpose of his letter was to instruct Bishop Ridley that the Reverend R.W. Gurd would not be returning as a missionary at Kitkatla: "the committee feel that Kitkatla ought to be served for the future by an Aboriginal Catechist [sic] under the superintendence of a European missionary."[71] Despite these instructions, the Reverend Gurd returned and continued his work. The society may have been sending pleas for more missionaries but Bishop

Mrs. Myra Moses, president, St. Luke's woman's auxiliary, Old Crow, and Mrs. Sarah Simon presenting to Bishop H.H. Marsh of the Yukon a beaded caribou purse and veil, 1963.

Ridley was a very persuasive solicitor. Nonetheless, the warning had been issued and it was clear that, as in other northern missions, the Diocese of Caledonia would have to begin to look elsewhere for funds and more aggressively pursue the idea of training Aboriginal converts for ministering to their own people.

The Yukon Diocese had to face this same fork in the road. Bishop Bompas was not a keen supporter of Aboriginal ministry. He argued that Aboriginal peoples themselves were opposed to this concept: "This is the view of the Indians themselves who do not much value one of their own countrymen as teacher for they have not sufficient trust in their attainments and they seem to view Christianity as a message from the White man's God."[72] He also felt that the Aboriginal peoples were so helpless and uncivilized that they could never maintain a Church. On the contrary, the Reverend Robert McDonald, a Canadian-born Métis, had more faith in Aboriginal ministry and was responsible for instructing a number of Vuntut Gwitchin in the northern Yukon in teaching Christianity. When the Reverend Stringer was appointed bishop in 1906, he took McDonald's lead and encouraged Aboriginal catechists. In fact, he wisely ordained a number of Aboriginal peoples to the diaconate, including Vuntut Gwitchin Julius Kendi, who worked at Old Crow, and Gwich'in Dene Richard Martin from Peel River. Bishop Stringer also ordained the first Inuit deacon, Thomas Umaok, who worked at Shingle Point in the early 1930s.

Aboriginal ministry has been crucial to the survival of the Anglican Church in northern Canada. The gradual accommodation of the church to Aboriginal culture has meant that churches in places like Old Crow became largely locally run. The transition from a remarkable intolerance for things Aboriginal to one of accommodation is probably the most interesting aspect of the history of Anglicanism in the north. Had it not been for the initiation of Aboriginal ministry, several churches would have closed permanently. The Church Missionary Society policy of Aboriginal ministry provided a context for individuals to become leading Christians in their communities. Although Aboriginal ministry was encouraged, there was a limit to its effectiveness imposed by those in the field. As was evident with the woman's auxiliary, White missionaries still felt the need to provide guidance to those spreading the word.[73]

One notable example of Aboriginal domination of the Anglican experience was the Church Army in northern British Columbia.[74] The most striking feature about the history of the Church Army was that Aboriginal peoples initiated it as a spontaneous movement. In his memoirs, the Reverend W.H. Collison claimed that he observed a rather sudden and "intense interest" in open air services and the use of musical instruments, among the Tsimshian, Nisga'a, and Haida. In his study of missionaries in Canada, John Webster Grant brilliantly concludes that there have been periods when this type of enthusiasm experienced success, but those moments remained overshadowed by a persistent paternalism among non-Aboriginal missionaries: "Such spontaneous movements were welcomed, but always the missionaries seemed to feel a compulsion to bring them under control and ultimately conform them to the safe patterns of European Christianity. There was always an eagerness to give Christianity to the Indians, seldom a willingness to allow them to receive it."[75] On the northwest coast, the Church Army became a contest for control. The Reverend W.H. Collison was urged when he observed the spontaneous desire for open air meetings to write away for the Church Army rules:

> Numbers of men and women were to be found preaching and praying out of doors, at the fisheries and other camps. Fearing some abuse might arise unless the movement was properly directed, I convened a public meeting to which I invited the leaders of the unusual movement. I informed them of the organization known as the Church Army, the headquarters of which was in London. As some of them were desirous to engage in open air methods and to use drum and other musical instruments which was in accordance with Church Army regulations, I was prepared to write and obtain the rules, should they desire to inaugurate a local branch.[76]

Synod at Aklavik, 1927. *Top, left to right:* Minnie Hackett, Reverend James H. Webster, J. Licekert, Sarah Stringer, Bishop I.O. Stringer, Ethel Catt. *Bottom:* Mr. Owen, Reverend E. Situchinli (ordained 1903), Reverend C.C. Harcott, and Reverend John Martin (ordained 1925).

The Reverend Collison revealed in this text anxieties over control of the ritual process and religious understanding. He was convinced, however, that, once the movement had received orders or rules of behaviour from England, it would be adequately reigned in. European surveillance and regulation had to constrain the Indigenous movement. He was persuaded that the Church Army would appeal to the "respect for rank" and love of music among Aboriginal peoples.

The Church Army, headquartered in London, was a strong part of the evangelical wing of the Anglican Church. To the outsider it would be comparable in appearance to the Salvation Army. It was founded in England in 1882 by the Reverend William Carlisle, who trained women and men to go into the slums of Westminster and preach the gospel. Evidence about the early days of the Church Army in the north is scanty, but it appears to have had instant appeal.

By 1892, there was a Church Army at Masset on the Queen Charlotte Islands (Haida Gwaii), and by the end of the decade there were branches among the Nisga'a in the Nass River (K'alii Aksim Lisims) valley. In his memoirs Bishop Ridley relates how he explained the rules of the Church Army to the Kitakshan of the Skeena River (Sginn). In the winter of 1896, Bishop Ridley was visited by a delegation of three Kitakshan who wanted to start a Church Army branch. In Ridley's usual hyperbolic way he responded to their questions:

> When we are ready to burst with emotion may we find relief in crying out in church "Amen" or "Alleluia"?" This I saw to be Salvationist infection, and asked, "Do you know the meaning of those words?" "No." "Then don't say words without meaning. God looks for sense from men and noise from dogs. Say aloud the responses for relief." "May women preach in a loud voice in the streets?" "Yes, if they speak wisely." "Then why not in Church?" "Because St. Paul says 'No.'" "Suppose men on the street laugh at us?" "Pay no heed." "Suppose they make a row in our house-meeting?" "Turn them out." "May we appoint men to do this." "Yes, the strong and good-tempered ones.[77]

Like the Reverend Collison, Bishop Ridley wanted to assure that the Kitakshans were aware of the Church Army's strict rules of adherence and that those rules were enforced by careful surveillance. By 1897, Bishop Ridley was able to report that there were 130 members of the Church Army at Port Simpson and, as he boasted, the adherents thought of him as their general. In the winter of 1897 he and other Army members travelled to Kitkatla to participate in a ceremony where Chief Sheuksh's wife was being inducted as an officer of the Church Army. Ridley placed a red ribbon around her neck and told her that it represented "a token of being bound as a servant to our Master." He then observed that Chief Sheuksh was "in the front pew all the time on his knees, his lips moving as if in prayer, and his eyes fountains of tears. What a contrast with the savage past."[78]

The Church Army seems to have had particular appeal because of its forms of celebration and because it gave Aboriginal peoples considerable leeway as participants. It was popular especially in villages along the Nass River, including Aiyansh, Gitlakdamiks, and LakGalzap. It also thrived at Kincolith (Gingolx), at Kitkatla on Dolphin Island, at Metlakatla and at Masset. The Army was promoted by the Reverend Collison and administered by the Reverend James McCullagh, who trained a large number of lay readers. One of them, Paul Mercer, became the first Aboriginal person to be ordained to the Anglican priesthood in British Columbia. The Army was revivalist in nature. Its leaders moved along the Nass, holding services wherever they could attract adherents.

In 1911, for example, the Reverend McCullagh reported that three Aboriginal officers, Stephen Allen, Alfred Mountain, and John Wesley, had stopped at Aiyansh. He described their trip from Kincolith as a "marching visit." Their evangelism then took them to Gwinoha, a nearby village. As a result, a Church was soon built there with about fifty members.[79] Lay reader, W.A. Myers volunteered to work in Gwinoha in the summer of 1911 and reported that by the winter of 1912 the Church was "in comfortable shape for worship." Adorned with Church Army flags, and furnished with a few benches, Myers was confident that the Aboriginal peoples were keen to make it a success: "We have an active Church organization, a reverent, modest, and humble body of worshippers, an enthusiastic Church Army and a busy Woman's Auxiliary."[80] In 1922 it was reported that Paul Mercer was teaching school and holding Sunday services at Gwinoha. The Church Army evangelists toured regularly, including Fishery Bay (Ts'imk'ol'hl Da oots'ip), where the Nisga'a gathered for their spring eulachon fishery. In 1912, they held an Easter service there: "The church was crowded: our native 'readers' A McKay and Paul Mercer, read the prayers and took the lessons, and a very reverent bright service we had, with good singing."[81] During the Army's tour of 1915 services were held at Fishery Bay, Port Essington (Kitsumkalum), and Port Simpson (Lax Kw'alaams).

Echoing the Reverend McCullagh's optimistic tone, the Reverend Collison described his impressions of Church Army services at Laxgalts'ap and Kincolith. At the former, where for several years an Aboriginal Church Army officer was the permanent Anglican representative, about 250 Nisga'a gathered. The Army officer received twenty-five dollars for eight months and spent the balance of the year in the salmon fishery. While Collison hoped that a permanent White missionary could be sent to Kincolith, he was impressed with the Army's work:

> We have had quite an inspiring time here (Kincolith) during the past month, dating from the "week of prayer." Nearly one hundred of the Indians arrived from the upper villages (Aiyansh, Giklakdamiks, &c), comprising the Church Army Bands. Meeting and services were held morning and evening during their stay. They have now passed on down the coast accompanied by our Church Army Band.[82]

Great excitement was aroused when Church Army followers in northern British Columbia were visited by Captain Casey from Army headquarters in London. He arrived in Prince Rupert in November 1927, to be greeted by an enthusiastic brass band. The Army conference which followed was reported to have attracted three hundred participants and lasted for three days. Open air services complete with inspiring testimonials were held. Casey was struck by the eagerness of the participants:

> Each evening, besides the Open-Air service which drew crowds of people, there was a Church Army Evangelistic Service held in the Cathedral which I conducted. A crowded church, an enthusiasm seldom seen in white people, messages burning with zeal from Native Church Army Captains, and singing which thrilled you, and the whole service closing with an appeal for rededication of life that was well responded to, made these services one of the happy spots of the conference.[83]

Casey visited the villages of Metlakatla, Kitwanga, and Kitwancool (Gitanyow). He described celebrations quite different from the usual Anglican church ceremony, ones that were musical, emotional, and dramatic.

Some missionaries criticized the Church Army's evangelistic style. Dr. Ardagh, for example, Bishop Ridley's first mission doctor and an ordained deacon, found the Army offensive. After having served in East Africa, Ardagh was sent to Metlakatla and, by 1916, had made his way to Gitwaingak. In one written report he expressed particular annoyance at the fact that Christian Aboriginal peoples were no longer interested in learning more about Christianity, seeming enthralled by little more than musical celebration and stirring testimonials:

> Over and above all they prefer a more noisy kind of service than we have in our church. In their own so-called "Church-Army" meetings, they will go on for hours to the accompaniment of drums and tambourines, then while in a state of abnormal excitement, they are induced to make

statements as if they were actually "converted." Alas! only too often, a fleeting experience. The Indian is naturally an extremist; hence our greatest difficulty in this work, viz., to get the Indians to have depth of character and to remain steady.[84]

Again we can see the degree of excitement caused by Church Army meetings and the appeal of them for the Nisga'a. They seem from Ardagh's comments to have directed the service themselves. While Aboriginal peoples usually built their own churches and Church Army halls and became lay readers, there were still some White missionaries like Ardagh who believed that they should continue to provide guidance or steadiness, and a deeper sense of Christian tradition. Even Alfred Price, a strong advocate of the Church Army, feared that feasts for the dead were still being held, proving that "sin dies hard." Anxieties over "heathenism" remained.[85] White missionaries were reluctant to surrender and continued to see an important role for themselves. The idea that the Aborginal peoples could maintain their own mission tested the limits of tolerance among an older generation of White missionaries.

By 1935, when Henry Flores was sent to Kitwanga, the Church Army had become a central part of the community. Flores claimed that he was "astonished to see the natives so much interested in church work." The Army meetings had evolved into Council meetings where community or family disputes were resolved:

> It is really wonderful to see that practically every man and woman is able to give ex tempore speeches during Church Army Services which are held twice a week. All family troubles are settled by the Church Council. If anyone has a quarrel with his neighbour or has done something wrong he is brought before the church council and the whole thing is settled and followed by prayers and the singing of hymns. These natives are very fond of long services, *the longer they are the better they enjoy them.* Revival services sometimes are kept going all night.[86]

Essentially, the revival meetings began to resemble tribal council assemblies. A clear expression of syncretism, the Nisga'a chose to resolve their community problems in the Anglican hall. Despite Flores's admiration for the church and his comments on the way problems were resolved, he was firm in his view that "with all this the missionary is absolutely responsible for their spiritual welfare."[87] Although it appeared that the Church Army was quite independent and could have survived without a White missionary, Flores was convinced that someone like himself had to be there to meet the spiritual needs of the Nisga'a. And there was the heart of the problem.

The Church Army played an integral role in the transition, from a time when the church in the Nass River (K'alii Aksim Lisims) valley was dominated by White missionaries with British cultural ideas, to a time when white ministers adopted many Nisga'a traditions. While White ministers are still part of the religious experience in the Nass, they are now more fully integrated into Nisga'a culture.[88] It is common to see Aboriginal art decorating churches and to see White priests wearing button blankets. During the 1940s and early 1950s, it was Aboriginal men such as lay reader Henry McKay of Greenville (Laxgalts'ap) and Paul Mercer at Aiyansh who continued to hold services.

In 1975, Archdeacon John Blyth, a White minister who lived in the Nass River valley for ten years, presented a report on ministry to the Diocese of Caledonia. Blyth addressed the question of what type of ministry would be most effective in the area. One of his responses recognized the role of Aboriginal women in the Anglican church:

> The ministerial role of women is important to the health of the Nishga community, both in respect to the ceremony of feasting, and also in clan relationships. The Anglican Church Women and the YWCA (of Aiyansh) are major sources of strength and oversight that express organizationally the psychological and sociological position of women in Nisga society. The women are described as "the mothers of the church" and their ministry of service is of utmost influence.[89]

It is most striking that the women were referred to as the "mothers of the church," a title which many White women missionaries had been given in the early years of the Anglican Church in the north. Like Sarah Simon, Aboriginal women had taken over the role of mothering their own people's children.

Establishment in the north of woman's auxiliary and Church Army memberships represent interfaces between the past cultural experiences of Aboriginal peoples and the missionaries. Their endurance represented new strategies adopted by missionaries when they recognized that the promise of heaven or the threat of hell were not enough to attract adherents to the missions. And from their perspective, the strategy worked because some Aboriginal peoples attended woman's auxiliary meetings and participated in Church Army revivals. This was a major transformation in the concept of mission work. In part, too, as Susan Neylan so ably demonstrates, the dichotomy between Christianity and Aboriginiality was not always so clear among Tsimshianic-speaking peoples, at least in the late nineteenth century: "They were both Native and Christian, at a time when secular battles over cultural practices and land issues saw only dichotomies. Christian identities were not subordinate or superior to Native ones, but they had become an important part of who Tsimshianic peoples had become after a few decades of missionization."[90] For a time, the Anglican Church in some villages and towns was – through the woman's auxiliary and the Church Army – well supported by Aboriginal Christians.

# Conclusion

No one today is purely *one* thing. Labels like Indian, or woman, or Muslim, or American are not more than starting-points, which if followed into actual experience for only a moment are quickly left behind. Imperialism consolidated the mixture of cultures and identities on a global scale. But its worst and most paradoxical gift was to allow people to believe that they were only, mainly, exclusively, white, or Black, or Western, or Oriental. No one can deny the persisting continuities of long traditions, sustained habitations, national languages, and cultural geographies, but there seems no reason except fear and prejudice to keep insisting on their separation and distinctiveness, as if that was all human life was about.

– Edward Said, *Culture and Imperialism*

When Agnes Deans Cameron visited northern Canada in the early twentieth century, she was struck by the need to categorize and understand the Aboriginal cultures in European terms: "Are these Eskimo Christians? Are they civilized? These are the questions which confront us when we speak of these Farthest North Canadians. It is an age of classification. You cannot find a flower nowadays that someone has not tacked a Latin name to, and it goes by inverse ratio – the smaller the flower the longer the name."[1] Just as natural landscapes, flora, and fauna were categorized, so too were individuals and cultural groups. Cameron questioned whether the people she encountered were really heathen. She reflected on specific cultural traditions that appeared to her to be reasonably sophisticated. While she viewed the Aboriginal peoples through imperial eyes and used terminology similar to that of the missionaries and more aggressive colonizers, she was aware of the ambiguities that existed with respect to categorization and racially motivated judgments.

Categories which seemed to be fixed became challenged or diminished in significance through experience. The mission field represented a contested terrain of shifting identities where preconceived attitudes and beliefs were used to view and comprehend – usually imperfectly – new environments and human conditions. While missionaries spent much of their time writing about Aboriginal peoples in terms typical of imperialists and colonizers, there were instances when they broke free of their world views and reflected on the deeper meaning of difference. In his memoirs, written in the 1950s, Archibald Fleming, who worked in the Arctic for forty years, first as a missionary and then as a bishop, captured this ambiguity. In his final chapter entitled "Reflections," he expressed what working with the Inuit had really meant to him: "During the past forty years many have asked me how I could love the Eskimo with all their dirty and degraded ways, their primitive life and pagan customs. The answer is quite simple. It is certainly not because I learned to like all aspects of life in an Eskimo snow village in winter or tent encampment in the summer. Much about life under such conditions is repulsive to any civilized man."[2] Fleming went on to say that his intention was not to romanticize the Inuit but to recognize that his relationship with them had evolved over time: "Time and time again they went out of their way to help me, an ignorant foreigner, and so I changed from holding the typical superiority attitude of the white man towards the native and I came to see him truly as equal. Whatever superior knowledge I possessed about some things the Eskimo had superior knowledge about other things."[3] Fleming juxtaposed descriptions of Inuit as dirty and degraded, and their lifeways as potentially "repulsive to any civilized man," with the declaration that his culture and theirs are equal. Two discourses were evident here. Most significantly, Fleming began to view himself as a "foreigner" and the Inuit as the holders of significant knowledge.

Like the protagonists in this book, Cameron and Fleming revealed tensions that focused on questions of identity. Concerns about categorization were central to every aspect of mission work. Their desire to categorize and establish identities was rooted in the philosophy of Christian mission, no doubt influenced by social Darwinism. Such questions as were Aboriginal peoples Christian or heathen, were Aboriginal mothers good responsible parents, were Aboriginal girls respectable, did Aboriginal behaviour measure up to European cleanliness, sobriety, and industry – and the anxieties that provoked them – revealed more about the Euro-Canadian world view and obsession with categorization than about Aboriginal peoples.

Daniel Francis argues convincingly that "the Indian is the invention of the European." For Francis, as for most Aboriginal people, there is no such thing as an "Indian." The stereotypes about Aboriginal peoples are Euro-Canadian constructs of what he refers to as "the imaginary Indian." The categorization of Aboriginal peoples – still evident – began early on this continent: "When Columbus arrived in America, there were a large number of different and distinct indigenous cultures, but there were no Indians."[4] Racial stereotypes were especially pervasive in Victorian England and were certainly reinforced in mission correspondence. Audiences at home enjoyed reading about and listening to tales of difference, savagery, and heathenism. They readily consumed and reproduced in their own minds a discourse of difference.

Just as much as static images of Aboriginal peoples can be discerned in mission correspondence, so too can stereotypical images of the missionaries themselves be perpetuated. In this view, the typical missionary would be culturally chauvinist and keen to assert power over Aboriginal peoples. They would be viewed as cruel interlopers, even child abusers. There is no doubt that some missionaries were in fact that way. The abuses perpetrated at residential schools throughout Canada have been well documented. Certainly, not all missionaries consciously set out to destroy Aboriginal culture. Yet, as they lived their lives out in the mission field, some became more, rather than less, convinced that they were representatives of a superior culture. The farther they got from their places of origin and the longer they were in the field, the more they romanticized their own culture and exaggerated the beauty and value of what they had left behind. They did not, however, romanticize Aboriginal culture, nor did they self-reflectively question their goals of assimilation. For the most part, they did not doubt that they were performing what they conceived as God's work nor that their objectives were legitimate.

What they did reflect upon however, were their differences. As Ruth Frankenberg has argued in relational terms, Europeans reformulated self-perceptions from the position of the colonized subject: "Equally significant, while discursively generating and marking a range of cultural and racial Others as different from an apparently stable Western or white self, the Western self is itself produced as an effect of the Western discursive production of its others."[5] While missionary women were constructing images of Aboriginal cultures they were simultaneously reconceptualizing themselves – perhaps for the first time from their particular standpoints in the mission field – as White, Christian, and superior. Through identifying such differences, White women began to define themselves in relation to others. They did not recognize that both the other and their White selves were being changed by cultural interaction. Rather, there was a tendency to reify moral and cultural differences. In some ways the articulation of difference created the space for imagined superiority and legitimized in the missionary's mind the actions taken to reinforce that superiority.

This feeling of superiority created a sense of power. Women missionaries evidently felt that they had power and influence over Aboriginal peoples, as Selina Bompas reminded White women: "there is power given you from on high which is intended you should use among them or any other race with whom you may be placed – it is the power of *influence*."[6] According to Bompas, White missionary women were to use their influence to model proper womanhood to Aboriginal women. Power was bestowed by God. Bompas did not question why White women were powerful and Aboriginal peoples powerless; for her, there was no debate about whose culture was superior. White women felt a sense of power in the mission field, but it was based on their continued efforts to write about and imagine the inferiority of the Aboriginal peoples – to keep the other in place while, ironically, trying to improve or elevate them through the message of Christianity. Quite apart from conceptions by missionaries of Aboriginality is the evidence of actual experiences in the mission field, which points to a much more fluid and conflicting dynamic. More than men, women's day-to-day lives were shaped by relations with Aboriginal peoples in their work as nurses and teachers, and in their efforts to create meeting spaces and celebrations. They developed intimate relations, especially with Aboriginal women. These relations were described in terms that would suggest closeness but not equality. They did get to know Aboriginal women and, more importantly from their perspective, came to rely on them for food and clothing, the necessities of daily living in the north. The extent to which White women appreciated their vulnerability or the charity of their Aboriginal hosts is difficult to discern. Nonetheless, the sharing of resources, the co-operative nature of life in the mission field – often overlooked by critics of the mission enterprise – is evident from the diaries and letters of women missionaries. So too is the fact that some Aboriginal peoples chose to convert to Christianity and assume leadership positions within the church.

While it is important for historians to try to remain objective, it is also critical to recognize the ironic position from which historians of colonization write today. How can we fail to judge the past in light of the present? The increasing evidence of the damage done by missions and residential schools, in sources such as the church's own publication, *Sins of the Fathers*, serve as reminders of the misplaced benevolence of colonizers who tried too hard to deliver the message of Christianity.[7] The women who went into mission work undoubtedly had good intentions and were themselves convinced that Christianity and the empire were inextricably linked and that "heathenism" had to be eradicated. For many women, mission work offered an empowering opportunity to work, see the world, and be independent. Many were enthralled by the chance to travel. Others, who dedicated their lives to mission work, no doubt had the calling, and others still were anxious to marry missionaries and go into the field as partners. Very few really questioned their own motives. No matter what enticed them to join the mission movement, their main objective was to improve Aboriginal peoples and cultures. Ironically, the missionaries themselves also became transformed through their experiences.

The Anglican Church still has a presence in the north and its missionaries are remembered, some fondly. It is also true that Aboriginal communities throughout Canada have been undergoing tremendous change. They are celebrating their survival and, at the same time, attempting to recover from the damaging elements of colonization. Aboriginal peoples of northern Canada have not become static or mired in the past. They have not stood still. The Anglican Church, however, did not move quickly enough toward change. Barbara Kingsolver concludes *The Poisonwood Bible* with the thought that "Africa swallowed the conqueror's music and sang a new song of her own." In the same way, the Aboriginal peoples in northern Canada are once again singing their own songs.

# Notes

## Introduction

1 Winifred Marsh, ed., *Echoes from a Frozen Land / Donald B. Marsh* (Edmonton: Hurtig, 1987), 13. In 1950, Donald Marsh was consecrated bishop of the diocese of the Arctic. He was sponsored initially by the Colonial and Continental Mission Society.

2 Winifred Petchey Marsh, *People of the Willow – The Padlimiut Tribe of Cariboo Eskimo Portrayed in Watercolours* (Toronto: Oxford University Press, 1976), 8. The people in the title refer to themselves as the Pallirmiut Inuit.

3 Marsh, ed., *Echoes from a Frozen Land*, 14.

4 The term "Aboriginal peoples" refers collectively to First Nations, Inuit, Inuvialuit, and Métis peoples, all of whom reside in communities within their ancestral lands in northwestern Canada and Nunavut.

5 Gender and race relations in western and northern Canada have received much warranted attention in recent scholarly and popular histories. See, for example: Jean Barman, "Taming Aboriginal Sexuality: Gender, Power and Race in British Columbia, 1850-1900," *BC Studies* 115-16 (Autumn/Winter 1997-98): 237-66; Sarah Carter, "Categories and Terrains of Exclusion: Constructing The 'Indian Woman' in the Early Settlement Era in Western Canada," *Great Plains Quarterly* 13 (Summer 1993): 147-61; Sarah Carter, *Capturing Women: The Manipulation of Cultural Imagery in Canada's Prairie West* (Montréal/Kingston: McGill-Queen's University Press, 1997); Barbara Eileen Kelcey, "Jingo Bells, Jingo Belles, Dashing Through the Snow: White Women and Empire in Canada's Arctic Frontier" (PhD diss., University of Manitoba, 1994); Adele Perry, "'Oh I'm Just Sick of the Faces of Men': Gender Imbalance, Race, Sexuality, and Sociability in Nineteenth-Century British Columbia," *BC Studies* 105-6 (Spring-Summer 1995): 27-45; Adele Perry, *On the Edge of Empire: Gender, Race and the Making of British Columbia, 1849-1871* (Toronto, ON: University of Toronto, 2001); Charlene Porsild, *Gamblers and Dreamers: Women, Men and Community in the Klondike* (Vancouver, BC: UBC Press, 1998); Myra Rutherdale, "Revisiting Colonization through Gender: Anglican Missionary Women in the Pacific Northwest and the Arctic, 1860-1945," *BC Studies* 104 (Winter 1994-95): 3-24. For popular treatments see Francis Backhouse, *Women of the Klondike* (Vancouver, BC: Whitecap, 1995); Kathryn Bridge, *By Snowshoe, Buckboard, and Steamer: Women of the Frontier* (Victoria, BC: Sono Nis, 1998); Bay Ryley, *Gold Diggers of the Klondike: Prostitution in Dawson City, Yukon* (Winnipeg, MB: J. Gordon Shillingford, 1997).

6 Kerry Abel, *Drum Songs: Glimpses of Dene History* (Montréal/Kingston: McGill-Queen's University Press, 1993); Clarence Bolt, *Thomas Crosby and the Tsimshian: Small Shoes for Feet Too Large* (Vancouver, BC: UBC Press, 1992); Kenneth S. Coates, *Best Left As Indians: Native-White Relations in the Yukon Territory, 1840-1973* (Montréal/Kingston: McGill-Queen's University Press, 1991); Brett Christophers, *Positioning the Missionary: John Booth Good and the Confluence of Cultures in Nineteenth-Century British Columbia* (Vancouver, BC: UBC Press, 1998); John Webster Grant, *Moon of Wintertime: Missionaries and Indians of Canada in Encounter since 1534* (Toronto, ON: University of Toronto Press, 1984); Peter

Murray, *The Devil and Mr. Duncan: A History of the Two Metlakatlas* (Victoria, BC: Sono Nis Press, 1985). Notable and welcome exceptions are the valuable work by Margaret Whitehead: "'Women Were Made for Such Things': Women Missionaries in British Columbia 1850s to 1940s," *Atlantis* 14 (Fall 1988): 141-50 and "'A Useful Christian Woman': First Nations Women and Protestant Missionary Work in British Columbia," *Atlantis* 18 (1992-93): 142-66.

7 Jean Usher, "Apostles and Aborigines: The Social Theory of the Church Missionary Society," *Histoire Sociale/Social History* 7 (April 1971), 28.

8 Cited in Grant, *Moon of Wintertime*, 221.

9 Grant, *Moon of Wintertime*, 101.

10 Frank A. Peake, *The Anglican Church in British Columbia* (Vancouver, BC: Mitchell Press, 1959),180.

11 A.G. Morice, *The History of the Northern Interior of British Columbia* (London: J. Lane, 1906; rpt. Smithers, BC: Interior Stationery, 1978), 224-40. See also Margaret Whitehead, *They Call Me Father: Memoirs of Father Nicolas Coccola* (Vancouver, BC: UBC Press, 1988).

12 The history of gender and Catholic missions in British Columbia has recently been the focus of scholarly attention. See especially the comprehensive study: Jacqueline Gresko, "Gender and Mission: The Founding Generations of the Sisters of Saint Ann and the Oblates of Mary Immaculate in British Columbia, 1858-1914" (PhD diss., University of British Columbia, 1999). See also Jo-Anne Fiske, "Pocahontas's Granddaughters: Spiritual Transition and Tradition of Carrier Women of British Columbia," *Ethnohistory* 43, 4 (1996), 663-81.

13 C.F. Pascoe, *Two Hundred Years of the S.P.G. 1701-1900*, vol. 1 (London: Society for the Propagation of the Gospel, 1901), 181-91.

14 Hugh McCullum and Karmel Taylor McCullum, *Caledonia 100 Years Ahead* (Toronto, ON: Anglican Book Centre, 1979), 19.

15 Archibald Lang Fleming, *Archibald the Arctic: The Flying Bishop* (New York, NY: Appleton-Century Crofts, 1956), 306.

16 The Missionary Society for the Church of England in Canada (MSCC) was formed in 1902 when all of the Anglican bodies involved in the promotion of mission work were brought under one organization. The Canadian Church Missionary Society, the Domestic and Foreign Board of Missions, and the Wycliffe Missions joined together to be part of the MSCC.

17 "The Most Northerly Residential School in the British Empire," *Northern Lights*, February 1933, 8.

18 See Kenneth S. Coates, *Canada's Colonies: A History of the Yukon and Northwest Territories* (Toronto, ON: James Lorimer, 1985).

19 Kenneth S. Coates, "'Betwixt and Between': The Anglican Church and the Children of the Carcross (Chooutla) Residential School, 1911-54," in *BC Studies* 64 (1984-85): 27-47. For a similar argument with respect to colonization and health care, see John D. O'Neil, "The Politics of Health in the Fourth World: A Northern Canadian Example," in *Interpreting Canada's North*, ed. Coates and Morrison, 279-98. See also Linda Hutcheon, "The Post Always Rings Twice: The Post Modern and the Post Colonial," *Material History Review* 41 (Spring 1995): 4-23, in which Hutcheon responds to the critics of the Royal Ontario Museum's exhibition entitled "Into the Heart of Africa." She argues that Canadians have traditionally seen themselves as colonials not as colonizers.

20 Kenneth S. Coates, *Best Left as Indians: Native-White Relations in The Yukon Territory, 1840-1973* (Montréal/Kingston: McGill-Queen's University Press, 1991), 112.

21 For a discussion of the critique of the efficacy of missions see Grant, *Moon of Wintertime*, esp. Ch. 9, The Onset of Doubt. The value of sustaining Aboriginal missions was debated in Toronto during the first decade of the twentieth century. Spearheaded by the prominent lawyer and evangelical executive member of the MSCC, Samuel Hume Blake, the proponents of abandoning missions essentially undertook a cost-benefit analysis and suggested cutting back. The Anglican Church, however, continued to send missionaries and in general were supported by the broader church community. Blake's outburst against missions are referred to as a "tempest in a teapot" by Grant but unquestionably his conclusions published in a pamphlet called "Don't You Hear the Red Man Calling,"

planted seeds of doubt with some MSCC members. In the late 1920s and early 1930s, these questions re-emerged in a broader context: see William Hocking, *Re-thinking Missions: A Layman's Inquiry After One Hundred Years* (New York, NY: Harper and Brothers, 1932).

22 See Torben Christensen and William R. Hutchison, eds., *Missionary Ideologies in the Imperialist Era: 1880-1920* (Copenhagen: Forlaget Aros, 1982). Gael Graham questions this dichotomy in her history of mission schools in China: *Gender, Culture, and Christianity: American Protestant Mission Schools in China 1880-1930* (New York, NY: Peter Lang, 1995).

23 "At Home and Abroad," *The Living Message* (July 1933), 214-15.

24 Jean Comaroff and John Comaroff, *Of Revelation and Revolution: Christianity, Colonialism and Consciousness in South Africa* (Chicago, IL: University of Chicago Press, 1991), vol. 1, 172.

25 Jean Usher, "Apostles and Aborigines: The Social Theory of the Church Missionary Society," *Histoire Sociale/Social History* 7 (April 1971), 31-2. See also Judith Rowbotham, "'Hear an Indian Sister's Plea': Reporting The Work of Nineteenth-Century British Female Missionaries," *Women's Studies International Forum* 21, 3 (1998): 247-61.

26 Usher, "Apostles and Aborigines," 32.

27 In her study of Methodist missionaries Rosemary Gagan notes the difficulty of finding information on women who worked in domestic missions. The Women's Missionary Society of the Methodist Church in Canada kept better records on women who went overseas. According to Gagan, the employment records on domestic missionaries are scanty: "Some files for home missionaries contain nothing but the location to which women were assigned." In some cases this is true for the Anglican Church of Canada as well. For her concerns on this subject see: *A Sensitive Independence: Canadian Methodist Women Missionaries in Canada and the Orient, 1881-1925* (Montréal/Kingston: McGill-Queen's University Press, 1992), 163.

28 See June Purvis, "From 'Women Worthies' to Poststructuralism? Debate and Controversy in Women's History in Britain," in *Women's History: Britain 1840-1945*, ed. June Purvis (London: UCL, 1995).

29 Denise Riley, *"Am I That Name?": Feminism and the Category of "Women" in History* (Minneapolis, MN: University of Minnesota Press, 1988), 6.

30 Ibid.

31 June Purvis, "Women's History and Poststructuralism," *Women's History Review* 5, 1 (1996), 7.

32 Edward W. Said, *Culture and Imperialism* (New York, NY: Alfred A. Knopf, 1993).

33 "The Arctic," *The Living Message*, July 1933, 214.

34 See, for example, Homi K. Bhabha, "Of Mimicry and Man: The Ambivalence of Colonial Discourse," *October* 28 (1984): 125-33.

35 Recent books by historical geographers Brett Christophers and Cole Harris, and by historians Adele Perry, Mary-Ellen Kelm, Charlene Porsild, and Elizabeth Vibert have all been informed by post-colonial and post-structural analyses. By placing at the centre of their analyses women, gender, and the shifting power dynamics between Aboriginal peoples and newcomers, these works contribute important reconceptualizations of the histories of northern and western Canada. Christophers, *Positioning the Missionary;* Cole Harris, *The Resettlement of British Columbia: Essays on Colonialism and Geographical Change* (Vancouver, BC: UBC Press, 1997); Perry, *On the Edge of Empire;* Porsild, *Gamblers and Dreamers;* Mary-Ellen Kelm, *Colonizing Bodies: Aboriginal Health and Healing in British Columbia* (Vancouver, BC: UBC Press, 1998); Elizabeth Vibert, *Traders' Tales: Narratives of Cultural Encounters in the Plateau, 1807-1846* (Norman, OK: University of Oklahoma Press, 1997).

36 Vron Ware, *Beyond The Pale: White Women, Racism, and History* (London: Verso, 1992), 230. As examples of popular representations of empire which include women in a number of complex relationships, she cites such television movies and films as *The Jewel in the Crown, A Passage to India*, and *Out of Africa*.

37 Nupur Chaudhuri and Margaret Strobel, eds., *Western Women and Imperialism: Complicity and Resistance* (Bloomington, IN: Indiana University Press, 1992), 3.

38 Anne McClintock, *Imperial Leather: Race, Gender, and Sexuality in the Colonial Context* (New York, NY: Routledge, 1995), 6.

39  Ware, *Beyond the Pale*, 37.
40  Antoinette M. Burton, "The White Woman's Burden: British Feminists and 'The Indian Woman,' 1865-1915," in *Western Women and Imperialism*, ed. Chaudhuri and Strobel, 152.
41  Ware, *Beyond the Pale*, 230.
42  See Katie Pickles, "Forgotten Colonizers: The Imperial Order of the Daughters of Empire (IODE) And The Canadian North," *The Canadian Geographer* 42, 2 (1998): 193-204; Julia Bush,"Edwardian Ladies and the 'Race' Dimensions of British Imperialism," *Women's Studies International Forum* 21, 3 (1998) 277.
43  Marta Danylewycz, *Taking the Veil: An Alternative to Marriage, Motherhood, and Spinsterhood in Quebec, 1840-1920* (Toronto, ON: McClelland and Stewart, 1987), 160.
44  Ruth Compton Brouwer, *New Women for God: Canadian Presbyterian Women and India Missions, 1876-1914* (Toronto, ON: University of Toronto Press, 1990), 188.
45  Gagan, *A Sensitive Independence*, 190.
46  For studies of this topic by scholars outside Canada, see: Patricia Grimshaw, *Paths of Duty: American Missionary Wives in Nineteenth-Century Hawaii* (Honolulu, HI: University of Hawaii Press, 1989); Patricia Hill, *The World Their Household: The American Women's Foreign Mission Movement and Cultural Transformation, 1870-1920* (Ann Arbor, MI: University of Michigan Press, 1985); Jane Hunter, *The Gospel of Gentility: American Women Missionaries in Turn-of-the Century China* (New Haven, CT: Yale University Press, 1984); Claudia Knapman, *White Women in Fiji 1835-1930: The Ruin of Empire*? (Sydney: Allen and Unwin, 1986); Ann Douglas, *The Feminization of American Culture* (New York, NY: Knopf, 1977); Caroll Smith-Rosenberg, *Disorderly Conduct: Visions of Gender in Victorian America* (New York, NY: Oxford University Press, 1985); Jane Haggis, "White Women and Colonialism: Towards a Non-Recuperative History," in *Gender and Imperialism*, ed. Claire Midgley (Manchester: Manchester University Press, 1998), 45-78; Rita Smith Kipp, "Emancipating Each Other: Dutch Colonial Missionaries' Encounter with Karo Women in Sumatra, 1900-1942," in *Domesticating the Empire: Race, Gender and Family Life in French and Dutch Colonialism*, ed. Julia Clancy-Smith and Frances Gouda (Charlottesville, WV: University Press of Virginia: 1998), 211-37; Margaret Tenant, "Sisterly Ministrations: The Social Work of Protestant Deaconess in New Zealand 1890-1940," *New Zealand Journal of History* 32, 1 (1998): 3-22; Barbara Welter, "The Feminization of American Religion, 1800-1860," in *Clio's Consciousness Raised: New Perspectives on the History of Women*, ed. Mary Hartman and Lois Banner (New York, NY: Harper and Row, 1974), 137-58.
    For Canadian religious women, see Christopher Headon, "Women and Organized Religion in Mid- and Late Nineteenth-Century Canada," *Journal of the Canadian Church Historical Society* 20 (March-June 1978): 3-18; Lynne Marks, "Working-Class Femininity and the Salvation Army: Hallelujah Lasses in English Canada, 1882-1892," in *Rethinking Canada: The Promise of Women's History*, ed. Veronica Strong-Boag and Anita Clair Fellman (Toronto, ON: Copp Clark Pitman, 1991), 182-205; Wendy Mitchinson, "Canadian Women and Church Missionary Societies in the Nineteenth-Century: A Step Towards Independence," *Atlantis* 2 (Spring, 1977): 57-75; Elizabeth Gillan Muir, *Petticoats in the Pulpit: The Story of Early Nineteenth-Century Methodist Women Preachers in Upper Canada* (Toronto, ON: United Church Publishing House, 1991); John D. Thomas, "Servants of the Church: Canadian Methodist Deaconess Work, 1890-1926," *Canadian Historical Review* 65 (September 1984): 371-95.
47  Wendy Fletcher-Marsh, *Beyond the Walled Garden* (Dundas, ON: Artemis, 1995); Brian Heeney, *The Women's Movement in the Church of England, 1850-1930* (Oxford: Clarendon, 1988).
48  Robin Fisher, *Contact and Conflict: Indian and European Relations In British Columbia* (Vancouver, BC: UBC Press, 1977); A.J. Ray and Donald Freedman, *Give Us Good Measure: An Economic Analysis of Relations Between the Indians and the Hudson's Bay Company before 1763* (Toronto, ON: University of Toronto Press, 1978); Sylvia Van Kirk, *"Many Tender Ties": Women in the Fur Trade Society in Western Canada, 1670-1870* (Winnipeg, MB: Watson and Dwyer, 1980).
49  Bolt, *Thomas Crosby and the Tsimshian*, 106.
50  Kenneth S. Coates, "Asking for All Sorts of Favours: The Anglican Church, the Federal

Government and the Natives of the Yukon Territory, 1891-1909," in *The Anglican Church and the World of Western Canada 1820-1970*, ed. Barry Ferguson (Regina, SK: University of Regina Press, 1991), 139.

## Chapter 1: Breaking Down the Barriers

1 J.B. McCullagh, "Impressions of a Crusader at Home," *North British Columbia News*, January 1915.
2 Eugene Stock, "Women Missionaries in C.M.S. Fields," *Church Missionary Intelligencer and Record*, May 1894, 343.
3 Stock, *The History of the Church Missionary Society, Its Environment, Its Men and Its Work*, vol. 3 (London: Church Missionary Society, 1899), 384.
4 Grace Hallenby, *Anglican Woman's Training College: A Background Document* (Toronto: AWTC History Committee, 1989), 69.
5 Eugene Stock, *The History of the Church Missionary Society*, vol. 1, 63.
6 Stock, *The History of the Church Missionary Society*, vol. 1, 56. John Venn, Rector of Clapham, was the first director of the Church Missionary Society. Thomas Scott was the first secretary. And Charles Simeon originated the idea of the creation of the Church Missionary Society.
7 Stock, *The History of the Church Missionary Society*, vol. 1, 60. The expression "enlarge the place of thy tent" is from William Carey, the founder of the Baptist Missionary Society, who in 1793 became the first Baptist missionary to visit India.
8 Stock, *The History of the Church Missionary Society*, vol. 1, 64.
9 Leonore Davidoff and Catherine Hall, *Family Fortunes: Men and Women of the English Middle Class 1780-1850* (London: Hutchinson, 1987), 82-3.
10 D.W. Bebbington, *Evangelicalism in Modern Britain: A History From the 1730s to the 1980s* (London: Unwin Hyman, 1989), 70.
11 Davidoff and Hall, *Family Fortunes*, 83.
12 Bebbington, *Evangelism In Modern Britain*, 76.
13 Cited in Bebbington, *Evangelicalism in Modern Britain*, 12.
14 George Dawson, *Soldier Heroes: British Adventure, Empire, and the Imagining of Masculinities* (London: Routledge, 1994), 61.
15 Grant, *Moon of Wintertime*, 105.
16 T.H. Canham, "The Diocese of Selkirk: Its Work and Its Workers," *Church Missionary Intelligencer*, January 1898, 16.
17 Stock, *The History of the Church Missionary Society*, vol. 3, 325.
18 Peake, *The Anglican Church in British Columbia*.
19 Kerry Abel, "Bishop Bompas and the Canadian Church," in *The Anglican Church and the World of Western Canada 1820-1970*, ed. Barry Ferguson (Regina, SK: University of Regina Press, 1991), 114.
20 Murray, *The Devil and Mr. Duncan*, 21.
21 Murray, *The Devil and Mr. Duncan*, 16. The Church Missionary Society was persuaded by Captain James C. Prevost of the necessity to establish a mission at Port Simpson. As a ship's captain, Prevost claimed to be familiar with the conditions of the Tsimshian who lived close to the fort. It struck him that they were in desperate need of Christianity. He approached the Church Missionary Society in the spring of 1856 and was first told that they could not afford to establish a mission station in northern British Columbia. He then prepared an article for the *Intelligencer* and contributions poured in. The mission was approved and Duncan left in December 1856 to fulfil the roles of school teacher and lay missionary.
22 Grant, *Moon of Wintertime*, 103.
23 Wycliffe College, *The Jubilee Volume of Wycliffe College 1877-1927-1937* (Toronto, ON: University of Toronto Press, 1937), 295. O'Meara was appointed second Principal of Wycliffe College in 1906 and held the position until 1930.
24 Patrick A. Dunae, "Boys Literature and the Idea of Empire, 1870-1914," *Victorian Studies* 24 (Autumn 1980), 120; Louis James, "Tom Brown's Imperialist Sons," *Victorian Studies* 17 (September 1973): 89-99.

25 Cited in J.A. Mangan, "Social Darwinism and Upper-Class Education in Late Victorian and Edwardian England," in *Manliness and Morality: Middle-Class Masculinity in Britain and America 1800-1940*, ed. J.A. Mangan and James Walvin (Manchester: Manchester University Press, 1987), 137.

26 Ibid.

27 Cited in John MacKenzie, "The Imperial Pioneer and Hunter and the British Masculine Stereotype in Late Victorian and Edwardian Times," in *Manliness and Morality: Middle-Class Masculinity in Britain and America 1800-1940*, ed. Mangan and Walvin, 177; Allen Warren, "Popular Manliness: Baden Powell, Scouting and the Development of Manly Character," in *Manliness and Morality*, ed. Mangan and Walvin, 199-219.

28 MacKenzie, "The Imperial Pioneer," 177.

29 "News From The Front: Diocese of Caledonia," *Across The Rockies* October 1911, 51.

30 Charles Lillard, ed., *In the Wake of the War Canoe: William Henry Collison* (Toronto: Musson Books, 1915; rpt. Victoria, BC: Sono Nis Press, 1981), 75.

31 Charles Lillard, ed., *Warriors of the North Pacific: Missionary Accounts of the Northwest Coast, the Skeena and Stikine Rivers and the Klondike, 1829-1900* (Victoria, BC: Sono Nis Press, 1984), 217.

32 Lillard, ed., *Warriors of the North Pacific*, 232.

33 Wycliffe College, *The Jubilee Volume of Wycliffe College 1877-1927-1937* (Toronto: University of Toronto Press, 1937), 156-8. The Reverend Thomas Marsh was originally from Clarksburg, Ontario, where his father was engaged as a private banker. Marsh later married and, with his wife and family, stayed in the north until 1926.

34 Ibid.

35 GSA, M74-3 Stringer Papers, Series 1-A-1 corr. outgoing 1888-1892, Letter from Stringer to Sarah Alexander, 6 July 1893. For a particularly effective treatment of masculinity, empire, and hunting see Elizabeth Vibert, *Traders' Tales: Narratives of Cultural Encounters in Columbia Plateau, 1807-1846* (Norman, OK: University of Oklahoma Press, 1997).

36 GSA, M74-3 Stringer Papers, Letter from Stringer to Sarah Alexander, 31 June 1894.

37 Grant, *Moon of Wintertime*, 228.

38 Stock, *The History of the Church Missionary Society*, vol. 3, 398.

39 Brian Heeney, *The Women's Movement in the Church of England* (Oxford: Clarendon Press 1988), 60.

40 Heeney, *The Women's Movement*, 11.

41 Barbara Caine, *Victorian Feminists* (Oxford and New York, NY: Oxford University Press, 1992), 43.

42 Caine, *Victorian Feminists*, 44.

43 Ann Douglas, *The Feminization of American Culture* (New York, NY: Knopf, 1977), 97.

44 Ibid., 110.

45 In her study of English women in the Middle East, Billie Melman argues that the practical aspects of evangelism blended neatly with the constructed image of separate sphere ideology and ostensibly gave women more freedom: "Woman's moral superiority, her generic spirituality, the very qualities that had made her the custodian of the 'home,' qualified her as a social and religious reformer" (*Women's Orients: English Women and the Middle East, 1718-1918* [Hampshire: MacMillan, 1995], 167). See also, Heeney, *The Women's Movement*, 19-45.

46 Dr. Herrick, "Missionaries' Wives," *The Canadian Church Magazine and Mission News*, October 1889, 226.

47 Ibid.

48 Georgina Gollock, "The Training of Women Missionaries," *Church Missionary Intelligencer* January 1898, 39-41.

49 Ibid., 40.

50 Ibid., 41.

51 Martha Vicinus, *Independent Women: Work and Community For Single Women, 1850-1950* (Chicago, IL: University of Chicago Press 1985), 47.

52 Quoted in Vicinus, *Independent Women*, 58.

53  Heeney, *The Women's Movement*, 69.
54  Vicinus, *Independent Women*, 60.
55  Wycliffe College, *The Jubilee Volume*, 282. Sybil Wilson was the daughter of Sir Daniel Wilson, a prominent Canadian educator.
56  Cited in Wycliffe College, *The Jubilee Volume*, 284.
57  Cited in Heeney, *The Women's Movement*, 72.
58  GSA, GS765, Mrs. Madeline Wodehouse, *Our Early Beginnings*, n.d., 2-3. See also Mrs. Emily Willoughby Cummings, *Our Story: Some Pages from the History of the Woman's Auxiliary to the Missionary Society of the Church of England in Canada 1885 to 1928* (Toronto: Garden City Press, n.d.).
59  Cummings, *Our Story*, 7.
60  "Churchwoman's Mission Aid of Toronto Diocese," *The Canadian Church Magazine and Mission News*, May 1887, 274.
61  While no details are provided about the nature of the Richmond Conference, it is safe to assume that it was a woman's auxiliary gathering.
62  Harriet Von Iffland, "The Ministry of Women," *Letter Leaflet*, March 1893, 254.
63  Von Iffland, 255.
64  "The Duty of the Woman's Auxiliary Towards Missions in the North-West," *Letter Leaflet*, May 1894, 106, 180, 249-51.
65  "Diocese of Caledonia," *The Canadian Church Magazine and Mission News*, May 1891, 118-19.
66  "Diocese of Caledonia," *New Era* April 1904, 121.
67  Alan L. Hayes, "Repairing the Walls: Church Reform and Social Reform 1867-1939," in *By Grace Co-Workers: Building the Anglican Diocese of Toronto 1780-1989*, ed. Alan. L. Hayes (Toronto: Anglican Book Centre, 1989), 66.
68  Address by Mrs. D.B. Donaldson, the Dominion Treasurer of the Woman's Auxiliary, to the members of the Synod of Algoma and the delegates to the annual meeting of the Woman's Auxiliary, at Sault Ste. Marie, June 1923. "The Woman's Auxiliary and its Work," *The Living Message*, November 1923, 354-5.
69  Gagan, *A Sensitive Independence*, 23.
70  Donaldson, 355.
71  Ibid., 354.
72  "Another Call for Nurses," *Letter Leaflet*, May 1920, 224-5.
73  Ibid.
74  "The Deaconess Order," *The Living Message*, September 1924, 260.
75  GSA, M82-12 Louise Topping Papers, The Story of "Louise Sutherland "Born Topping" (in this manuscript called "Hope") of St. Stephen, NB, 14.
76  Fleming, *Archibald the Arctic*, 309-10.
77  It should be noted, however, that Eleanor Lennox, M.D. who was a woman's auxiliary missionary, worked in Prince Rupert during the 1920s and 1930s for the Japanese mission. Another woman, Dr. Isabel Greenwood, was trained as a doctor, and worked at Fort McPherson (Tetlit'zheh) from 1934 to 1936; her husband, the Reverend Thomas Greenwood, was hired by the MSCC and, in 1951, was consecrated bishop of the Yukon.
78  GSA, M75-27, Anglican Women's Training College, 2-D Graduates, 1894-99, Box 7. Sadie Alexander's progress at the college was recorded in the following terms:

> Sadie Alexander from ... Huron Diocese entered ... March 22, 1895 for a short term in order to be better fitted for a missionary life in the Mackenzie River Diocese where she expects to go as the wife of the Reverend I.O. Stringer Missionary to the Esquimaux. Sadie derived much benefit from all the lectures she was able to attend during her stay in the house and made good use of the time being a very good stenographer she took down the lectures verbatim – which will we trust be a great help to her in her work as a missionaries wife. Sadie was a great earnest Christian girl and was a great favorite with the other probationers notwithstanding all the hardships and privations she so often heard of other missionaries enduring she felt sure that by the Grace of God she would be able to endure all for the sake of her master.

79  GSA, Stringer Papers, Series 2 2-B, Sarah Ann Stringer Talks, Addresses, Address to the United Church Woman's Missionary Society in Toronto, 9 October 1930.
80  Lillard, ed., *In the Wake of the War Canoe*, 19.
81  Province of British Columbia Archives, Tape 1227: 1-2, Transcript of Interview with Mrs. Robert Tomlinson, 14-15.
82  Transcript of Tomlinson interview, 6.

### Chapter 2: Perceptions and Interpretations of the "Other"

1  Church Missionary Society Papers, G1 Series, Reel A 122, Letters from the Society, 4 October 1895, Miss Carleton's Instructions.
2  H.F. Hyatt, "The Ethics of Empire," *The Nineteenth Century* XLI (April 1897): 529.
3  Albert Memmi, *The Colonizer and the Colonized* (Boston, MA: Beacon Press, 1965), 79.
4  Ibid., 70.
5  Frederick Cooper and Ann L. Stoler, "Introduction Tensions of Empire: Colonial Control and Visions of Rule," *American Ethnologist* 16 (November 1989): 609.
6  See Hayden White, *Tropics of Discourse: Essays in Cultural Criticism* (Baltimore, MD: Johns Hopkins University Press, 1978), 194.
7  Anne McClintock, *Race, Gender, and Sexuality in the Colonial Contest*, 211.
8  Mary Louise Pratt, *Imperial Eyes: Travel Writing and Transculturation* (London: Routledge, 1992).
9  S.A. Archer, ed., *Heroine of the North Pacific: Memoirs of Charlotte Selina Bompas (1830-1917)* (London, ON: Macmillan, 1929), xii.
10  Quoted in Jean Johnston, *Wilderness Women: Canada's Forgotten History* (Toronto, ON: Peter Martin, 1973), 181.
11  Archer, ed., *Memoirs of Charlotte Selina Bompas*, 27.
12  Ibid., 43.
13  Ibid., 38.
14  Ibid., 157.
15  Church Missionary Society Papers, North Pacific Mission, C.2 British Columbia C.2/0 orig. letters to 1900, Letter from Florence Appleyard to the parent committee, 7 July 1893.
16  GSA, GS76-15, Series 7.4, Box 19, women's auxiliary Corresponding Secretary Mrs. Caroline M Patterson Hall, Letter from Mary Mellish to Mrs. Caroline M. Patterson Hall, 27 January 1905.
17  "Mackenzie River," *The Living Message*, January 1922, 38.
18  William L. Morton, ed., *God's Galloping Girl: The Peace River Diaries of Monica Storrs, 1929-1931* (Vancouver, BC: UBC Press, 1979), 172.
19  Ibid.
20  GSA, M88-4, Adelaide Jane Butler Papers, Letter from Adelaide Butler to Mary Butler, 9 September 1934.
21  McClintock, *Race, Gender, and Sexuality in the Colonial Contest*, 253.
22  Mariana Valverde, *The Age of Light, Soap, and Water: Moral Reform In English Canada, 1885-1925* (Toronto, ON: McClelland and Stewart, 1991).
23  White, *Tropics of Discourse*, 194.
24  See GSA, Register of Missionaries, Clerical Lay and Female and Native Clergy from 1804-1904, In Two Parts, Church Missionary Society, n.d.; "Hazelton," *North British Columbia News*, July 1916, 27.
25  GSA, Stringer Papers, Series 2 2-B, Sarah Ann Stringer, Talks, Addresses, Women's United Church Missionary Society, Toronto, 9 October 1930.
26  Miss F.A.T. Copeland, "Kincolith," *North British Columbia News*, April 1911, 72; Archer, ed., *Memoirs of Charlotte Selina Bompas*, 41.
27  Cited in Isaac O. Stringer, "The Esquimaux of the Mackenzie River Delta," *Canadian Church Magazine and Mission News*, October 1892, 222-3.
28  Bishop William Ridley, "The Indians of British Columbia," *Canadian Church Magazine and Mission News*, December 1896, 273.
29  Church Missionary Society Papers, C.2. British Columbia, North British Columbia Mission, Reel A 123, Letter from Miss Carleton to the parent committee, 28 February 1896.

30 GSA, Stringer Papers, Series 2 2-C, Sarah Ann Stringer, Diaries 1-17, 15 to 22 November 1897.
31 GSA, Stringer Papers, February 1900.
32 Archer, ed., *Memoirs of Charlotte Selina Bompas*, 46.
33 "Selkirk-Carcross," *Letter Leaflet,* May 1907, 181.
34 Mrs. Bentley, "Moosehide," *Northern Lights,* February 1930, 10.
35 John Comaroff and Jean Comaroff, *Of Revelation and Revolution*, 218-19.
36 GSA, Bessie Quirt Papers, Diary, 12 January 1930; GSA, Adelaide Butler Papers, Letter from Adelaide Butler to Mary Butler, 22 April 1934.
37 "Selkirk and Coffee Creek," *Northern Lights,* 1923.
38 Lee Sax and Effie Linklater, ed., *Gikhyi: The True and Remarkable Story of Arctic Kutchin Christian Leaders* (Whitehorse, YT: Diocese of Yukon, 1990), 79.
39 *Canadian Church Magazine and Mission News*, March 1887, 221.
40 Bhabha "Of Mimicry and Man," 125-33.
41 Archer, ed., *Memoirs of Charlotte Selina Bompas*, 31.
42 Ibid., 58.
43 GSA, M88-4, Adelaide Jane Butler Papers, Adelaide Jane Butler to Mary Butler, 8 January 1933. "Husky" was the term often used by missionaries to describe an Inuk. The missionaries claimed that "Eskimo" was a derogatory name used by First Nations and so chose to call Inuit "Huskies."
44 Ibid.
45 Jane Hunter, "The Home and the World: The Missionary Message of U.S. Domesticity," in *Women's Work for Women: Missionaries and Social Change in Asia*, ed. Leslie A. Flemming (Boulder, CO: Westview, 1989), 159-60.
46 GSA, GS76-15, Woman's Auxiliary Papers, Series 71, Box 18, Woman's Auxiliary Corresponding Secretary Miss L.H. Montizambert, Letter from Mrs. (Sarah) Sadie Stringer to Mrs. Montizambert, 10 February 1897.
47 Ibid.
48 Ibid.
49 Archer, ed., *Memoirs of Charlotte Selina Bompas*, 71.
50 Ibid., 75.
51 Ibid.
52 Ibid., 76.
53 Denise Riley, *Feminism and the Category of "Women" in History*, 6.
54 Hudson's Bay Company Archives, E.78, Augusta E. Morris Papers, Diary, Corr., 1881-1883. Diary, 22 April 1883. I would like to thank Anne Morton for bringing this collection to my attention.
55 Selina Bompas, "Our Women of the North," *Canadian Churchman,* 14 November 1907, 737.
56 Ibid.
57 GSA, Stringer Papers, Series 2 2-B, Sarah Ann Stringer, Talks, Addresses, Ladies of the Canadian Club in Winnipeg, November 1931.
58 "Yukon," *The Living Message,* February 1926, 319.
59 Mildred McCabe, "At Home and Abroad-Aklavik," *The Living Message,* October 1928, 323.
60 McCabe, "At Home and Abroad-Aklavik," 324.
61 "Canada," *The Living Message,* March 1937, 72.
62 "Old Crow," *The Living Message,* May 1938, 136.
63 Ibid.
64 "Mackenzie River," *The Living Message,* February 1926, 34.

### Chapter 3: Gender Relations in the Mission Field

1 Murray, *The Devil and Mr. Duncan*, 62.
2 Lillard, ed., *In the Wake of the War Canoe*, 16.
3 Separate sphere ideology has received the attention of many scholars who have studied Victorian culture and society. See for example, Linda Kerber, "Separate Spheres, Female Worlds, Woman's Place: The Rhetoric of Women's History," *Journal of American History* 75 (June 1988): 9-39; Leonore Davidoff and Catherine Hall, *Family Fortunes*, 149-93.

4   Catherine Hall, *White, Male and Middle Class: Explorations in Feminism and History* (New York, NY: Routledge, 1992), 230.
5   "Missionary Wives," *Canadian Church Magazine and Mission News,* January 1897, 18.
6   Lillard, ed., *In the Wake of the War Canoe,* 18-19.
7   Ibid., 19.
8   "The Diocese of Mackenzie River," *The New Era,* August 1904, 262.
9   Quoted in Kenneth S. Coates, "Send Only Those Who Rise a Peg: Anglican Clergy in the Yukon 1858-1932," *Journal of the Canadian Church Historical Society* 28 (Spring 1986): 7.
10  YTA, Provincial Synod of British Columbia 88/147 corr. 346, Bompas/Naylor corr., 14 July 1896.
11  YTA, Anglican Church Series 1-1A Box 3, Folder 16, corr. 251, Letter from Stringer to Venn. Arch Warren, 15 January 1920.
12  Selina Bompas, "Our Women of the North," *Canadian Churchman,* November 1907, 739.
13  Rev. J.B. McCullagh, "Aiyansh," *Aiyansh Notes,* April 1908, 5. His first wife died of typhoid fever while in the mission field.
14  Ibid.
15  Miss F. Copeland, "Kincolith," *North British Columbia News,* April 1911, 73.
16  Jane Hunter, "The Home and the World: The Missionary Message of U.S. Domesticity," in *Women's Work For Women: Missionaries and Social Change in Asia,* ed. Leslie A. Flemming (Boulder, CO: Westview, 1989), 160.
17  I.S. MacLaren and Lisa N. LaFramboise, eds., *The Ladies, the Gwich'in, and the Rat: Travels on the Athabasca, Mackenzie Rat, Porcupine, and Yukon Rivers in 1926* (Edmonton, AB: University of Alberta Press, 1998), 93.
18  GSA, M74-3, Stringer Papers, Series 1-A-1 corr. outgoing, 1888-1892, Letter from Isaac Stringer to Sarah Alexander, 6 July 1893.
19  Other missionary wives spent long periods working on their own in the field. In 1904, for example, the Reverend J. Lucas reported to the *Letter Leaflet* that he had been away from Fort Simpson (Líídli Kųé) for seven months during which time his wife held burial and Sunday services. See *Letter Leaflet,* August 1904, 395.
20  "Bishop Ridley and the North Pacific Mission," *Church Missionary Intelligencer and Record* IX: 99 (March 1884), 166.
21  "Caledonia," *Canadian Church Magazine and Mission News,* May 1899, 120.
22  Stock, *The History of the Church Missionary Society,* vol. 4, 639.
23  Church Missionary Society Papers, C.2 British Columbia, C.2/0 orig. letters to 1900 North Pacific Mission G.1 C.2/03 1897, Letter from Collison to parent committee, 6 January 1897.
24  Cited in Stock, *The History of the Church Missionary Society,* vol. 4, 638.
25  GSA, M71-4, Diocese of the Arctic Collection, St. Luke's Mission, Pangnirtung, Florence Hirst Journals, 17 July 1937. Florence (Flossie) Hirst, originally from Yorkshire, England, started her mission career at Shingle Point (Tapqaq) in 1929 and stayed in the north until 1955. In the late 1930s, she married the Reverend George Nicholson, a graduate of Islington College.
26  Church Missionary Society Papers, Reel A 125, Letter from Price to parent committee, 3 September 1889.
27  Church Missionary Society Papers, Class C C.2 North Pacific Mission C.2/ orig. letters, etc., incoming 1857-1880, Letter from Tomlinson to parent committee, 15 June 1872.
28  GSA, M74-3, Stringer Papers, Series 2 2-C, Sarah Ann Stringer, Diary, 24 December 1896.
29  GSA M74-3, Stringer Papers, July 1898.
30  GSA, M74-3, Stringer Papers, 2-A-1, corr. outgoing, Letter from Stringer to Mrs. Newton, 16 July 1899.
31  From Rev. C.E. Whittaker, Peel River to Mrs. Kuhring, Church of Ascension, Toronto, 19 January 1899, *Letter Leaflet,* September 1899.
32  Archdeacon C.E. Whittaker, *Recollections of an Arctic Parson* (Toronto, ON: General Synod Archives, n.d.), 24.
33  Fleming, *Archibald the Arctic,* 287.
34  Church Missionary Society Papers, corr. outgoing, Reel 105, Letters from Doolan to parent committee, 8 September 1866; 20 October 1866.

35  V.C. Sim, for example, neglected his health to such an extent that he died in service. See Coates, "Anglican Clergy in the Yukon 1858-1932," 8.
36  Lillard, ed., *In the Wake of the War Canoe*, 81.
37  YTA, Anglican Church Series, 1-1A, Box 4, Folder 3, corr. 252, Letter from C. Hoare to Bishop Stringer, 11 January 1922.
38  YTA, Anglican Church Series, Letter from Stringer to Hoare, 2 June 1922.
39  Church Missionary Society Papers, corr. outgoing, Reel A 123, Letter from Ridley to parent committee, 16 June 1896.
40  Church Missionary Society Papers, corr. outgoing, Reel A 125, Letter from Ridley to parent committee, 28 October 1898.
41  Church Missionary Society Papers, corr. outgoing, Reel A 123, Letter from Ridley to parent committee, 17 August 1891.
42  Church Missionary Society Papers, Reel A 123, 4 August 1890.
43  Church Missionary Society Papers, Reel A 123, 11 November 1891.
44  Church Missionary Society Papers, corr. outgoing, Reel A 122, Letter from parent committee to Bertha Davies, 30 March 1900.
45  Sara Mills, *Discourses of Difference: An Analysis of Women's Travel Writing and Colonialism* (London: Routledge, 1991), 42.
46  Cited in Stock, *History of the Church Missionary Society*, vol. 4, 638.
47  Ibid.
48  Church Missionary Society Papers, corr. outgoing, Reel A 123, Letter and Diary from Beeching to parent committee, 14 July 1895.
49  Church Missionary Society Papers, corr. outgoing, Reel A 123, Letter from Carlton to parent committee, 21 February 1896.
50  GSA, Bessie Quirt Papers, Diary, 27 August 1929; 26 September 1929; 16 September 1929.
51  GSA, Bessie Quirt Papers, 15 January 1930.
52  "Caledonia," *Canadian Church Magazine and Mission News*, April 1896, 83.
53  For a discussion on female friendships in nineteenth-century America, see: Carroll Smith-Rosenberg, "The Female World of Love and Ritual: Relations Between Women in Nineteenth-Century America," *Disorderly Conduct: Visions of Gender in Victorian America* (New York, NY: Oxford University Press, 1985), 53-77.
54  Vicinus, *Independent Women*, 202.
55  GSA, M89-3-N4, Bompas Papers, Letter from C.S. Bompas to S.A. Bompas, n.d.
56  YTA, Anglican Church Series 1V.1, Reference Files Personnel, Box 51, Bowen Biography File.
57  Cited in Diocese of the Yukon Woman's Auxiliary, Five Pioneer Women of the Anglican Church in the Yukon (Whitehorse: Star Printing, 1975), 1.
58  Archer, ed., *Memoirs of Charlotte Selina Bompas*, 144-5.
59  For example, in a letter to her sister-in-law Bompas told her about visiting the "kind and hospitable" Bowens in Whitehorse and staying with them for one week. GSA, M89-3-N4, Bompas Papers, Letter from C.S. Bompas to S.A. Bompas, October 1900.
60  Archer, ed., *Memoirs of Charlotte Selina Bompas*, 167.
61  In 1900, for example, Mrs. Spendlove, originally from England, wrote to the *Letter Leaflet* to describe her most recent news. She was at that time in her twentieth year of service: "My husband and I left our home, Fort Norman, three weeks since, he to attend the Missionary Conference at Peel River, I to attend a Missionary wife in her confinement" ("Letters from Our Missionaries – Domestic," *Letter Leaflet*, September 1900, 363).
62  YTA, Anglican Church of Canada: Provincial Synod of British Columbia, 88/147 corr. 346, Bompas/Naylor corr. file, Letter from Bompas to Naylor, 28 November 1899.
63  Ibid.
64  YTA, Letter from Bompas to Naylor, February 1900.
65  GSA, M66-1, Stringer Letters from Mrs. Bompas, Letter from Bompas to Bishop Stringer, 2 August 1910.
66  GSA, M66-1, Letter from Bompas to Stringer, n.d.
67  GSA, Quirt Diary, 21 December 1930. Quirt befriended many of the missionary women. She was godmother to the children of missionary Marguerite Latham Shepherd.

68   Rosenberg, Disorderly Conduct, 60.
69   This is not to say, however, that men did not have similarly intimate friendships. For an illuminating study of male friendships in Victorian society see, Jeffrey Richards, "'Passing the love of women's': Manly Love and Victorian Society," in *Manliness and Morality: Middle-Class Masculinity in Britain and America 1800-1940*, ed. J.A. Mangan and James Walvin (Manchester: Manchester University Press, 1987), 92-122.
70   Morton, ed., *The Peace River Diaries of Monica Storrs*, xxv-xxvi.
71   Ibid., 180.
72   Ibid., 229.
73   Church Missionary Society Papers, Reel A 125, corr. outgoing, Letter from Hall to parent committee, 4 January 1898; Letter from Carleton to parent committee, 22 November 1898.
74   Church Missionary Society Papers, Reel A 125, Letter from Ridley to parent committee, 7 December 1896.
75   Church Missionary Society Papers, Reel A 125, Letter from Margaret West to parent committee, 11 December 1896.
76   "The Late Miss Margaret West," *North British Columbia News*, July 1931, 70; "Children in British Columbia," *North British Columbia News*, May 1929, 182.
77   GSA, M88-4, Adelaide Jane Butler Papers, Letter from Adelaide Butler to Dollie Butler, 7 January 1933.
78   Ibid.
79   In the spring of 1904, when Selina Bompas went to the Rupert's Land Diocese annual meeting of the women's auxiliary in Winnipeg, she was greeted with a standing ovation. She addressed the meeting and, according to the *Letter Leaflet*, "dwelt on the teachability of the Indians and their desire to imitate the white men. Often they were led by his conduct to imitate him in wrong-doing, as for instance giving way to drink. The greater therefore was the responsibility laid upon us, who now possessed their land, to teach them what was right, alike by precept and example" ("Rupert's Land Diocese," *Letter Leaflet*, June 1904, 332). In July 1904, she addressed the Montreal Diocese Women's Auxiliary annual meeting ("Montreal Diocese," *Letter Leaflet*, July 1904, 357).
80   "Ontario," *Letter Leaflet*, July 1905, 234.
81   *Canadian Churchman*, 4 March 1937, 138.
82   GSA, M82-12, Louise Topping Papers, The Story of Louise Sutherland Born "Topping" (in this manuscript called "Hope") of St. Stephen, NB, 26.
83   Fleming, *Archibald the Arctic*, 321.

**Chapter 4: Making a Home Away from Home**

1   Helen Callaway, *Gender, Culture, and Empire: European Women in Colonial Nigeria* (London: Macmillan, 1987), 57.
2   See especially Mills, *Discourses of Difference;* and Alison Blunt and Gillian Rose, ed., *Writing Women and Space: Colonial and Postcolonial Geographies* (London: Guildford, 1994); Alison Blunt, *Travel, Gender, and Imperialism: Mary Kingsley and West Africa* (London: Guildford, 1994).
3   Pratt, *Travel Writing and Transculturation*, 61.
4   Karen M. Morin, "British Women Travellers and Constructions of Racial Difference Across the Nineteenth-Century American West," *Transactions* 23, 3 (1998): 312.
5   Memmi, *The Colonizer and the Colonized*, 60.
6   Ibid., 59.
7   Archer, ed., *Memoirs of Charlotte Selina Bompas*, 24.
8   Morton, ed., *The Peace River Diaries of Monica Storrs*, Introduction (n.p.), 7, and 151.
9   Morton, ed., *The Peace River Diaries of Monica Storrs*, August 1876, 67.
10  Morton, ed., *The Peace River Diaries of Monica Storrs*, September 1881, 100.
11  GSA, M71-4, Diocese of the Arctic, Box 12, St. Luke's Mission Pangnirtung, Florence Hirst Journals, Journal #2 1936-1937, 27 April 1937.
12  Melman, *Women's Orients: English Women and the Middle East*, 210.
13  "Yukon," *The Living Message*, February 1928, 42.

14  "Mackenzie River," *The Living Message,* October 1928, 356.
15  "A Letter from Aiyansh," *North British Columbia News,* July 1926, 210.
16  Patricia Jasen, *Wild Things: Nature, Culture, and Tourism in Ontario 1790-1914* (Toronto, ON: University of Toronto Press, 1995).
17  Mills, *Discourses of Difference,* 181.
18  Linda S. Bergmann, "Women against a Background of White: The Representation of Self and Nature in Women's Arctic Narratives," *American Studies* 34 (Fall 1993): 53.
19  "From Mrs. Stringer," *Letter Leaflet,* November 1898, 6.
20  Ibid.
21  Catherine Hoare, *The Mission World* XIX, 5 (May 1921): 166-7.
22  GSA, M71-4, Series 5-1-1, no. 13, Box 16, Diocese of the Arctic, D. B. Marsh Series, Diaries etc., Letter from Winifred Petchey Marsh to her sisters, May 1938.
23  Ibid.
24  Marsh, *People of the Willow,* 11.
25  *Letter Leaflet,* September 1900, 328.
26  Mrs. Field, *Letter Leaflet,* April 1898, 182. Despite these complaints, she and her husband served in Caledonia for thirty-two years.
27  For an American treatment of this topic, see Frances E. Karttunen, *Between Worlds: Interpreters, Guides, and Survivors* (New Brunswick NJ: Rutgers University Press, 1994).
28  Diocese of the Yukon Woman's Auxiliary, *Five Pioneer Women of the Anglican Church in the Yukon* (Whitehorse: Star Printing, 1975), 35.
29  GSA, M88-4, Butler Papers, Letter from Adelaide Butler to Dollie Butler, 19 November 1932.
30  Archer, ed., *Memoirs of Charlotte Selina Bompas,* 27.
31  GSA, M88-4, Butler Papers, Letter from Adelaide Butler to Dollie Butler, 2 March 1934.
32  YTA, Canham Personnel File, Letter from Mrs. Canham to Miss Large at Southsea, September 1896.
33  Rev. Thorman, "Tahl Tan," *North British Columbia News,* October 1917.
34  Mrs. Thorman, "Tahl Tan," *North British Columbia News,* January 1921, 3-4.
35  GSA, Quirt Diary, 26 October 1929.
36  Ibid.
37  Marsh, ed., *Echoes from a Frozen Land,* 16.
38  GSA, M74-3, Stringer Papers, Series 2 2-A, Sarah Ann Stringer, Diary, 7 May to 14 June 1897.
39  Diocese of the Yukon Woman's Auxiliary, *Five Pioneer Women,* 36.
40  YTA, Charlotte Selina Bompas, "Mission Work on the Upper Yukon," *Pamphlet Collection,* 737.
41  YTA, Charlotte Selina Bompas, "Mission Work on the Upper Yukon," 738.
42  Archer, ed., *Memoirs of Charlotte Selina Bompas,* 18.
43  GSA, M89-3 N4 Bompas Papers, Letter from Charlotte Selina Bompas to her sister-in-law Selina Anne Bompas, 13 August 1882.
44  YTA, Letter from Mrs. Canham to Miss Large at Southsea, September 1896.
45  Yukon Diocesan Women's Auxiliary, *Five Pioneer Women,* 36.
46  Glenbow Museum, M4745, files 24 and 25, E.P. Hockin corr. files, 8 December 1931.
47  GSA, Butler Papers, Letter from Adelaide Butler to Dollie Butler, 27 April 1935.
48  Diocese of Caledonia Synod Archives, Monica Storrs Diary, week ending 2 January 1932, 41.
49  L.K. Worley, "'Through Others' Eyes': Narratives of German Women Travelling in Nineteenth-Century America," *Yearbook of German-American Studies* 21 (1986): 40.
50  John J. Mannion, *Irish Settlements in Eastern Canada: A Study of Cultural Transfer and Adaptation* (Toronto, ON: University of Toronto Press, 1974), 3.
51  John Comaroff and Jean Comaroff, *Ethnography and the Historical Imagination* (Boulder, CO: Westview, 1992), 281.
52  Ibid., 280-1.
53  Ibid., 272.
54  Alison Blunt, "Imperial Geographies of the Home: British Domesticity in India, 1886-1925," *Transactions* 24, 4 (1999): 438.

55  Oswald Wynd, *The Ginger Tree* (New York, NY: Harper and Row, 1977), 146. Alicia Bassett-Hill is a fictional missionary from the Society For the Propagation of the Christian Gospel.
56  Archer, ed., *Memoirs of Charlotte Selina Bompas*, 132-3.
57  GSA, M71-4, Bessie Quirt Papers, Diary, 12 August 1929.
58  GSA, M71-4, Bessie Quirt Papers, Diary, 2 October 1929.
59  Morton, ed., *The Peace River Diaries of Monica Storrs*, 39-47.
60  GSA, M71-4, Diocese of the Arctic Hirst Journals, 9 October 1935.
61  Ibid.
62  Archer, ed., *Memoirs of Charlotte Selina Bompas*, 38.
63  Mr. J.W. Bilby, "The Eskimo Mother at Home," *Canadian Church Magazine and Mission News*, March 1902, 63-4.
64  GSA, Stringer Papers, Series 2 2-C, Sarah Ann Stringer, Diaries 14 to 21 March 1898.
65  GSA, Stringer Papers, Series 2 2-C, Sarah Ann Stringer, Diaries, 20 to 27 December 1897.
66  GSA, Butler Papers, Letter from Adelaide Butler to Dollie Butler, 27 April 1935.
67  GSA, Butler Papers, Letter from Adelaide Butler to Dollie Butler, 15 January 1935.
68  Miss Ida E. Collins, "Report of the Junior Auxiliary of Carcross Mission 1910 to 1911," *Fourth Annual Report of the Yukon Diocesan Branch of the Woman's Auxiliary,* Dawson, 7 and 8 August 1911, 22.
69  "The Coronation in Caledonia," *North British Columbia News,* January 1938, 360.
70  GSA, Hirst Journal, 21 April 1937.
71  Nupur Chaudhuri, "Shawls, Jewelry, Curry, and Rice in Victorian Britain," in *Western Women and Imperialism: Complicity and Resistance,* ed. Nupur Chaudhuri and Margaret Strobel (Bloomington, IN: Indiana University Press, 1992), 242. Chaudhuri argues that British women in India often sent cultural materials home but, while they were there, they did not show outward signs of respect or admiration for things Indian. She found that only after the memsahibs returned to Britain could they promote and participate in the popularity of Indian culture. See also Archer, ed., *Memoirs of Charlotte Selina Bompas,* 125 and 136.
72  Doreen Massey, *Space, Place, and Gender* (Minneapolis, MN: University of Minnesota Press, 1994), 265.

## Chapter 5: Motherhood and Morality

1  This ditty was meant to mimic the music hall melodies of the late nineteenth century and was originally from "Aladdin, or Love Will Find A Way," by V.C. Clinton-Baddeley, London, 1949. Quoted in John MacKenzie, *Propaganda and Empire* (Manchester: Manchester University Press, 1984), 57.
2  Hunter, "The Home and the World: The Missionary Message of U.S. Domesticity," 159.
3  Margaret Jolly, "Colonizing Women: The Maternal Body and Empire," in *Feminism and the Politics of Difference,* ed. Sneja Gunew and Anna Yeatman (Boulder, CO: Westview, 1993), 104.
4  Peggy Pascoe, *Relations of Rescue: The Search for Female Moral Authority in the American West, 1874-1939* (New York, NY: Oxford University Press, 1990), 209.
5  Davin, "Imperialism and Motherhood," 10-12.
6  Caine, *Victorian Feminists,* 43.
7  Ibid., 44.
8  Lillard, ed., *In the Wake of the War Canoe,* 18.
9  "Diocese of Caledonia," *The New Era,* April 1904, 123.
10  "Death of Mrs. Du Vernet," *North British Columbia News,* January 1929, 916.
11  GSA, Stringer Papers, Series 1 1-A-5, Stringer Martin/Cowaret corr., Letter from Martin to Stringer, 9 February 1916; Letter from Stringer to Martin, 15 March 1916.
12  GSA, Stringer Papers, Letter from Martin to Stringer, 6 August 1923.
13  GSA, Stringer Papers, Letter from Martin to Stringer, 15 October 1928.
14  "Letter from Mrs. Bompas – (Continued)," *Letter Leaflet,* December 1893, 59.
15  Archer, ed., *Memoirs of Charlotte Selina Bompas,* 76.
16  Ibid., 69.
17  Ibid., 136.
18  Ibid., 165.

19  GSA, M71-4, Box 12, Diocese of the Arctic Collection, St. Luke's Mission, Pangnirtung, Florence Hirst Journals, 20 February 1936.
20  GSA, M71-4, Florence Hirst Journals, 23 February 1936.
21  GSA, M71-4, Florence Hirst Journals, 21 April 1936.
22  GSA, M71-4, Florence Hirst Journals, 10 January 1938.
23  "Life at Hay River Mission," *The New Era*, August 1907, 274.
24  David Richeson, ed., *The New North: An Account of a Woman's 1908 Journey through Canada to the Arctic. Agnes Deans Cameron* (Saskatoon, SK: Western Producer Prairie Books, 1986), 131.
25  Church Missionary Society Papers, corr. outgoing, Reel A 123, Letter from Hogan to parent committee, July 1893.
26  Church Missionary Society Papers, Reel A 125, Letter from Tyte to parent committee, 1 March 1898.
27  Selina Bompas, "The Carcross School Children," *The New Era*, July 1908.
28  "Mackenzie River," *The Living Message*, 12 May 1928, 149.
29  "Yukon," *The Living Message*, February 1928, 41.
30  See Coates, "Betwixt and Between" 27-47; Celia Haig-Brown, *Resistance and Renewal: Surviving the Indian Residential School* (Vancouver, BC: Tillacum, 1988).
31  "The Arctic: Bishop Fleming Visits Anglican Eskimo Children at Shingle Point," *The Living Message*, October 1934, 312.
32  "Indian Girls and Women," *North British Columbia News*, October 1912, 38-9.
33  GSA, Stringer Papers, Series 2 2-B, Sarah Ann Stringer Talks, Addresses, Address to Winnipeg's Canadian Club Women, November 1931.
34  For an illuminating treatment of the education of Aboriginal girls in an all-girls mixed-race school in Yale, British Columbia, see Jean Barman, "Separate and Unequal: Indian and White Girls at All Hallows School, 1884-1920," in *Rethinking Canada: The Promise of Women's History*, ed. Veronica Strong-Boag and Anita Clair Fellman (Toronto, ON: Copp Clark Pitman, 1991), 215-24.
35  Church Missionary Society Papers, corr. outgoing, Reel A 123, Letter from Hogan to parent committee, July 1893.
36  J.H. Keen, "Children At Metlakatla," *The New Era*, June 1905, 218.
37  "Caledonia," *Letter Leaflet*, January 1906, 71.
38  "Caledonia," *Letter Leaflet*, January 1906, 72.
39  Blackman, *During My Time*, 88.
40  Cited in Julie Cruikshank with Angela Sidney, Kitty Smith, and Annie Ned, *Life Lived Like a Story: Life Stories of Three Yukon Elders* (Vancouver, BC: UBC Press, 1990), 113-14.
41  "Hay River – Needs and Anxieties," *The New Era*, April 1908, 141-2.
42  "Mackenzie River," *Letter Leaflet*, June 1917, 244-5.
43  GSA, Stringer Papers, Series 1 1-A-5, Stringer Martin/Cowaret corr., Letter from Martin to Stringer, 10 January 1924.
44  *Canadian Church Magazine and Mission News*, May 1895, 104.
45  "Miners and Indians," *Canadian Church Magazine and Mission News*, December 1900, 267.
46  "Hazelton" *North British Columbia News*, July 1916, 27.
47  GSA, Stringer Papers, Series 1 1-A-5, Stringer Martin/Cowaret corr., Letter from Martin to Stringer, 26 January 1918.
48  "Letter from Mrs. Bompas – July 1900," *Letter Leaflet*, January 1901, 74.
49  "St. Andrew's Selkirk," *Northern Lights*, 1921, 4.
50  "Dawson, St. Paul's Hostel," *Northern Lights*, May 1929, 11-12.
51  "Selkirk," *The New Era*, October 1905, 377.
52  "Selkirk," *Letter Leaflet*, April 1905, 155.
53  *Letter Leaflet*, 1923.
54  "Rampart House and Old Crow," *Northern Lights*, 1927, 4.
55  When Bishop Bompas retired, there were stations at Carcross, Whitehorse, Selkirk, Dawson, Moosehide, Bonanza, Forty Mile, Rampart House, and Herschel Island. By 1926 new stations had started at Champagne, Teslin, Little Salmon, Carmacks, Ross River, Mayo town and the Mayo Reserve, Old Crow, and Shingle Point. Some of these stations were

served by itinerants during the 1920s ("Presentation to Bishop Stringer," *Northern Lights,* May 1926, 3).

56 GSA, Stringer Papers, Series 3-J-17, Geddes to Mr. and Mrs. Morris, 17 July 1936.
57 Ibid.
58 "At Home and Abroad," *The Living Message,* October 1928, 322.
59 B. Shearman, *North British Columbia News,* July 1930.
60 Cited in Joan Jacobs Brumberg, *Mission for Life: The Story of the Family of Adoniram Judson, the Dramatic Events of the First American Foreign Mission, and the Course of Evangelical Religion in the Nineteenth Century* (New York: Free Press, 1980), 80.
61 "Hay River – 'Mother,'" *Arctic News* 1953, 10.
62 "Hay River – 'Mother,'" *Arctic News* 1953, 11.
63 "The News – Mackenzie River Deanery," *Arctic News* 1952, 7.
64 For a closer look at concepts of heroism in the mission field see Judith Rowbotham, "'Soldiers of Christ'? Images of Female Missionaries in Late Nineteenth-Century Britain: Issues of Heroism and Martyrdom," *Gender and History* 12, 1 (2000): 82-106.

**Chapter 6: Contesting Control while Encouraging Zeal**

1 Niel Gunson, *Messengers of Grace: Evangelical Missionaries in the South Seas, 1797-1860* (Melbourne; New York: Oxford University Press, 1978), 221.
2 H.G. Barnett, "Personal Conflicts and Cultural Change," *Social Forces* 20 (December 1941) 160-71.
3 Abel, *Drum Songs: Glimpses of Dene History,* 143.
4 Enrico Carlson Cumbo, "'Impediments to the Harvest': The Limitations of Methodist Proselytization of Toronto's Italian Immigrants, 1905-1925," in *Catholics at the 'Gathering Place': Historical Essays on the Archdiocese of Toronto, 1841-1991,* ed. Mark George McGowan and Brian P. Clarke (Toronto, ON: Canadian Catholic Historical Association, 1993), 165.
5 Pioneer missionaries were often referred to as saints. Bishop Ridley, for example, spoke of Bishop Bompas as "one of our modern saints and heroes" (Lillard, ed., *Warriors of the North Pacific,* 257).
6 Comaroff and Comaroff, *Ethnography and the Historical Imagination,* 238.
7 According to Daniel Francis, government officials also sought success stories to demonstrate that assimilation was possible. See *The Imaginary Indian: The Image of the Indian in Canadian Culture* (Vancouver, BC: Arsenal Pulp Press, 1992), 206.
8 Rev. R.W. Gurd, "The Passing of an Indian Chieftess [sic]," *North British Columbia News,* January 1914, 3.
9 "Widow of Late Archdeacon Mcdonald Passes Away in St. Mary's Hospital, Dawson," *Northern Lights,* August 1938, 6.
10 Cited in Margaret Blackman, *During My Time: Florence Edenshaw Davidson, a Haida Woman* (Seattle, WA: University of Washington Press, 1982), 66. Harrison himself had a difficult relationship with the Anglican church. He resigned from the Church Missionary Society in 1890. Charles Lillard describes him as a "Dostoyevskian character." He stayed on the Queen Charlotte Islands until 1919 (see Lillard, ed., *Warriors of the North Pacific,* 125).
11 Blackman, *During My Time,* 91-2.
12 Ibid., 144.
13 I.O. Stringer, "Herschel Island, Arctic Ocean," *Letter Leaflet,* August 1898, 328.
14 GSA, Stringer Papers, Series 3-J-17, "Annual Report, Diocese of Yukon, 1909."
15 "Hay River," *Letter Leaflet,* January 1916, 84.
16 "Telegraph Creek," *North British Columbia News,* January 1920, 45.
17 GSA, Stringer Papers, Series 1-A-5, Stringer Martin/Cowaret Corr., Martin to Stringer, 26 January 1918.
18 GSA, M88-4, Adelaide Jane Butler Papers, Letter from Adelaide Butler to Dollie Butler, 18 November 1933.
19 Terrence L. Craig, *The Missionary Lives: A Study in Canadian Missionary Biography and Autobiography* (Leiden: Brill, 1997), 105.
20 Rev. J.B. McCullagh, "Aiyansh," *Aiyansh Notes,* April 1908, 4.
21 Miss F.A.T. Copeland, "Kincolith," *Aiyansh Notes,* April 1911, 73.

22 Church Missionary Society Papers, Reel A121, 14 February 1900, Letter from Miss Bertha Davies to the parent committee.

23 Church Missionary Society Papers, Reel A122, 30 March 1900, Letter from parent committee to Miss Davies.

24 Church Missionary Society Papers, Reel A121, Letter from Rose Davies to the parent committee, 6 December 1899.

25 Church Missionary Society Papers, Reel A 122, Letter from G.A. Gollock to Davies, February 1904.

26 GSA, Bessie Quirt Diary, 9 March 1930.

27 Archer, ed., *Memoirs of Charlotte Selina Bompas*, 48.

28 Ibid., 57.

29 Ibid., 148.

30 "Hay River," *Letter Leaflet*, April 1916, 180.

31 Gertrude Thorne, "A Letter From Aiyansh," *North British Columbia News*, July 1926, 210.

32 Church Missionary Society Papers, Reel A 121, Letter from Miss Carleton to parent committee, 22 November 1898.

33 Miss Wilgress, "Hay River," *Letter Leaflet*, July 1905, 252.

34 Jo-Anne Fiske, "Carrier Women and the Politics of Mothering," in *British Columbia Reconsidered: Essays on Women,* ed. Gillian Creese and Veronica Strong-Boag (Vancouver, BC: Press Gang, 1992), 204.

35 Bridget Moran, *Stoney Creek Woman: The Story of Mary John* (Vancouver, BC: Tillacum Library, 1988).

36 The same argument has been made about turn-of-the-century southern women's involvement in the Women's Christian Temperance Union. Women who joined initially to lobby for prohibition often ended up supporting the suffrage campaign. Along the way, they learned organizational skills and became more politically active. See Wendy Mitchinson, "The WCTU: 'For God, Home and Native Land': A Study in Nineteenth Century Feminism," in *A Not Unreasonable Claim: Women and Reform in Canada, 1880s to 1920s,* ed. Linda Kealey (Toronto, On: Women's Educational Press, 1979), 169-211.

37 *Second Annual Report of the Selkirk Diocesan Branch,* 4; *Fifth Annual Report of the Yukon Diocesan Branch of the Woman's Auxiliary,* 28 August 1912, 7. For example in 1906 the executive of the Yukon Women's Auxiliary consisted of Honorary President Mrs. Commissioner McInnes, President Mrs. Bompas, Vice-Presidents Wives of Clergy, Corresponding Secretary Miss Ellis, Recording Secretary F. G. de Gex, Treasurer Mrs. Astley, Dorcas Secretary, and Superintendent of Junior Branches of the Woman's Auxiliary Miss Ellis. Most of these women were with the mission. Later women like Mrs. George Black would join their ranks. In 1912, Mrs. Black invited all the women back to tea at the Government house after the annual meeting.

38 Bompas was proud to be the first president and compared herself to Mrs. Tilton and the other six women who began the national Woman's Auxiliary. She claimed to take "motherly interest" in the organization (*Third Annual Report of the Yukon Diocesan Branch of the Woman's Auxiliary,* 9 and 10 September 1910, 9).

39 YTA, Anglican Church Records, Series 111.5 a Box 50, Folder 1 of 11 corr. 298, *Selkirk Diocesan Branch Woman's Auxiliary, Second Annual Report,* "Annual Address of Mrs. Bompas, President Delivered at Dawson Y.T. August 13, 1906," 9.

40 YTA, "Annual Address of Mrs. Bompas, President Delivered at Dawson Y.T. August 13, 1906," 7.

41 YTA, Woman's Auxiliary to the Missionary Society of the Church of England in Canada, Diocese of the Yukon, Letter from (Sarah) Sadie Stringer to Mrs. Plumptre, 22 November 1915. The women's auxiliary branch generally decided on a mission or cause to contribute to and set an annual pledge. These pledges changed regularly based on need. During the First World War, for example, the women of the Dawson women's auxiliary chose to spend their treasury moneys in the following way: "$25.00 towards our share of the Diocesan Pledges; $250.00 towards Rector's stipend; $30.00 for St. Paul's share of support of Indian boy at Chooutla Indian School; $100.00 towards Belgian Relief Fund; $83.00 towards furnishings for the Rectory; $161.00 towards M.S.C.C Fund, $100.00 of which

donation is for 1914 and the remainder for 1915; $10.00 for Yukon Endowment Fund, etc." The branch claimed to have made $850.00 in a sale of their work.

42  Ida Collins also reported that between 1906 to 1910 some of the Aboriginal children who belonged to the Junior Auxiliary had died. In letters sent to the parents, Collins stated that she believed it was "a cause of thanksgiving that each died in the Christian faith." YTA, *Third Annual Report of the Yukon Diocesan Branch of the Woman's Auxiliary Missionary Society of the Church of England in Canada, Report of Carcross Junior W.A. for 1906-1910*, 20.

43  Alfred Ellis and Margaret Johnson "Report of Junior Branch, Carcross," 34.

44  Selina Totty, "Report of the Moosehide Branch of the W.A.," *Fourth Annual Report of the Yukon Diocese Branch of the Woman's Auxiliary*, Dawson, 7 and 8 August 1911, 21.

45  Ibid.

46  Selina Totty, "Report of the Moosehide Branch of the W.A.," Yukon Diocesan Branch of the Woman's Auxiliary, *Report of the Sixth Annual Meeting*, Whitehorse, August 8th and 9th 1913, 31.

47  Minutes of the Eighth Diocesan Meeting of the Woman's Auxiliary, Dawson July 16th, 1915, 23. By this time there were 119 members in the Yukon women's auxiliary including the junior members.

48  Mrs. Totty "Report of the Moosehide Branch, 1915-1916," *Report of the Ninth Annual Meeting*, Dawson, 15 and 16 August, 15.

49  Mrs. Totty, "Report of the Moosehide Branch of The Women's Auxiliary from June, 1916, to June, 1917," in the *Report of the Tenth Annual Meeting*, Whitehorse, 4 August 1917, 38.

50  Harriet Knight, "St. Paul's Branch Dorcas Secretary's Report," Minutes of the Ninth Diocesan Meeting of the Yukon Woman's Auxiliary, Dawson, 15 and 16 August 1916, 14-15.

51  YTA, Yukon Diocesan Branch of the Woman's Auxiliary, *Report of the Twenty-Third Annual Meeting*, Dawson, 5-7 July 1931, 6.

52  Charlotte Imogene McCullum was from a prominent Anglican family in Chapleau, Ontario, whose father was a lumber baron and a federal politician.

53  YTA, Yukon Diocesan Branch of the Woman's Auxiliary, *Report of the Twenty-Third Annual Meeting*, Dawson, 5-7 July 1931, 5.

54  Ibid., 19. A very revealing photograph taken at the 1931 annual meeting shows several white women all wearing similarly styled hats standing with Mrs. McDonald and Mrs. Kendi.

55  While the parish of Old Crow has been without priests at times in the mid-twentieth century, the woman's auxiliary has continued to be a central organization for women in the community. The Bishop of the Yukon in an interview recalled that, as a young clergyman in the early 1970s, he was stationed at Old Crow. In recognizing the power of the Woman's Auxiliary he claimed to be very careful to "never cross the W.A." (interview with Bishop Ron Ferris, 10 February 1993).

56  Laura Beatrice Berton, *I Married the Klondike* (Toronto, ON: McClelland and Stewart, 1954), 59.

57  Berton, *I Married the Klondike*, 60.

58  Glenda Riley, *Women and Indians on the Frontier, 1825-1915* (Albuquerque, NM: University of New Mexico Press, 1993).

59  GSA, M71-4, Diocese of the Arctic, Hirst Journals, 2 January 1936.

60  GSA, M71-4, Hirst Journals, 21 April 1937.

61  GSA, M71-4, Hirst Journals, 5 August 1938.

62  Leslie A. Flemming, "A New Humanity: American Missionaries' Ideals for Women in North India, 1870-1930," in *Western Women and Imperialism: Complicity and Resistance,* ed. Nupur Chaudhuri and Margaret Strobel (Bloomington, IN: Indiana University Press, 1992), 9. In her study of American missionary women in India, Leslie Flemming has argued that missionaries did not offer Indian women radically different alternatives from domestic work. But, in their encouragement of "education, physical well being and voluntary activities," Indian women began to assume roles that had previously been denied them.

63  GSA, M71-4, Series 5-6-1, Box 21, Diocese of the Arctic Typescript draft of Mrs. Fleming's trip on the Nascopie in 1942 with her husband, 87-88.

64  GSA, Diocese of the Arctic Collection, D.B. Marsh Series, Diaries, Circulars, Letters, etc., M71-4, Series 5-1-1, Box 16, 5 November 1940.
65  GSA, M71-4, Arctic II 2-1-j, Folder 2, *WA Minute Books*, 1923-1948, 4 October 1926.
66  GSA, M71-4, *WA Minute Books*, 6 December 1926.
67  GSA, M71-4, Diocese of the Arctic Collection, Series II 2c, Box 10, Mission Material Woman's Auxiliary, The Story of the Early Days of the W.A. at Fort McPherson told by Mrs. Sarah Simon and Mrs. McDonald, July 1941 at the annual meeting.
68  "Report from the Ven. D.B. Marsh, Archdeacon of Aklavik," *Arctic News*, May 1949, 12.
69  "Canada," *The Living Message*, 152.
70  Church Missionary Society Papers, A 122, Letter from Baring-Gould to Ridley, 24 May 1901.
71  Ibid.
72  Cited in Abel, "Bishop Bompas and the Canadian Church," 119.
73  Bishop Fleming of the Arctic claimed that it was important to train Aboriginal ministers but believed that it was a slow process: "It is of course the ultimate desire of every missionary to raise up in due course a native priesthood that can minister to its own. With a primitive people this can only be done little by little as first one man and then another proves his capacity" (*Archibald the Arctic*, 286). This attitude was far more typical than either Stringer's or McDonald's.
74  Although Bishop Bompas was a low church evangelistic, it never occurred to him to introduce the evangelical Church Army to the Yukon. However, he would have rejected some of its aspects, including the acceptance of Aboriginal Christians as leaders.
75  John Webster Grant, *Moon of Winter Time*, 262.
76  Lillard, ed., *In the Wake of the War Canoe*, 229.
77  Lillard, ed., *Warriors of the North Pacific*, 228.
78  Ibid., 243.
79  J.B. McCullagh, "Gwinoha!" *North British Columbia News*, April 1911, 74-5.
80  J.B. McCullagh, "Gwinoha!" *North British Columbia News*, February 1912.
81  "Six Months At Lak-Galzap – Easter Day at Fishery Bay," *North British Columbia News*, October 1913, 49; "Church Army Indians On Active Service," *North British Columbia News*, October 1915, 89-90.
82  "Lak Gal Zap," *North British Columbia News*, April 1920, 51.
83  "A Visit to the Canadian West and the Indian Church Army," *North British Columbia News*, October 1928, 302.
84  "The Doctor at Kitwingak," *North British Columbia News*, April 1916, 17.
85  Alfred E. Price, "Kitiwingak, Skeena River," *North British Columbia News*, May 1910, 35.
86  H. Flores, "Floods At Kitwanga," *North British Columbia News*, July 1936, 303.
87  Ibid.
88  McCullum and McCullum, *Caledonia 100 Years Ahead*, 89.
89  Cited in McCullum and McCullum, *Caledonia 100 Years Ahead*, 144.
90  Susan Neylan, "'The Heavens are Changing': Nineteenth-Century Protestant Missionization on the North Pacific Coast" (PhD diss., University of British Columbia, 1999).

**Conclusion**

1  Richeson ed., *Agnes Deans Cameron*, 210.
2  Fleming, *Archibald the Arctic*, 373.
3  Ibid., 375.
4  Francis, *The Imaginary Indian*, 4.
5  Ruth Frankenberg, *White Women, Race Matters: The Social Construction of Whiteness* (Minneapolis, MN: University of Minnesota Press, 1993), 16-17.
6  Selina Bompas, "Our Women of the North," *Canadian Churchman*, November 1907, 739.
7  David Napier, *Anglican Journal Residential School Special Report: Sins of the Fathers*, Anglican Church of Canada, May 2000.

# Bibliography

**Primary Sources**

Archival Sources

*Whitehorse*
Yukon Territorial Archives (YTA)
Yukon Anglican Church Records

Correspondence from Bishop W.C. Bompas to the Reverend H.A. Naylor, 1896-1906
Diocesan Woman's Auxiliary Annual Minutes and Reports, 1906-72
Hilda Hellaby Papers
Journals and Annual Reports of the Sunday School Caravan Mission
Lilian Lucey Papers
Parish Records for Dawson, Fort Selkirk, and Mayo
Personnel Files
Records, St. Paul's Hostel in Dawson
Synod Files

*Toronto*
General Synod Archives of the Anglican Church of Canada (GSA)

Adelaide Jane Butler Papers
Anglican Women's Training College, Day Books, 1902-16
Anglican Women's Training College, Minute Books, Candidate Committee Meetings, 1914-34
Bessie Quirt Papers
Bishop Donald Marsh Papers
Bishop I.O. Stringer Papers
Bishop Bompas Papers
Correspondence between Bishop James R. Lucas [Mackenzie River Diocese] and Miss Halson [W.A. Dorcas Secretary], 1914-25
Diocese of the Arctic Papers
F.H. Eva Hasell Papers
Florence Hirst Papers
Louise Topping Papers
Records of the Missionary Society For the Church of England in Canada, 1904-40
Records of the Woman's Auxiliary to the Missionary Society of the Church of England in Canada
T.H. Canham Papers

Woman's Auxiliary Records, Arctic Diocese: Woman's Auxiliary Minute Books, St. Peter's
    Mission, Hay River, 1923-48; Woman's Auxiliary Arctic Reports
Women's Work in the Church Report on Certain Resolutions of the Lambeth Conference,
    by a Committee of the House Bishops, 1935.

*Prince Rupert*
Diocese of Caledonia Archives

Annual Reports of the Synod of Caledonia
Clergy Register
Letters from the Superintendent of Ridley House Nora Bird to England, 1939-43
Minutes of the Board of Trustee
Monica Storrs Diary, 1935-39
Woman's Auxiliary Reports

*Edmonton*
Provincial Archives of Alberta

Bishop Lucas Papers
Mackenzie River Diocese Records

*Victoria*
Province of British Columbia Archives

Church Missionary Society Records
Deacon Robert Tomlinson and Family: *Wayside Log 1879 Chronicle of trip taken from Kin-
    colith on the Nass to Skeena River and Kispiox*
Oral Interview: Alice Tomlinson's daughter-in-law Mrs. Robert Tomlinson, Sound and
    Moving Image Tapes, 1962.

*Ottawa*
National Archives of Canada
R.J. Bowen Papers
William Duncan Papers

*Vancouver*
Vancouver School of Theology
British Columbian and Yukon Church Aid Society Collection 1902-40

*Winnipeg*
Hudson's Bay Company Archives
Photograph Collection 1945/5 Augusta E. Morris
E. 78 Augusta E. Morris – Diary, Correspondence, 1881-83

*Calgary*
Glenbow Museum
M4745 Files 24 and 25, E.P. Hockin Correspondence Files

**Books**
Archer, S.A., ed. *A Heroine of the North: Memoirs of Charlotte Selina Bompas (1830-1917)*.
    London: Macmillan, 1929.
Berton, Laura Beatrice. *I Married the Klondike*. Toronto, ON: McClelland and Stewart, 1954.
Church Missionary Society. *Register of Missionaries (Clerical, Lay and Female) and Native
    Clergy from 1804 to 1904*. London: Church Missionary Society, 1904.
Cody, H.A. *An Apostle of the North: Memoirs of the Right Reverend William Carpenter Bompas*.
    London: Seely and Co., 1908.

Cummings, Emily Willoughby. *Our Story: Some Pages from the History of the Woman's Auxiliary to the Missionary Society of the Church of England in Canada 1885 to 1928*. Toronto, ON: Garden City Press, n.d.

Diocese of the Yukon Woman's Auxiliary. *Five Pioneer Women of the Anglican Church in the Yukon*. Whitehorse: Star Printing, 1975.

Du Vernet, Sylvia., ed. *Portrait of a Personality – Archbishop Frederick Hubert Du Vernet*. Toronto: Du Vernet, 1987.

Fleming, Archibald Lang. *Archibald the Arctic: The Flying Bishop*. New York, NY: Appleton-Century Crofts, 1956.

Hallenby, Grace. *Anglican Women's Training College: A Background Document*. Toronto, ON: AWTC History Committee, 1989.

Hasell, F.H.E. *Canyons, Cans, and Caravans*. London: Society for Promoting Christian Knowledge, 1930.

Janvrin, Alice., ed. *W. Ridley: Snapshots of the North Pacific*. London: Church Missionary Society, 1904.

Lillard, Charles, ed. *In the Wake of the War Canoe: William Henry Collison*. 1915; rpt. Victoria, BC: Sono Nis Press, 1981.

–, ed. *Warriors of the North Pacific: Missionary Accounts of the Northwest Coast, the Skeena and Stikine Rivers, and the Klondike, 1829-1900*. Victoria, BC: Sono Nis Press, 1984.

Marsh, Winifred Petchey. *People of the Willow: The Padlimiut Tribe of Caribou Eskimo Portrayed in Watercolours*. Toronto, ON: Oxford University Press, 1976.

–, ed. *Echoes from a Frozen Land / Donald B. Marsh*. Edmonton: Hurtig, 1987.

Morton, W.L., ed. *God's Galloping Girl: The Peace River Diaries of Monica Storrs, 1929-1931*. Vancouver: UBC Press, 1979.

Richeson, David., ed. *The New North: An Account of a Woman's 1908 Journey through Canada to the Arctic. Agnes Deans Cameron*. Saskatoon, SK: Western Producer Prairie Books, 1986.

Ridley, William. *Not Myth but Miracle*. London: Seeley, 1900.

Wycliffe College, *The Jubilee Volume of the Wycliffe College, 1877-1927-1937*. Toronto, ON: University of Toronto Press, 1939.

## Newspapers and Periodicals

*Across The Rockies*
*Aiyansh Notes*, 1907-09
*Arctic News*
*Canadian Churchman*
*Church Missionary Gleaner*
*Church Missionary Society, The Intelligencer*
*Evangelical Churchman*
*Letter Leaflet*
*Nineteenth Century*
*North British Columbia News*, 1909-39
*Northern Lights*, 1913-present
*The Canadian Church Magazine and Our Mission News*
*The Living Message*
*The Mission World*
*The New Era*

## Pamphlets

Bompas, Charlotte Selina. "Mission Work on the Upper Yukon," Pamphlet Collection, Yukon Territorial Archives.

Middleton, Charles. "A Voice from the Yukon Gold District: A Chat with the Venerable T.H. Canham, Archdeacon of Selkirk." *The Sunday Magazine 1898* (London: Ibister and Co. Limited): 180-9. Pamphlet Collection, Yukon Territorial Archives.

Whittaker, C.E. *"Recollections of An Arctic Parson,"* General Synod Archives, n.d.

Wodehouse, Madeline. *"Our Early Beginnings."* Woman's Auxiliary Papers. General Synod Archives.

Wright, Allen. *"Fortymile and Charlotte Bompas."* Pamphlet Collection, MSS-155. Yukon Archives.

**Oral Interviews**
Bishop T. Ferris, Bishop of the Yukon, February 1993.
Mrs. Faith Cronk, Grand Manan, New Brunswick, February 1996. [daughter of Marguerite Latham Shepherd]
Mrs. Yvonne MacDonald, Coxheath, Nova Scotia, March 1996. [niece of Mildred McCabe]

**Secondary Sources**

**Published**
Abel, Kerry. Bishop Bompas and the Canadian Church. In *The Anglican Church and the World of Western Canada*. ed. Barry Ferguson. 113-25. Regina, SK: University of Regina Press, 1991.
–. *Drum Songs: Glimpses of Dene History*. Montréal/Kingston: McGill-Queen's University Press, 1993.
Austin, Alvyn J. *Saving China: Canadian Missionaries in the Middle Kingdom, 1888-1959*. Toronto, ON: University of Toronto Press, 1986.
Backhouse, Frances. *Women of the Klondike*. Vancouver, BC: Whitecap, 1995.
Barber, Marilyn. The Fellowship of the Maple Leaf Teachers. In *The Anglican Church and the World of Western Canada*. ed. Barry Ferguson. 154-67. Regina, SK: University of Regina Press, 1991.
Barman, Jean. Separate and Unequal: Indian and White Girls at All Hallows School, 1884-1920. In *Rethinking Canada: The Promise of Women's History*. ed. Veronica Strong-Boag and Anita Clair Fellman. 215-33. Toronto, ON: Copp Clark Pitman, 1991.
–. Taming Aboriginal Sexuality: Gender, Power, and Race in British Columbia, 1850-1900. *BC Studies* 115-16 (Autumn/Winter 1997-98): 237-66.
Barnett, H.G. Personal Conflicts and Cultural Change. *Social Forces* 20 (December 1941): 160-71.
Bebbington, D.W. *Evangelicalism in Modern Britain: A History from the 1730s to the 1980s*. London: Unwin Hyman, 1989.
Bergmann, Linda S. Women against a Background of White: The Representation of Self and Nature in Women's Arctic Narratives. *American Studies* 34 (Fall 1993): 53-68.
Best-Lindstrom, Varpu. *Defiant Sisters: A Social History of Finnish Immigrant Women in Canada*. Toronto, ON: Multicultural History Society of Ontario, 1988.
Bhabha Homi K. Of Mimicry and Man: The Ambivalence of Colonial Discourse. *October* 28 (1984): 125-33.
–, ed. *Nation and Narration*. London: Routledge, 1990.
Blackman, Margaret B. *During My Time: Florence Edenshaw Davidson, a Haida Woman*. Seattle: University of Washington Press, 1982.
Blunt, Alison. Imperial Geographies of the Home: British Domesticity in India, 1886-1925. *Transactions* 24, 4 (1999): 421-40.
–. *Travel, Gender, and Imperialism: Mary Kingsley and West Africa*. London: Guildford, 1994.
Blunt, Alison, and Gillian Rose, ed., *Writing Women and Space: Colonial and Postcolonial Geographies*. London: Guildford, 1994.
Bolt, Clarence. *Thomas Crosby and the Tsimshian: Small Shoes for Feet Too Large*. Vancouver, BC: UBC Press, 1992.
Boyd, Lois. Presbyterian Ministers' Wives: A Nineteenth Century Portrait. *Journal of Presbyterian History* 59, 1 (Spring 1981): 3-17.
Bridge, Kathryn. *By Snowshoe, Buckboard, and Steamer: Women of the Frontier*. Victoria, BC: Sono Nis, 1998.
Brouwer, Ruth Compton. *New Women for God: Canadian Presbyterian Women and India Missions, 1876-1914*. Toronto, ON: University of Toronto Press, 1990.
–. Opening Doors through Social Service: Aspects of Women's Work in the Canadian

Presbyterian Mission in Central India, 1877-1914. In *Women's Work for Women: Missionaries and Social Change in Asia.* ed. Leslie Flemming. 11-34. Boulder, CO: Westview, 1989.

–. Transcending the "Unacknowledged Quarantine": Putting Religion into English-Canadian Women's History. *Journal of Canadian Studies* 27 (Fall 1992): 47-61.

Brownlee, Robin, and Mary-Ellen Kelm. Desperately Seeking Absolution: Native Agency as Colonialist Alibi. *Canadian Historical Review* 75 (December 1994): 543-56.

Brumberg, Joan Jacobs. *Mission for Life: The Story of the Family of Adoniram Judson, the Dramatic Events of the First American Foreign Mission, and the Course of Evangelical Religion in the Nineteenth Century.* New York, NY: Free Press, 1980.

Burton, Antoinette. *Burdens of History: British Feminists, Indian Women, and Imperial Culture, 1865-1915.* Chapel Hill, NC: University of North Carolina Press, 1994.

Bush, Julia. Edwardian Ladies and the "Race" Dimensions of British Imperialism. *Women's Studies International Forum* 21, 3 (1998): 277-90.

Caine, Barbara. *Victorian Feminists.* New York: Oxford University Press, 1992.

Callaway, Helen. *Gender, Culture, and Empire: European Women in Colonial Nigeria.* London: Macmillan, 1987.

Carlson, Joyce, and Alf Dumont. *Bridges in Spirituality: First Nations Christian Women Tell Their Stories.* Toronto, ON: United Church Publishing House, 1997.

Carter, Sarah. *Capturing Women: The Manipulation of Cultural Imagery in Canada's Prairie West.* Montréal/Kingston: McGill-Queen's University Press, 1997.

–. Categories and Terrains of Exclusion: Constructing the "Indian Woman" in the Early Settlement Era in Western Canada. *Great Plains Quarterly* 13 (Summer 1993): 147-61.

Cavanaugh, Catherine A., and Randi R. Warne, eds. *Standing on New Ground: Women in Alberta.* Edmonton: University of Alberta Press, 1993.

Chaudhuri, Nupur. Shawls, Jewelry, Curry, and Rice in Victorian Britain. In *Western Women and Imperialism: Complicity and Resistance.* ed. Nupur Chaudhuri and Margaret Strobel. 231-46. Bloomington: Indiana University Press, 1992.

Christensen, Torben, and William R. Hutchison, eds. *Missionary Ideologies in the Imperialist Era: 1880-1920.* Copenhagen: Forlaget Aros, 1982.

Coates, Kenneth S. Asking All Sorts of Favours: The Anglican Church, the Federal Government, and the Natives of the Yukon Territory, 1891-1909. In *The Anglican Church and the World of Western Canada, 1820-1970.* ed. Barry Ferguson. 126-43. Regina, SK: University of Regina Press, 1991.

–. *Best Left as Indians: Native White Relations in the Yukon Territory, 1840-1973.* Montréal/Kingston: McGill-Queen's University Press, 1991.

–. "Betwixt and Between": The Anglican Church and the Children of Carcross (Chooutla) Residential School, 1911-1954. *BC Studies* 64 (1984-85): 27-47.

–. *Canada's Colonies: A History of the Yukon and the Northwest Territories.* Toronto, ON: James Lorimer, 1985.

–. "Send Only Those Who Rise a Peg": Anglican Clergy in the Yukon, 1858-1932. *Journal of the Canadian Church Historical Society* 28 (Spring 1986): 1-17.

Cole, Douglas, and Ira Chaikin. *An Iron Hand Upon the People.* Vancouver, BC: Douglas and McIntyre, 1990.

Comaroff, Jean, and John Comaroff. *Of Revelation and Revolution: Christianity, Colonialism and Consciousness in South Africa.* Vol. 1. Chicago, IL: University of Chicago Press, 1991.

–. *Ethnography and the Historical Imagination.* Boulder, CO: Westview, 1992.

Cook, Jenny. Bringing the Outside In: Women and the Transformation of the Middle-Class Maritime Canadian Interior, 1830-1860. *Material History Review* 38 (Fall 1993): 36-49.

Cooper, Carol. Native Women of the Northern Pacific Coast: An Historical Perspective 1830-1900. *Journal of Canadian Studies* (Winter 1993): 44-75.

Cooper, Frederick, and Ann L. Stoler. Tensions of Empire: Colonial Control and Visions of Rule. *American Ethnologist* 16 (November 1989): 609-21.

Coutts, Robert. Anglican Missionaries as Agents of Acculturation: The Church Missionary Society at St. Andrew's, Red River, 1830-1870. In *The Anglican Church and the World of Western Canada.* ed. Barry Ferguson. 50-60. Regina: Canadian Plains Research Center, University of Regina Press, 1991.

Christophers, Brett. *Positioning the Missionary: John Booth Good and the Confluence of Cultures in Nineteenth-Century British Columbia*. Vancouver, BC: UBC Press, 1998.

Craig, Terrence L. *The Missionary Lives: A Study in Canadian Missionary Biography and Autobiography*. Leiden: Brill, 1997.

Cruikshank, Julie, with Angela Sidney, Kitty Smith, and Annie Ned. *Life Lived Like a Story: Life Stories of Three Yukon Elders*. Vancouver, BC: UBC Press, 1990.

Cumbo, Enrico Carlson. "Impediments to the Harvest": The Limitations of Methodist Proselytization of Toronto's Italian Immigrants, 1905-1925. In *Catholics at the "Gathering Place": Historical Essays on the Archdiocese of Toronto, 1841-1991*. ed. Mark George McGowan and Brian P. Clarke. 155-77. Toronto, ON: Canadian Catholic Historical Association, 1993.

Danylewycz, Marta. *Taking the Veil: An Alternative to Marriage, Motherhood, and Spinsterhood in Quebec, 1840-1920*. Toronto, ON: McClelland and Stewart, 1987.

Davidoff, Leonore, and Catherine Hall. *Family Fortunes: Men and Women of the English Middle Class 1780-1850*. London: Hutchinson, 1987.

Davin, Anna. Imperialism and Motherhood. *History Workshop Journal* 5 (Spring 1978): 9-67.

Dawson, George. *Soldier Heroes: British Adventure, Empire, and the Imagining of Masculinities*. London: Routledge, 1994.

Devens, Carol. *Countering Colonization: Native American Women and Great Lakes Missions, 1630-1900*. Berkeley: University of California Press, 1992.

Dickason, Olive Patricia. *Canada's First Nations: A History of Founding Peoples from Earliest Times*. Toronto, ON: McClelland and Stewart, 1992.

Douglas, Ann. *The Feminization of American Culture*. New York, NY: Knopf, 1977.

Dunae, Patrick. Boys Literature and the Idea of Empire, 1870-1914. *Victorian Studies* 24 (Autumn 1980): 105-21.

Fast, Vera. *Missionary on Wheels: Eva Hasell and the Sunday School Caravan Missions*. Toronto, ON: Anglican Book Centre, 1979.

Ferguson, Barry., ed. *The Anglican Church and the World of Western Canada 1820-1970*. Regina, SK: Canadian Plains Research Centre, University of Regina Press, 1991.

Fisher, Robin. *Contact and Conflict: Indian and European Relations in British Columbia*. Vancouver, BC: UBC Press, 1977.

Fisher, Robin, and Kenneth S. Coates, eds. *Out of the Background: Readings on Canadian Native History*. Toronto, ON: Copp Clark Pittman, 1988.

Fiske, Jo-Anne. Carrier Women and the Politics of Mothering. In *British Columbia Reconsidered: Essays on Women*. ed. Gillian Creese and Veronica Strong-Boag. 198-217. Vancouver, BC: Press Gang, 1992.

–. Pocahontas's Granddaughters: Spiritual Transition and Tradition of Carrier Women of British Columbia. *Ethnohistory* 43, 4 (1996): 663-81.

Flemming, Leslie A. A New Humanity: American Missionaries' Ideals for Women in North India, 1870-1930. In *Western Women and Imperialism: Complicity and Resistance*, ed. Nupur Chaudhuri and Margaret Strobel. 191-207. Bloomington, IN: Indiana University Press, 1992.

–, ed. *Women's Work for Women: Missionaries and Social Change in Asia*. Boulder, CO: Westview, 1989.

Francis, Daniel. *The Imaginary Indian: The Image of the Indian in Canadian Culture*. Vancouver, BC: Arsenal Pulp Press, 1992.

Frankenberg, Ruth. *White Women, Race Matters: The Social Construction of Whiteness*. Minneapolis, MN: University of Minnesota Press, 1993.

Furniss, Elizabeth. *The Burden of History: Colonialism and the Frontier Myth in a Rural Canadian Community*. Vancouver, BC: UBC Press, 1999.

–. *Victims of Benevolence: The Dark Legacy of the Williams Lake Residential School*. Vancouver, BC: Arsenal Pulp Press, 1995.

Gagan, Rosemary R. *A Sensitive Independence: Canadian Methodist Women Missionaries in Canada and the Orient, 1881-1925*. Montréal/Kingston: McGill-Queen's University Press, 1992.

Getty, Ian. The Failure of the Native Church Policy of the CMS in the North-West. In *Religion and Society in the Prairie West*. ed. Richard Allen. 19-34. Regina, SK: University of Regina Press, 1974.

Gough, Barry. A Priest versus the Potlatch: The Reverend Alfred James Hall and the Fort Rupert Kwakiutl, 1878-80. *Journal of the Canadian Church Historical Society* 24 (October 1982): 75-90.

Graham, Gael. *Gender, Culture, and Christianity: American Protestant Mission Schools in China, 1880-1930*. New York, NY: Peter Lang, 1995.

Grant, John Webster. *Moon of Wintertime: Missionaries and the Indians of Canada in Encounter Since 1534*. Toronto, ON: University of Toronto Press, 1984.

Green, Rayna. The Tribe Called Wannabee: Playing Indian in America and Europe. *Folklore* 99 (Winter 1988): 30-51.

Grimshaw, Patricia. "Christian Woman, Pious Wife, Faithful Mother, Devoted Missionary": Conflicts in Roles of American Missionary Women in Nineteenth Century Hawaii. *Feminist Studies* 9 (1983): 489-522.

–. *Paths of Duty: American Missionary Wives in Nineteenth-Century Hawaii*. Honolulu, HI: University of Hawaii Press, 1989.

Guildford, Judith, and Suzanne Morton, eds. *Separate Spheres: Women's Worlds in the 19th-Century Maritimes*. Fredericton: Acadiensis, 1994.

Gunson, Niel. *Messengers of Grace: Evangelical Missionaries in the South Seas, 1797-1860*. Melbourne/New York: Oxford University Press, 1978.

Haggis, Jane. "Good Wives and Mothers" or "Dedicated Workers"? Contradictions of Domesticity in the "Mission of Sisterhood," Travancore, South India. In *Maternities and Modernities: Colonial and Postcolonial Experiences in Asia and the Pacific*. ed. Kalpana Ram and Margaret Jolly. 81-113. Cambridge, UK: Cambridge University Press, 1998.

–. White Women and Colonialism: Towards a Non-Recuperative History. In *Gender and Imperialism*. ed. Claire Midgley. 45-78. Manchester: Manchester University Press, 1998.

Haig-Brown, Celia. *Resistance and Renewal: Surviving the Indian Residential School*. Vancouver, BC: Tillacum, 1988.

Hall, Catherine. *White, Male, and Middle Class: Explorations in Feminism and History*. New York, NY: Routledge, 1992.

Harkin, Michael. Engendering Discipline: Discourse and Counterdiscourse in the Methodist-Heiltsuk Dialogue. *Ethnohistory* 43, 4 (1996): 642-61.

Harris, Cole. *The Resettlement of British Columbia: Essays on Colonialism and Geographical Change*. Vancouver, BC: UBC Press, 1997.

Hayes, Alan L. Repairing the Walls: Church Reform and Social Reform 1867-1939. In *By Grace Co-Workers: Building the Anglican diocese of Toronto 1780-1989*. ed. Alan L. Hayes. 43-96. Toronto, ON: Anglican Book Centre, 1989.

Headon, Christopher. Women and Organized Religion in Mid and Late Nineteenth-Century Canada. *Journal of the Canadian Church Historical Society* 20 (March/June 1978): 3-18.

Heeney, Brian. *The Women's Movement in the Church of England, 1850-1930*. Oxford: Clarendon, 1988.

Hill, Patricia. *The World Their Household: The American Women's Foreign Mission Movement and Cultural Transformation, 1870-1920*. Ann Arbor, MI: University of Michigan Press, 1985.

Hocking, William. *Re-thinking Missions: A Layman's Inquiry After One Hundred Years*. New York, NY: Harper and Brothers, 1932.

Hughes, Thomas. *Tom Brown's School Days*. London: Penguin, 1857; rpt. 1971.

Hunter, Jane. *The Gospel of Gentility: American Women Missionaries in Turn-of-the-Century China*. New Haven, CT: Yale University Press, 1984.

–. The Home and the World: The Missionary Message of U.S. Domesticity. In *Women's Work for Women: Missionaries and Social Change in Asia*. ed. Leslie A. Flemming. 159-66. Boulder, CO: Westview, 1989.

Hutcheon, Linda. The Post Always Rings Twice: The Post Modern and the Post Colonial. *Material History Review* 41 (Spring 1995): 4-23.

Jackel, Susan, ed. *A Flannel Shirt and Liberty: Emigrant British Gentlewomen in the Canadian West, 1880-1914*. Vancouver, BC: UBC Press, 1982.

Jacobs, Jane, ed. *A Schoolteacher in Old Alaska: The Story of Hannah Breece*. Toronto, ON: Random House, 1995.

James, Louis. Tom Brown's Imperialist Sons. *Victorian Studies* 17 (September 1973): 89-99.

Jasen, Patricia. *Wild Things: Nature, Culture, and Tourism in Ontario 1790-1914*. Toronto, ON: University of Toronto Press, 1995.

Johnston, Jean. *Wilderness Women: Canada's Forgotten History*. Toronto, ON: Peter Martin, 1973.

Jolly, Margaret. Colonizing Women: The Maternal Body and Empire. In *Feminism and the Politics of Difference*. ed. Sneja Gunew and Anna Yeatman. 103-27. Boulder, CO: Westview, 1993.

Karttunen, Frances E. *Between Worlds: Interpreters, Guides, and Survivors*. New Brunswick, NJ: Rutgers University Press, 1994.

Kelm, Mary-Ellen. *Colonizing Bodies: Aboriginal Health and Healing in British Columbia, 1900-50*. Vancouver, BC: UBC Press, 1998.

Kemper, Alison. Deaconess As Urban Missionary and Ideal Woman: Church of England Initiatives in Toronto, 1890-1895. In *Canadian Protestant and Catholic Missions, 1820s-1960s Historical Essays In Honour of John Webster Grant*. ed. John S. Moir and C.T. McIntire. 171-90. New York, NY: Peter Lang, 1988.

Kerber, Linda. Separate Spheres, Female Worlds, Woman's Place: The Rhetoric of Women's History. *Journal of American History* 75 (June 1988): 9-39.

Kingsolver, Barbara. *The Poisonwood Bible*. New York, NY: HarperCollins, 1998.

Kipp, Rita Smith. Emancipating Each Other: Dutch Colonial Missionaries' Encounter with Karo Women in Sumatra, 1900-1942. In *Domesticating The Empire: Race, Gender and Family Life in French and Dutch Colonialism*. ed. Julia Clancy-Smith and Frances Gouda. 211-37. Charlottesville, WV: University Press of Virginia, 1998.

Knapman, Claudia. *White Women in Fiji 1835-1930: The Ruin of Empire?* Sydney: Allen and Unwin, 1986.

Krech, Shepard, III. On the Aboriginal Population of the Kutchin. In *Interpreting Canada's North: Selected Readings*. ed. Kenneth S. Coates and William R. Morrison. 53-76. Toronto, ON: Copp Clark Pitman, 1989.

Lane, Hannah M. "Wife, Mother, Sister, Friend": Methodist Women in St. Stephen, New Brunswick, 1861-1881. In *Separate Spheres: Women's Worlds in the Nineteenth-Century Maritimes*. ed. Janet Guildford and Suzanne Morton. 93-118. Fredericton: Acadiensis, 1994.

Lay, Jackie. To Columbia on the Tynemouth: The Immigration of Single Women and Girls in 1862. In *In Her Own Right: Selected Essays on Women's History in B.C.* 19-41. Victoria: Camosun College, 1980.

Leacock, Eleanor. Montagnais Women and the Jesuit Program for Colonization. In *Rethinking Canada: The Promise of Women's History*. ed. Veronica Strong-Boag and Anita Clair Fellman. 11-27. Toronto, ON: Copp Clark Pitman, 1991.

Mangan, J.A. Social Darwinism and Upper-Class Education in Late Victorian and Edwardian England. In *Manliness and Morality: Middle-Class Masculinity in Britain and America 1800-1940*. ed. J.A. Mangan and James Walvin. 135-59. Manchester: Manchester University Press, 1987.

Mangan, J.A., and James Walvin, ed. *Manliness and Morality: Middle-Class Masculinity in Britain and America, 1800-1940*. Manchester: Manchester University Press, 1987.

Mannion, John J. *Irish Settlements in Eastern Canada: A Study of Cultural Transfer and Adaptation*. Toronto, ON: University of Toronto Press, 1974.

Marks, Lynne. Working Class Femininity and the Salvation Army: Hallelujah Lasses in English Canada, 1882-1892. In *Rethinking Canada: The Promise of Women's History*. ed. Veronica Strong-Boag and Anita Clair Fellman. 182-205. Toronto, ON: Copp Clark Pitman, 1991.

Marsh-Fletcher, Wendy. *Beyond the Walled Garden*. Dundas: Artemis, 1995.

–. The Limitation and Opportunity of Gender: Women and Ecclesiastical Structures in Canadian Anglicanism, 1920-55. *Journal of the Canadian Church Historical Society* 37 (April 1995): 41-54.

Marshall, David. *Secularizing the Faith: Canadian Protestant Clergy and the Crisis of Belief, 1850-1940*. Toronto, ON: University of Toronto Press, 1992.

Massey, Doreen. *Space, Place and Gender*. Minneapolis, MN: University of Minnesota Press, 1994.

McCarthy, Mary. *From the Great River to the Ends of the Earth: Oblate Misions to the Dene, 1847-1921*. Edmonton, AB: University of Alberta Press, 1995.

McClellan, Catharine. *A History of the Yukon Indians: Part of the Land, Part of the Water*. Vancouver, BC: Douglas and McIntyre, 1987.

McClintock, Anne. *Imperial Leather: Race, Gender, and Sexuality in the Colonial Contest*. London: Routledge, 1995.

McCullum, Hugh, and Karmel Taylor McCullum. *Caledonia 100 Years Ahead*. Toronto, ON: Anglican Book Centre, 1979.

MacKay, Douglas. *The Honourable Company*. Toronto, ON: McClelland and Stewart, 1936; rpt. 1966.

MacKenzie, John. The Imperial Pioneer and Hunter and the British Masculine Stereotype in Late Victorian and Edwardian Times. In *Manliness and Morality: Middle-Class Masculinity in Britain and America 1800-1940*. ed. J.A. Mangan and James Walvin. 176-98. Manchester: Manchester University Press, 1987.

–. *Propaganda and Empire*. Manchester: Manchester University Press, 1984.

MacLaren, I.S., and Lisa N. LaFramboise, eds. *The Ladies, the Gwich'in, and the Rat: Travels on the Athabasca, Mackenzie, Rat, Porcupine, and Yukon Rivers in 1926*. Edmonton, AB: University of Alberta Press, 1998.

MacLean, Eva. *The Far Land*. Prince George, BC: Caitlin, 1993.

Melman, Billie. *Women's Orients: English Women and the Middle East, 1718-1918*. Hampshire: MacMillan, 1992.

Memmi, Albert. *The Colonizer and the Colonized*. Boston, MA: Beacon Press, 1965.

Miller, J.R. *Shingwauk's Vision: A History of Native Residential Schools*. Toronto, ON: University of Toronto Press, 1996.

Mills, Sara. *Discourses of Difference: An Analysis of Women's Travel Writing and Colonialism*. London: Routledge, 1991.

Mitchinson, Wendy. Canadian Women and Church Missionary Societies in The Nineteenth-Century: A Step Towards Independence. *Atlantis* 2 (Spring 1977): 57-75.

–. The WCTU: "For God, Home, and Native Land": A Study in Nineteenth-Century Feminism. In *A Not Unreasonable Claim: Women and Reform in Canada, 1880s to 1920s*. ed. Linda Kealey. 169-211. Toronto, ON: Women's Educational Press, 1979.

Moran, Bridget. *Stoney Creek Woman: The Story of Mary John*. Vancouver, BC: Tillacum Library, 1988.

Morice, A.G. *The History of the Northern Interior of British Columbia*. London: J. Lane, 1906. rpt. Smithers, BC: Interior Stationary, 1978.

Morin, Karen M. British Women Travellers and Constructions of Racial Difference Across The Nineteenth-Century American West. *Transactions* 23, 3 (1998): 311-30.

Muir, Elizabeth Gillan. *Petticoats in the Pulpit: The Story of Early Nineteenth-Century Methodist Women Preachers in Upper Canada*. Toronto, ON: United Church Publishing House, 1991.

Murray, Peter. *The Devil and Mr. Duncan: A History of the Metlakatlas*. Victoria, BC: Sono Nis Press, 1985.

O'Neil, John D. The Politics of Health in the Fourth World: A Northern Canadian Example. In *Interpreting Canada's North: Selected Readings*, ed. Kenneth S. Coates and William R. Morrison. 279-98. Toronto, ON: Copp Clark Pitman, 1989.

Owen, Michael. Lighting the Pathways for New Canadians: Methodist and United Church Missions in Eastern Alberta, 1904-1940. In *Standing On New Ground: Women in Alberta*. ed. Catherine A. Cavanaugh and Randi R. Warne. 1-18. Edmonton, AB: University of Alberta Press, 1993.

Palmer, Albert W. *The Minister's Job*. New York, NY: Harper and Brothers, 1936.

Parr, Joy. Gender History and Historical Practice. *Canadian Historical Review* 76 (September 1995): 354-76.

Pascoe, C.F. *Two Hundred Years of the S.P.G. 1701-1900*. Vol. 1. London: Society for the Propagation of the Gospel, 1901.

Pascoe, Peggy. *Relations of Rescue: The Search for Female Moral Authority in the American West, 1874-1939*. New York, NY: Oxford University Press, 1990.

Patterson, E. Palmer, II. *Mission on the Nass: The Evangelization of the Nishga (1860-1890)*. Waterloo, ON: Eulachan, 1982.

Peake, Frank. *The Anglican Church in British Columbia*. Vancouver, BC: Mitchell Press, 1959.

–. *The Bishop Who Ate His Boots*. Don Mills, ON: Anglican Church of Canada, 1966.

Perry, Adele. "Oh, I'm Just Sick of the Faces of Men": Gender Imbalance, Race, Sexuality and Sociability in Nineteenth-Century British Columbia. *BC Studies* 105-6 (1995): 27-45.

–. *On the Edge of Empire: Gender, Race and the Making of British Columbia*. Toronto, ON: University of Toronto, 2001.

Pickles, Katie. Forgotten Colonizers: The Imperial Order of the Daughters of Empire (IODE) and the Canadian North. *The Canadian Geographer* 42, 2 (1998): 193-204.

Pierson, Ruth Roach. Experience, Difference, Dominance, and Voice in the Writing of Canadian Women's History. In *Writing Women's History: International Perspectives*. ed. Karen Offen, Ruth Roach Pierson, and Jane Rendall. 79-107. Bloomington, IN: Indiana University Press, 1991.

Pierson, Ruth Roach, and Nupur Chaudhuri, ed. *Nation, Empire, Colony: Historicizing Gender and Race*. Bloomington, IN: Indiana University Press, 1998.

Porsild, Charlene. *Gamblers and Dreamers: Women, Men,and Community in the Klondike*. Vancouver, BC: UBC Press, 1998.

Pratt, Mary Louise. *Imperial Eyes: Travel Writing and Transculturation*. London: Routledge, 1992.

Purvis, June. Women's History and Poststructuralism. *Women's History Review* 5, 1 (1996): 5-7.

–, ed. *Women's History: Britiain 1850-1945*. London: UCL Press, 1995.

Raibmon, Paige. Theatres of Contact: The Kwakwaka'wakw Meet Colonialism in British Columbia and at the Chicago World's Fair. *Canadian Historical Review* 81, 2 (2000): 157-90.

Ray, A.J., and Donald Freedman. *Give Us Good Measure: An Economic Analysis of Relations Between the Indians and the Hudson's Bay Company before 1763*. Toronto, ON: University of Toronto Press, 1978.

Richards, Jeffrey. "Passing the love of women's": Manly Love and Victorian Society. In *Manliness and Morality: Middle-Class Masculinity in Britain and America 1800-1940*, ed. J.A. Mangan and James Walvin. 92-122. Manchester: Manchester University Press, 1987.

Ridout, Katherine. A Woman of Mission: The Religious and Cultural Odyssey of Agnes Wintemute Coates. *Canadian Historical Review* 71 (June 1990): 204-44.

Riley, Denise. *"Am I That Name?": Feminism and the Category of "Women" in History*. Minneapolis, MN: University of Minnesota, 1988.

Riley, Glenda. *Women and Indians on the Frontier, 1825-1915*. Albuquerque, NM: University of New Mexico Press, 1984.

Roberts, Barbara. Ladies, Women and the State: Managing Female Immigration 1880-1920. In *Community Organization and the Canadian State*. ed. Rozana Ng, Gillian Walker, and Jacob Muller. 108-30. Toronto, ON: Garamond Press, 1990.

Rowbotham, Judith. "Hear an Indian Sister's Plea": Reporting the Work of Nineteenth-Century British Female Missionaries. *Women's Studies International Forum* 21, 3 (1998): 247-61.

–. "Soldiers of Christ?" Images of Female Missionaries in Late Nineteenth-Century Britain: Issues of Heroism and Martyrdom. *Gender and History* 12, 1 (2000): 82-106.

Rutherdale, Myra. Revisiting Colonization Through Gender: Anglican Missionary

Women in the Pacific Northwest and the Arctic, 1860-1945. *BC Studies* 104 (Winter 1994-95): 3-24.

Ryley, Bay. *Gold Diggers of the Klondike: Prostitution in Dawson City, Yukon.* Winnipeg, MB: J. Gordon Shillingford, 1997.

Said, Edward W. *Culture and Imperialism.* New York, NY: Alfred A. Knopf, 1993.

–. *Orientalism: Western Representations of the Orient.* London: Routledge and Kegan Paul, 1978.

Sandwell, Ruth, ed. *Beyond the City Limits: Rural British Columbia.* Vancouver, BC: UBC Press, 1998.

Sax, Lee, and Effie Linklater, eds. *Gikhyi: The True and Remarkable Story of Arctic Kutchin Christian Leaders.* Whitehorse, YT: Diocese of Yukon, 1990.

Silverman, Elaine Leslau. *Last Best West: Women on the Alberta Frontier, 1880-1930.* Montreal: Eden, 1984.

Smith, Donald B. *Sacred Feathers: The Reverend Peter Jones (Kahkewaquonaby) and the Mississauga Indians.* Toronto, ON: University of Toronto Press, 1987.

Smith-Rosenberg, Caroll. *Disorderly Conduct: Visions of Gender in Victorian America.* New York, NY: Oxford University Press, 1985.

Stock, Eugene. *History of the Church Missionary Society: Its Environment, Its Men, and Its Work.* Vols. 1-4. London: Church Missionary Society, 1899.

Strobel, Margaret. *European Women and the Second British Empire.* Bloomington, IN: Indiana University Press, 1991.

Strong-Boag, Veronica, and Carole Gerson. *Paddling Her Own Canoe: The Times and Texts of E. Pauline Johnson Tekahionwake.* Toronto, ON: University of Toronto, 2000.

Tenant, Margaret. Sisterly Ministrations: The Social Work of Protestant Deaconess In New Zealand 1890-1940. *New Zealand Journal of History* 32, 1 (1998): 3-22.

Thomas, John. Servants of the Church: Canadian Methodist Deaconess Work, 1890-1926. *Canadian Historical Review* 65 (September 1984): 371-95.

Trigger, Bruce. *Natives and Newcomers: Canada's "Heroic Age" Reconsidered.* Montréal/ Kingston: McGill-Queen's University Press, 1985.

–. *The Children of Aataentsic: A History of the Huron People to 1660.* 2 vols. Montréal/ Kingston: McGill-Queen's University Press, 1976.

Tucker, Cynthia Grant. *Prophetic Sisterhood: Liberal Women Ministers of the Frontier, 1880-1930.* Bloomington, IN: Indiana University Press, 1990.

Usher, Jean. Apostles and Aborigines: The Social Theory of the Church Missionary Society. *Histoire Sociale/Social History* 7 (April 1971): 28-53.

Valverde, Mariana. *The Age of Light, Soap, and Water: Moral Reform In English Canada, 1885-1925.* Toronto, ON: McClelland and Stewart, 1991.

Van Kirk, Sylvia. A Vital Presence: Women in the Cariboo Gold Rush 1862-1875. In *British Columbia Reconsidered.* ed. Gillian Creese and Veronica Strong-Boag. 21-48. Vancouver, BC: Press Gang, 1992.

–. *"Many Tender Ties": Women in the Fur Trade Society in Western Canada, 1670-1870.* Winnipeg, MB: Watson and Dwyer Publishing Company, 1980.

Vibert, Elizabeth. *Traders' Tales: Narratives of Cultural Encounters in the Columbia Plateau, 1807-1846.* Norman, OK: University of Oklahoma Press, 1997.

Vicinus, Martha. *Independent Women: Work and Community for Single Women, 1850-1920.* Chicago: University of Chicago Press, 1985.

Ware, Vron. *Beyond the Pale: White Women, Racism, and History.* London: Verso, 1992.

Warren, Allen. Popular Manliness: Baden Powell, Scouting and the Development of Manly Character. In *Manliness and Morality: Middle-Class Masculinity in Britain and America 1800-1940.* ed. J.A. Mangan and James Walvin. 199-219. Manchester: Manchester University Press, 1987.

Welter, Barbara. The Feminization of American Religion: 1800-1860. In *Clio's Consciousness Raised: New Perspectives on the History of Women.* ed. Mary Hartman and Lois W. Banner. 137-58. New York, NY: Harper and Row, 1974.

Westfall, William. *Two Worlds: The Protestant Culture of Late Nineteenth-Century Ontario.* Montréal/Kingston: McGill-Queen's University Press, 1989.

White, Hayden. *Tropics of Discourse: Essays in Cultural Criticism*. Baltimore, MD: Johns Hopkins University Press, 1978.

Whitehead, Margaret. *The Cariboo Mission: A History of the Oblates*. Victoria, BC: Sono Nis Press, 1981.

–. *They Call Me Father: Memoirs of Father Nicolas Coccola*. Vancouver, BC: UBC Press, 1988.

–. "A Useful Christian Woman": First Nations Women and Protestant Missionary Work in British Columbia. *Atlantis* 18 (1992-93): 142-66.

–. "Women Were Made for Such Things": Women Missionaries in British Columbia 1850s to 1940s. *Atlantis* 14 (Fall 1988): 141-50.

Worley, L.K. "Through Others' Eyes": Narratives of German Women Travelling in Nineteenth-Century America. *Yearbook of German-American Studies* 21 (1986).

Wynd, Oswald. *The Ginger Tree*. New York, NY: Harper and Row, 1977.

Zaslow, Morris. *The Northward Expansion of Canada, 1914-67*. Toronto, ON: McClelland and Stewart, 1988.

### Theses and Dissertations

Gresko, Jacqueline. Gender and Mission: The Founding Generations of the Sisters of Saint Ann and the Oblates of Mary Immaculate in British Columbia, 1858-1914. PhD diss., University of British Columbia, 1999.

James, Cathy. "An Opportunity for Service": Women of the Anglican Mission to the Japanese in Canada, 1903-1957. Master's thesis, University of British Columbia, 1990.

Kelcey, Barbara. Lost in the Rush: The Forgotten Women of the Klondike Stampede. Master's thesis, University of Victoria, 1989.

–, Jingo Belles, Jingo Belles, Dashing through the Snow: White Women and Empire on Canada's Arctic Frontier. PhD diss., University of Manitoba, 1994.

Neylan, Susan. "The Heavens Are Changing": Nineteenth-Century Protestant Missionization on the North Pacific Coast. PhD diss., University of British Columbia, 1999.

# Index